DEMOCRAZY

DEMOCRAZY

A POLITICAL SPOOF

ATULYA MAHAJAN

JAICO PUBLISHING HOUSE
Ahmedabad Bangalore Bhopal Bhubaneswar Chennai
Delhi Hyderabad Kolkata Lucknow Mumbai

Published by Jaico Publishing House
A-2 Jash Chambers, 7-A Sir Phirozshah Mehta Road
Fort, Mumbai - 400 001
jaicopub@jaicobooks.com
www.jaicobooks.com

© Atulya Mahajan

DEMOCRAZY
ISBN 978-81-8495-656-6

First Jaico Impression: 2015

No part of this book may be reproduced or utilized in
any form or by any means, electronic or
mechanical including photocopying, recording or by any
information storage and retrieval system,
without permission in writing from the publishers.

Page design and layout: SÜRYA, New Delhi

Printed by

To the ones I love the most in the world – my family, my readers and *aloo paranthas*. What would I be without you?

Also to the various scams India has seen over the years. Every time news breaks of a scam worth lakhs of crores, my chest swells with pride. We must be a rich nation to afford such mega-scams.

CONTENTS

Foreword	*ix*
Acknowledgements	*xi*
DAY 1: Last Man Standing	1
DAY 2: The Great Leaders	13
DAY 3: Cobwebs of the Mind	41
DAY 4: Fire in The Belly	63
DAY 5: Right to Metro Seats	85
DAY 6: Badi Sarkar Smart Children Yojna	103
DAY 7: The Media Circus	119
DAY 8: Himalayan Problems	145
DAY 9: Better than BB	169
DAY 10: One Thousand Push-Ups	187
DAY 11: The Talking Parrot	201
DAY 12: Who Will Ring the Bell?	219
About the Author	232

FOREWORD

Democrazy is a wonderful satirical look at our democracy at work through the prism of fickle social media peppered with prime time news, caricatures of politicians and of course WE the people. You have to be living under a rock to not recognize the inspiration behind all the characters in the book – 'fictional' as they are. With every page I turned I was half afraid that I would stumble upon a character 'inspired' by me.

Over the years I have enjoyed reading Atulya's work. He touches the right chords every time with effortless ease and this book is an extension of it.

When something bothers you so much and you are upset with your inability to fix it, satire is usually the answer. Often while reading *Democrazy*, I didn't know whether to laugh or cry. Laugh because of the humor or cry because how close to reality his portrayals are. The writing is hilarious and the lines spoken by the characters are ingenuously funny. In fact, at times, poignant because we have heard so much of what is written here in reality that the easier way to swallow it is with a jug full of satire. There's a lot being said between the lines too for the discerning political observer.

While our young Democracy is no doubt a work in progress, Atulya conditions you to enjoy the process and laugh with it! Whether you are a media person, a social media user or a politician, this book will make you laugh while forcing you to take a long hard look at yourself.

#Mustread!

Gul Panag

Gul Panag is an actor and activist who contested the 2014 General Elections and watched the hussle-bussle of electioneering from close quarters.

ACKNOWLEDGEMENTS

While there is no doubt that this book is the result of my incredible genius and jaw-dropping sense of humor, there are some people who also helped in this work of art come to life.

Thanks to my family for allowing me to live the life of a bachelor, hidden away from view, mostly whiling away my time on Twitter and Facebook with occasional breaks to work on the manuscript. Thanks to my lovely wife Kiran for being so cool and ensuring that she laughs at everything I write, even when I intentionally give her something truly terrible just to test her commitment. Thanks to my mom, herself a prolific writer, for being the one who has perhaps read every revision of the manuscript and provided prompt feedback. Thanks to my dad for being a constant pillar of support and encouragement. Thanks to my two children Aditya and Ananya; 4-year old Aditya for telling me to go do my work on the rare nights when I came by to sleep early and Ananya for waiting to be born, until I was done with the final round of edits. Thanks also to my big sister Divya for saying she loved the book without even reading it. You're not getting a copy of the next one by the way.

Thanks to the folks at Jaico for making this dream come true. I have enjoyed working with Akash, Sandhya, Nita and Srija. It is their efforts that have resulted in this masterful piece of art.

Thanks to the people who helped with the initial reviews and their feedback on the manuscript. Amit, Anurag, Smriti and Rahul – you've helped make the world a better place.

Thanks to all the fans and lovers who send me the occasional note about how much they adore my work, thereby making my day. You should do this more often.

Thanks also to the millions of readers who did not read my first book. Hopefully you will read this one and send me gushing emails about how you've never read anything this amazing ever before. Just so you are aware, you will encounter sudden great fortune if you read this book and tell five people about it. The benefits could include anything from a promotion at work, getting a friend request from that hot girl you fancy, or a Twitter follow from Modiji. In some cases, it may even stop hair-loss.

Finally, thanks to our great nation and the various leaders it has produced over the years, great and not-so-great. This book would have never happened without their invaluable efforts at sustaining our amazing Democrazy. Keep the scams coming!

Needless to say, all characters in this book are mere figments of my imagination and any resemblance to anybody dead or alive is a mere coincidence. No politicians, journalists, religious gurus or industrialists were hurt in the writing of this book.

DAY 1

LAST MAN STANDING

AdarshBharatiya@AdarshBharatiya

If you thought your job was tough, try being a party spokesman defending the government on Buddhi's show.

FerozWriter@FerozWriterIIMA

The missus shouted at me for 20 minutes for leaving dirty socks on the sofa. She went Buddhi on me.

MeraKaamJoker@MeraKaamJoker

Apparently, today is World Hypertension Day. We should all celebrate by watching Buddhi on TV.

Chhicchora@Chhicchora

BB walks into a bar. The bar breaks into tears.

Swamy@Swamy1959

I have confirmed news that Buddhi changes into his Superman costume after the show and flies off to save the world.

'Good evening, ladies and gentlemen. Elections are round the corner. The ruling party seems confident of returning to power on the back of an anti-anti-incumbency factor, which they claim has been proven by the National Laboratory of Election Wind Analysis. Meanwhile, the leader of opposition is so sure of winning the elections that he has vowed to give up watching his favorite *Harry Potter* movies if he loses.

'But tonight we want to look at the day's biggest news. Has Chhote Sarkar outdone himself with his suggestion for regularized corruption? Are official bribe rate-cards the answer to our problems? You are watching B for Buddhi, brought to you tonight by Scream, the energy drink that will leave you screaming for more. I am your host Buddhiman Buddhiraja. Tonight we will look at the implications of Chhote Sarkar's announcement'.

Buddhiman Buddhiraja, popularly known as BB, stared into Camera #2, one of the six cameras dedicated to making sure that each of his expressions was captured from various angles for the benefit of the audience, while four others covered the participants of his nightly 'B for Buddhi' show. His bespoke Armani suit, in a resplendent shade of purple, seemed to shine in the glare of the burning lights. BB was a rock star, the darling of the bosses and protector of the masses. A gold medallist in journalism from Baroda University, BB had gone on to complete his Master's degree from the prestigious Harvard University and had been handpicked to the newsroom of Bow Wow by the channel's founder.

Bow Wow was the newest, most radical news channel in town; the channel that claimed that its mission was to bring tears to viewers' eyes with its unadulterated, super-charged news coverage. Buddhiman Buddhiraja was the channel's crown jewel, making people on his show cry night after night with his unrelenting interrogations.

'We will start today's discussion with Dr Mohammad Panja, widely acknowledged as the most secular person in the country. Dr Panja is the honourable Minister of Mobile Phones as well as the spokesperson for the ruling We Will We Will Rock You party. Dr Panja was born into the religion-that-cannot-be-named but converted to the other religion-that-cannot-be-named to prove his secular credentials to the party. The rest, as we all know, is history.' BB looked up into Camera #3 and flashed his pearly off-whites.

'Dr Panja, would you mind summarizing Chhote Sarkar's idea for the benefit of our viewers?' BB looked over his left shoulder and addressed Mohammad Panja, all of 81 years of age. The name change had worked well for the wrinkly old man, helping him win the affections of the party leaders back in the day.

Camera #5 panned to Panja, who flashed a grandfatherly smile before answering. 'My dear Buddhi, let me tell you a story from when I was a child…'

BB stopped him mid-sentence with a wave of the hand and a serious look on his face. 'I beg your pardon sir but we don't have time on the show for stories. Can you just answer the question you are being asked?'

The other panel members smiled and the tension in the room eased a little, only for the status quo to be restored as Camera #5 focused on the disappointed look on BB's face – a look often seen on the face of school teachers when they leave the class for a few minutes to get the *gajar halwa* recipe from the teacher next door and return to find the classroom turned into a fish market.

'Dr Panja, go ahead.' He signalled to the secular minister to talk, with the other hand gesturing the other three panelists to maintain decorum.

'Buddhi ji, it is very simple. Corruption is killing our country and the only way to wipe out this cancer, is to legalize it. Hereafter, all government offices will have a rate-list clearly indicated at the entrance. Get a new passport for Rs 10,000, get it renewed for 5,000, get a driving license for 4,000, a fake birth certificate for two lakhs, and so on. This is an ingenious plan that only the kind Chhote Sarkar could have come up with. It is beautiful. People will know clearly what they need to pay. They won't need to go through the hassle of negotiations. They would have the confidence in their hearts that they can officially bribe government officers without any sense of guilt and shame – two emotions that often afflict some of our citizens.' Panja smiled at BB as he finished and then turned around to look at his fellow panelists, seeking supporting nods.

BB looked at Panja with a disgusted expression, his eyes burning with anger. 'Are you saying, Dr Panja, venerable MP for over half a dozen terms, beacon of secularity, that we are now going to make bribery official?'

Camera #2 and #4 panned to the pained expression on BB's face. The show's producers would project a split screen for viewers, with BB's distressed eyes staring at them from the left panel, and his left cheek on the right half of their TV screens.

BB spoke with pain in his voice. 'What next, sir? Government approved murderers and robbers, available for an officially published price to extract revenge on your enemies, or gangs of horse-mounted dacoits that you can rent from the District Collector's office? Where does this end, kind sir?'

BB swallowed the lump that had formed in his throat and continued. 'Sir, do you know how much money I paid to get my driving license?' He stared at Panja, daring him to answer.

The man sitting next to Panja cleared his throat and answered BB's question. 'BB ji, of course you didn't pay anything. I can't even imagine you doing something so preposterous. A bee only drinks the nectar it extracts himself.'

BB looked at the man who had dared interrupt him. Ravikant Girpade was the Chief Rally Officer and spokesperson for the opposition party. A double PhD in psychology and criminology from Pune University made him the perfect person to provide insights into the minds of his co-panelists. He was a regular on BB's show, whose viewers loved him for his earthy one-liners and sharp dressing sense. Today, he was attired in a black three-button suit made from the finest wool available on Savile Row and a lustrous red tie done in a perfect double-Windsor Knot. He spoke like a politician but dressed like a corporate honcho.

BB set in position the lock of hair, that had strayed onto his forehead, with practiced flourish and looked at Girpade. 'Unfortunately, Dr Girpade, I was young and stupid and had no idea that the going rate was 300. I ended up giving Rs 2,000. Dad had been really mad at me that night.' His eyes were full of remorse, as he gingerly touched his cheek, reliving the beating from many years ago.

Girpade looked shocked, while Panja punched the air in delight. 'There you go, BB ji. If they had a rate-list you would have never got cheated and your dad would have not been angry at you.'

BB held up a hand in Panja's direction asking him to stop talking and addressed Girpade. 'To Dr Girpade and all my viewers, let me publicly apologize for that childhood mistake. I was seventeen then, and under the influence of MTV, communism and local liquor. But that was a one-time mistake. Ever since, I have not paid any bribe. My home has not had any water for the last month because the babus at the water department need a bribe to fix my broken meter and I have not given in. I've gone through four cans of my Fair & Square underarm-whitening deodorant already.'

'Dear BB ji, that's more like it. You had me worried for a minute. After all, if you become corrupt what hope does the rest of the nation have?' Girpade heaved a sigh of relief, before coming up with another of his gems, 'He who takes a naked picture of himself cannot complain if his mother finds it on the Internet.'

BB looked at Girpade with the look of affection he usually reserved for people who either slept with him, or could come up with intelligent statements such as this one. 'Well said, sir. Well said. Thank you for your kind words.'

Girpade grinned at this acknowledgement from the great BB and continued, his tone more charged this time. 'I am very saddened by the attitude of the learned Dr Panja. How will a common man afford a passport if it costs Rs 10,000? As the announcement suggests, they won't even accept cards or cheques. Only cash. Can you imagine how much of a hassle this is? Who carries that much money on them? If people are forced to carry huge bundles of cash, it will only lead to an increase in robberies and pickpocketing. Maybe next they

Day 1: Last Man Standing

will come up with a scheme to allow registered thieves to rob your house once a month!'

Girpade thumped the desk in anger, his clean-shaven face contorted by the anguish arising due to this contemptuous statement of the old man who was sitting next to him, looking on happily, in part because he was busy scratching his itchy testicles, his hands working away, hidden from the cameras by the desk.

Girpade raised a hand and pronounced, 'I am just disappointed with this proposal. It is appalling that Chhote Sarkar and Panjaji would bear such a contemptuous attitude towards an issue so close to so many hearts. He is getting old; maybe he should retire and spend time playing carom-board with Chhote Sarkar, who has no business to be in politics anyway.'

He continued. 'Bribery is against Indian culture. Why do you think Lord Ram did not bribe his mother to avoid going for his *vanvaas*? Why was it that his army had to struggle so much to defeat Raavan, when they could have just bribed the evil king's generals to bowl a few no-balls so that they could score some easy runs, sorry wins. Why?'

A bearded saffron-clad man sitting next to Girpade coughed deliberately and cut him off. 'BB ji, Indian culture gave us the wondrous Neem, king of herbs. Bribery, non-veg, and computers are all Western concepts that have invaded Indian culture today. Our country is a land of peace, purity and calm. I would like to tell your viewers about my latest Neem-based cooking oil that is guaranteed to teach our children the right moral values, decrease the risk of heart attack and help your stock investments double in six months.'

The producers played a loud sound of a drum roll and zoomed in on BB's angry face, before he burst into a tirade. 'Baba Neemacharya, how many times have I told you to not plug your products on my show. How hard is it for you to understand that?'

Baba Neemacharya held his ears in a reconciliatory gesture and said, 'Sorry BB ji, I forgot. I think I must have missed taking my Neemnemonic memory fortification tonic last night. It does wonders for your brain power and is especially useful for children preparing for IIT-JE...'

'ENOUGH!' BB slammed the pen on the floor and pressed a buzzer on his desk. Immediately, four bouncers came rushing, held up the Baba from his shoulders and carried him to a corner of the studio where a steel door with vertical bars opened up to reveal what looked like a prison cell. The Baba was deposited in the BB jail and the door duly locked with a massive lock that weighed no less than five kilos and could be opened only with BB's finger scan.

'Now you stay there and think about what you did wrong. I sentence you to two hours in the BB Jail.' BB slammed a hammer on his desk and pronounced the verdict.

The show broke for commercials as a team of doctors rushed to BB to check his blood pressure, pulse rate and blood sugar level to make sure that he wasn't too enraged. Satisfied that he was doing fine, they retreated to their section of the studio as the show resumed.

'BB ji, I am sorry to see Baba Neemacharya breaking the rules of your show so casually. I hope he comes out of BB Jail a more mature person. Remember, my friend,' Girpade pointed his fingers heavenwards and proclaimed, 'A train that runs on the wrong track and a man who talks back to his wife – nobody can save them from a painful end.'

BB raised his left hand at Girpade like a traffic policeman regulating a busy intersection and pointed his right one at the fourth person on the panel, who was a young man with a stubble and a receding hairline, wearing a crumpled black Che Guevara T-shirt, and busy typing away on his phone.

'Let's move to the fourth guest for today – 30-year-old Adarsh Pandey, who is a social media celebrity. Adarsh has close to 50,000 Twitter followers who hang on to each of his key insights into modern politics and what ails our nation.'

'Adarsh, what are your thoughts on this discussion? I notice you've been tapping away on your phone. I presume you've been live-tweeting today's proceedings. Isn't that what you guys call it?'

BB then looked into Camera #7 and let out a deep sigh. 'I was never much of a technology person. In our days we would get out, stick posters in the middle of the night and go door-to-door for campaigning during the Baroda University elections. We now live in a very different world, with Twitter and Facebook and all of this computer stuff.'

He looked at Adarsh and repeated his question, 'So Adarsh, my dear friend, what do you think?'

Adarsh looked up from his phone, visibly excited. 'This is awesome! The Big Bee just retweeted me!' The incredulous looks from the others made him return to the room and the discussion at hand.

'Chhote Sarkar,' he said, settling into the chair as he rolled his eyes, 'is a joke. The government wants to legalize corruption while millions of people are rotting away in hunger and lakhs of young students are sitting jobless at home playing pirated versions of *Call of Duty-free* and *Grand Theft Autorickshaw*. Do you have any idea how they will be able to afford even a bribe for a petty traffic offense if they remain unemployed?'

Panja peered in Adarsh's direction, and cut him off saying, 'Young man, don't worry. We will make sure everybody gets employment. As a responsible and secular government, we will ensure that the minority communities get special discounts on the published rate-cards so that they don't feel victimized and everybody can afford to bribe to get their work done. In fact, we will bring out the Right to Bribery Bill in the next Parliament session when our government gets back to power.'

Adarsh laughed loudly and continued, his voice shaky from the excitement of being on television for the first time in his life, discussing a topic close to his heart. 'Are you serious, sir? This is your answer? What have we achieved, so many years after independence? We are at the bottom of the list on most world rankings – per-capita income, health, corruption, education, to name a few. Half the country is wallowing in poverty while the rich keep getting richer. The government clearly doesn't want poor people to get out of poverty, because they are the vote-banks, to be given false assurances and alcohol bottles that buy their silence. How will legalizing corruption help? I fail to understand!'

He wasn't done yet. He looked at BB as he spoke now. 'This government has failed us. Democracy has failed us. The Great

Liberator was a bloody liar. We are a complete and utter mess. I feel we should just ask the army to take over the country. That is our only hope.'

Panja got up from his desk, quickly retracting his fingers from their warm comfort zone inside his pajamas. The fingers were soon redeployed to point in Adarsh's direction. 'This is treason. This boy has no idea what he is talking about. He should be sent to jail for disrespecting our democracy. You ungrateful young man! How dare you talk so disrespectfully of the Great Liberator? WE WILL NOT TAKE THIS LYING DOWN!'

Girpade also got up and kept a hand on Panja's shoulder, 'Sir ji, let's not get carried away. It is the misdeeds of your government that have made the youth so distrustful of the democratic process. It is all your fault.'

'You scoundrel, Girpade. Mind your language,' Panja's face was red with anger and his breathing laboured. He swung his right hand in the general direction of Girpade's torso and – much to BB's delight – found his target. Girpade was a modest man, a veritable size zero, five feet six inches tall, with a 29-inch waist and a gross weight of 60 kilos. Panja was taller but almost as frail. His body shook from the effort of hitting Girpade and he himself nearly collapsed.

The blow caught Girpade by surprise and he fell backwards, landing at the base of the chair upon which Adarsh was sitting. Not to be outdone, he recovered quickly and charged at Panja. Both men were soon on the ground and there were four pairs of limbs flying around as Cameras #7, #8, #9 and #10 kept a close watch, telecasting live images of the accomplished PhDs slugging it out.

BB looked at the latest fist-fest in his studio, sighed, stared into Camera #2 with the despair of a man who has just seen his wife in bed with the ugly neighbour who stole their newspaper every morning and said, 'Ladies and gentlemen, these are representatives of the two main political parties in the country. If this is our future, then God save the nation.'

The cameras kept rolling for the next 30 minutes, recording the tearing of Panja's *kurta*, Panja grabbing Girpade's tie and spinning him around like a frantic rat and Adarsh frantically live-tweeting every moment of the encounter.

This episode would see a massive jump in the TRP ratings of B for Buddhi. Adarsh would end up getting plenty of new Twitter followers. Baba Neemacharya would sell some more of his Neem products, even if it had meant serving time in the slimy cell of BB Jail. Girpade would make a trip to the hospital to get a tetanus shot after Panja bit him on his nose but they would both be back on the show soon. They always came back, like naughty but loyal puppies.

BB's Blackberry buzzed. It was a text message.

'My dear Buddhu. You can't imagine how hot I am for you right now. So proud of you! XOXO'

DAY 2

THE GREAT LEADERS

AdarshBharatiya@AdarshBharatiya

Ultimately, elections in our country just boil down to voting for the party you hate less.

BhaktLal@BhaktLalMP

I hope that Badi Sarkar becomes my mother in my next life.

PatliiKamar@PatliiKamar

Chhote Sarkar is soooo hawt. I literally peed my pants after watching him speak.

FerozWriter@FerozWriterIIMA

Eat your thoughts, Chhote Sarkar says. I hope he doesn't end up eating his words.

Chhichhora@Chhichhora

@PatliiKamar No you didn't.

Swamy@Swamy1959

I have confirmed news that Badi Sarkar is not Chhote Sarkar's real mother.

BowWowBreaking@ BowWowBreaking

Tonight at 11, we look at how Indian government bought toothless submarines without a single weapon for 83,000 crores.

The alarm went off at 5AM, just as it had for the last 35 years. Ambika Pandey was already up, just as she had been on most days of her three decades of service. Early to bed and early to rise was the mantra that her dad had taught her many years ago. Not that she had a choice. Her school commenced at 7AM and as the principal she couldn't afford to be late. The buck stopped with her and she would lose the right to shout at her staff if she became one of them. There was still a year to go before she retired.

She went through her morning chores of yoga, packing lunchboxes for her husband, son and daughter and was pouring out steaming hot cups of tea, laced with tulsi and ginger, low on sugar for the diabetic husband, more milk than water the way she liked it. This meant as a corollary that the men had also learnt to like their tea that way.

The husband retrieved the newspaper from the balcony of their modest apartment in the suburbs of Indraprastha and picked up his cup of tea. Last night, both of them had been full of pride as they sat down in front of the television to watch their son achieve something that nobody in their extended family ever had but she had ended up disappointed. He had been on national television – on the most hyped news show in the country – even though she was not particularly fond of the inherent sensationalism of the show and the arrogance of its anchor. Their very own Adarsh had been invited to B for Buddhi, via an email from the host Buddhiman Buddhiraja.

'Look at him,' she had commented. 'So casual in his approach to everything. So careless! We've just spoiled him with our love. He looks like a destitute. He hasn't even bothered to shave before going on television! God alone knows when he last took a shower. He could have worn a nice shirt and trousers on this special day but look at what he has chosen instead – that stupid Che Gerara T-shirt. Who is that man anyway? Some *adivaasi* (tribal)?'

The two had retired for the night without getting the chance to talk to Adarsh, who must have returned around midnight after the live show had ended and he got dropped off all the way from Gurgone, on the other side of town, the Indraprastha suburb where only cows and pigs dared to tread after hours.

As the couple sat at the dining table sipping their tea, Adarsh emerged from his room, clad in the same T-shirt and jeans from the night before, rubbing his eyes, his long hair in disarray, his gaze riveted to the phone in his hand as he walked towards the washroom.

'Look at him – no good morning. No *namaste*. Nothing! Are these the manners we've taught our son?' Madam frowned as she watched him go past, half-asleep, ignoring his parents.

The husband grabbed her hand to calm her down and looked lovingly at his wife of 33 years. She looked at him, surprised by the sudden show of affection. Her hair was tied up in an elegant bun. She had stopped dyeing her hair a few years back and it now lay atop her pretty face as a thick mass of silver. She was approaching 60 but her features were still sharp. He used to call her his very own Sharmila Tagore when they got married. He believed she looked just as pretty even now.

'Let him be. He is just a child,' he said. 'You need to stop worrying so much. You've just recovered from that terrible typhoid. Be calm and go to school peacefully. God knows what mess awaits you there.'

'Child? He is 30! Very soon he will marry and have his own children. How long can he continue to behave so immaturely? We aren't going to be around forever.'

Adarsh emerged out of the washroom a few minutes later, still fidgeting with his phone. His mother asked him to come to the table.

'Sir, may I offer you some tea?'

'*Ma*...why are you two making such a racket this morning? What does a man need to do to get some sleep in this house?' He threw up his hands in despair, but soon returned to typing away frantically on the phone.

'Did you apply that neem paste last night for your hair?' She

Day 2: The Great Leaders

asked him. He made a face to show that he couldn't care less about it.

'Did you recharge my mobile? I don't have any balance left at all.'

He gave her an apologetic look. 'Sorry *ma*, I forgot.'

'Of course you forgot. The only thing you remember is Twitter. When your parents are too old to fend for themselves you should pack us off to an old-age home. You clearly have enough to worry about already – how many 'likes' you've got on Facebook or how many Twitter followers you added last night. And just look at your hair – it's all falling off! This is all because you don't step away from the computer. And you won't even take the medicine I get for you.'

'Come on, ma. Don't start lecturing me so early in the morning; you'd much rather save some for your school. I will recharge your phone online right away.' He started moving towards his room when he suddenly remembered the previous night's show. 'Oh, did you guys watch B for Buddhi last night?'

Madam looked at dad and then at Adarsh. 'Yes, we did. I think you should be more careful about making such bold statements on national television. They will take you away and put you in a jail if you keep messing with such powerful people. Why did you need to say all that about senior people such as Panja and Chhote Sarkar? And couldn't you find a better shirt to wear on national television?'

'Che Guevara, *ma*. He was a Marxist revolutionary. I was trying to make a statement with it.'

The wall clock's pendulum swung to signal it was 6:30AM. Madam sighed.

'I have to go to school now but we need to talk, Adarsh. I am worried. You need to start showing signs of maturity now.'

She grabbed the car keys, picked up her bag and marched off, the black cotton sari with Rajasthani motifs on the border swishing around her ankles as she walked. Adarsh went back to bed while his father proceeded to read the newspaper for the next one hour. There was a picture of Panja slapping Girpade on B for Buddhi's latest episode on page 5, with the caption 'The War Begins'.

*

Ambika Madam reached the gate of the school and honked. It was ten minutes to 7AM. The guard should have opened the gate by now.

'I take two weeks off from school and these people forget everything. Idiots!' She honked impatiently again.

It was a few minutes before the guard came running to open the gate. He was not wearing his uniform and from his dishevelled look it was clear that he was not expecting any visitors at this time. He looked at Madam's car with disbelief. She had said she would join work on Wednesday. Today was only Monday. The old fox had returned early to catch the staff by surprise.

'Ram Prasad, Madam was away so you have forgotten the school protocols?' She rolled down the window of her car to scold the watchman.

'No, no, Madam ji. I just got a little late in waking up today. It is getting so cold these days.' He was wrapped in the brown shawl she had gifted him last year on Diwali and she could smell the alcohol on his breath.

She drove in and parked the car in the slot reserved for the principal. After two weeks away, she did not want to start the day with an argument with the watchman. There was going to be more to fix for sure.

She reached her desk and watched the teaching staff trickle in one-by-one to sign their attendance on the register in her office. A few were on time while most of the others sauntered in at least half-an-hour late. The last one, a particularly difficult chemistry teacher, gasped when she strolled into the office at 9AM humming a Yo Yo Funny Singh song and noticed Madam sitting there. 'Madam I had loose motions this morning,' she said sheepishly. Madam had already marked her absent for the day.

During the school assembly, she addressed the students and staff.

'Good morning, children.' She loved starting the day with a greeting. Students liked her, especially when she was in a good mood. Children in trouble were known to tremble with fear at the prospect of being taken to her office. And it was not just students

Day 2: The Great Leaders

but also the teachers who were afraid to confront her most of the time. Of course, on occasion, they would gang up against her and use the power of democracy to overrule the strict disciplinarian in her. But such occasions were few and far between.

'Good morning, Madam,' the two thousand students of the school responded.

'It is December. In a few months you will be taking the final exams. Our school has been among the best schools in the city for the last ten years and I am sure we will continue the tradition this year, too.

'Are you all studying hard for the exams?' She asked. The students responded with a chorus of yeses. Madam smiled. She loved addressing her students every morning. They were the secret to her energy.

'I want to talk to you today about an important event that is going to take place soon. Our school is one of the voting centres for the upcoming elections and your teachers and I will be on election duty. I hope you all understand the importance of democracy. It is a government *of the people, for the people* and *by the people*. Our forefathers gave up their lives to attain independence to make way for democracy. It is very important that your generation appreciates their sacrifices and uses your power of voting when you are adults. The youth are this country's future and it is in your hands that the country can flourish. Always believe in the power of a billion people casting their votes and choosing the government they want. This is the most peaceful and fair way of electing a government of our choice. Violence leads to anarchy, remember that. Revolutions may look good in movies but they are not desirable in real life.'

She paused to catch her breath. Earlier she could speak on and on for hours. The advancing age had reduced her stamina.

She continued, 'Democracy isn't just about the government. It is about all of us in every sphere of life; at school, in our homes, with friends and family. The important thing is not to impose your decisions on others but to try to take everybody along, build consensus, and listen to everybody's viewpoints before taking a decision. That is the key. Nobody likes dictatorships.'

Some of the teachers standing in the crowd smirked. Dictatorship was exactly what they called her style of working. But then, the way she saw it, there was only so much democracy one could practice with a bunch of undisciplined teachers who differed from monkeys only in not being able to swing from trees. Madam had tried being democratic but it just meant that no decisions got taken and people never took ownership of their work.

*

'So who can tell me how we can get more collaboration across our divisions and improve the productivity of our organization? Adarsh?'

Adarsh awoke from his slumber with a start. The meeting had been dragging on for two hours and he was bored of the new division head rambling on and on about his boring agenda. They changed these senior managers every six months to introduce fresh blood into the mix and every time the new person would launch some big initiatives that fizzled out almost before they had been rolled out properly. Adarsh found it especially tiresome to sit through such strategy sessions. He felt jealous of his colleague and buddy Samarth, who had an uncanny ability to sleep with his eyes open.

To make matters worse, he couldn't take his phone out of the pocket during the session. That was a recipe for disaster, especially now that many of his colleagues knew that he was very active on social media platforms. It was nothing less than torture especially on a day when his phone was abuzz with one notification after another. The picture he had tweeted last night – of Girpade and Panja grappling with each other's flailing limbs on the floor of BB's studio – had gone viral and had already crossed one lakh views and received 1462 RTs (re-tweets) when he walked into the conference room. Every time the phone vibrated with a notification, his fingers twitched to look into his phone screen to see the latest score, or check out his newest celebrity follower. This was the stuff social media enthusiasts dreamt of. He had been at the right place at the right time. Only 12 hours had passed since the episode was aired live and he had already gained 7,000 new followers. He couldn't wait to check his latest TwitterRat score and his updated rank in the

Day 2: The Great Leaders

list of top Twitter users in the country. He would easily crack the top 50 now…he was really excited!

However, for now, there was the question raised by the boss that had to be answered. 'Sure, Amit. We need to improve collaboration across divisions so that people are able to better relate their work to the bigger picture and understand the vision of the organization to maximize their full potential,' he blurted out the stock statement they always liked to hear.

'Err, that doesn't really answer the question, but okay. Anybody else?'

Adarsh tuned out of the conversation and stared at his watch. There was another half-an-hour to go. He was tired, starving and anxious to check out his Twitter account but he couldn't afford a mistake here. The last director had fired a manager on-the-spot for yawning during one such strategy-making session. However, his boredom resurfaced within a few minutes and his thoughts began to drift.

Mom had given him a lecture on discipline and focus early in the morning but that was okay. Democracy had failed the country and the hoopla around the power of the vote was meaningless, given that all politicians were corrupt. The situation was hopeless and democracy was just making jt worse.

Adarsh didn't always understand his parents. They were so naive; always ranting about Twitter and Facebook and other assorted things. Adarsh had become a rebel over the years, stifled by his parents' constant need for discipline and honesty. He had not told them of the first time he had bribed a traffic policeman with Rs 20 to let him off when caught riding his motorcycle without a helmet, or how he would sneak into his girlfriend's hostel room on Saturday nights while his parents were asleep at home assured that their son was in a study group at a friend's place.

Thanks to last night's TV appearance, he had become a minor celebrity. Congratulatory messages were pouring in from friends who had seen him on the controversial show whose clips were now running all over the news channels. He had been a part of history. He had counted at least 20 'real' celebrities who had started following him on Twitter, including the Big Bee.

But then last night had been an experience so unique that he couldn't stop thinking about it. He still vividly remembered walking into the studio where he found BB, Panja, Neemacharya and Girpade chatting over tea and *paneer pakodas*. They were laughing and backslapping each other like college buddies at an alumni meet. Neemacharya had even clicked a selfie of the group with everyone holding a *pakoda* in their hands.

The one whose personality seemed to tower above all else had been BB. Adarsh had never seen anyone quite like him. The man had the fashion sense of a Bollywood hero, the swagger of a rock star, and the confidence of the Australian cricket team of the 90s. Adarsh noticed the arrogance with which he spoke to his staff and wondered if the human resources team at his own office would allow even a senior director to talk to a member of staff with such condescension. There would be immediate complaints filed and matters escalated. Nobody accepted that kind of behaviour these days but with BB it seemed different. Adarsh had seen him summon a young girl who was probably an intern, tear a report she had prepared and throw the torn bits of paper on her face and then tell her that she would not be writing any reports for the next two weeks but her only job would be to fetch tea for him every three hours. She burst into tears, but politely asked him if he liked masala tea or ginger, before running away sobbing into the collar of her top.

His followers on Twitter wanted him to confirm rumors that even though BB wore a fancy jacket on camera, he only wore pajamas underneath but Adarsh couldn't comment on such questions. They had made him sign a 50-page non-disclosure agreement. What happened in the Bow Wow studio clearly had to remain within the confines of the Bow Wow studio.

As the meeting dragged on, Adarsh's eyes started getting uncontrollably droopy. There was a moment's silence in the room as everybody turned to watch the 30-year-old manager of a team of ten developers snore loudly, oblivious to his surroundings.

*

Day 2: The Great Leaders

Madam's phone rang. It was the Big Boss from their central office. 'Hello, Madam. How are you? *Typhoid theek ho gaya?*'

'Good morning, sir. Yes I am feeling much better now, all thanks to your blessings,' she said. They liked their egos to be massaged a little.

'Okay, very good.' He paused for a few seconds. 'How are the students looking for the finals? We want to target best results. *Ekdum* top results for this year.' We have got instructions straight from Badi Sarkar who would not be happy with anything less than perfect.

She responded with an optimistic answer, 'Sir, the students are looking good. God willing, we might even be able to achieve a 100% pass percentage this year.'

'No, Madam. We can't wait for God this time. You need to work your magic and do whatever it takes.' Another pregnant pause before he proceeded. 'You are smart. I am sure you understand. Do *whatever* it takes. We just want the numbers.'

Madam sighed with frustration. She fully understood what he wanted. This was happening in most schools, as she had heard from reliable sources. Teachers would walk into classrooms during exams and drop a few hints here and there. The children were happy to get the easy way out. Parents were happy that their kids were being looked after. Big Boss was happy to report increasing pass percentages. Badi Sarkar was happy that her government had literacy numbers to show off. No one seemed to care that the schools were producing students who couldn't solve basic math problems to save their lives.

'No, sir. I don't think I understand what you mean. I will ask the teachers to spend more time in their classes and make sure the students understand the concepts before the exams begin.'

There was no response on the other side for a few seconds.

'Hello? Sir, are you there?'

He sighed. 'Yes. Yes, I am still here. I have to go now. You think about this. I will try to stop by some time.'

She put the phone down. Things were getting worse with every passing year but this was a new low. She had just been asked to participate in institutionalized cheating. She had heard of how the principal in Great Liberator Nagar School had herself walked into classrooms and written down answers on the blackboard during the final exams last year. They had given her a trophy for her great performance in improving the results of the school but even then she had ended up behind Madam's school. Madam was untouchable. She didn't need cheating to deliver results. That was not how Madam rolled.

She would never participate in such a disgusting activity. Ambika Madam was clear about that.

No sooner than she had hung up the phone, she heard the clatter of footsteps on the hallway leading to her office.

The sound grew louder and she could soon hear heavy leather boots on the concrete floor outside her office and then the scarred face of Ram Manohar Bisht, the contractor, who had built the auditorium in the Great Liberator Nagar School, appeared. The buzz was that they had received a sanction of Rs 50 lakhs for the building out of which he took five, the principal took ten, Big Boss got ten and with the remaining money, he had built an auditorium without a stage.

Bisht entered the room and bowed his head in a *namaste*, 'Good morning, Madam ji. May you have a long life.' He was bent double almost to the stomach and Ambika could see the balding crown of his head.

'Watch out, Bisht ji! You'll hit the table.'

Bisht straightened himself and flashed a nervous smile at Madam. His teeth were decaying and stained from years of chewing tobacco. His moustache needed trimming. His grey safari suit was in need of dry-cleaning. His dirty shoes needed polishing. His entire demeanour screamed needy. Madam wished someone would invent a washing machine in which you could put such people on a thirty-minute cycle and they'd come out neat and clean, inside and out.

'Madam ji. How have you been? I heard your enemies had some illness. Typhoid, was it?'

She smiled. 'I wish my enemies had typhoid, but it was me this time.'

Day 2: The Great Leaders

He laughed loudly, filling the room with the smell of pan masala. 'Madam ji, I just love your sense of humor.'

'What brings you here, Bisht ji?' She leaned back in her chair and peered at him from behind her glasses, the legs fastened to her person with a pearl chain that went around her neck.

'Madam ji, I heard you have got a sanction to build a swimming pool in your school. This is so great. The poor kids from our area will also be able to enjoy swimming like the rich children of public schools.'

She frowned. The sanction had come in just last evening, and the officer in-charge had informed her on the phone. How did this guy know already?

She continued staring at him, daring him to say what he really wanted to.

He leaned forward and placed his elbows on the table. 'Madam ji, I thought I will talk to you about the swimming pool. I was wondering if we could work together on the project.'

'Have you ever made a swimming pool before?'

'*Arre* Madam ji, what is there in a swimming pool? Dig a big hole, put tiles and fill with water.' Surely Ram Manohar Bisht can manage that.'

'Very well, then. We will send out a request for proposals and you could submit yours then.'

He pulled his chair closer to the table. 'Madam ji, why go through the hassle of tender-*wender*? We can work something out ourselves, if you don't mind.'

She took a deep breath and replied. 'Oh so you want a deal. What's the going rate?'

'Madam ji, it is standard. You keep twenty per cent and I'll keep ten per cent. Big Boss ji will want his cut, too. If the money runs short, we will build a smaller pool. These poor people will be happy with anything. Nobody will know.'

She exploded.

'BISHT JI, HOW DARE YOU TRY TO BRIBE ME? GET OUT OF MY OFFICE BEFORE I CALL THE POLICE!'

Her peon and a security guard came running as she rang the bell and escorted the contractor out. Madam helped herself to a glass of water and did *Pranayaam* for the next ten minutes to get her breathing back to normal.

*

The imported SUV cruised through the highway towards its destination, a dusty settlement of about 500 Broccoli farmers. They were three hours from Indraprastha and had a few more hours to go.

'*Bhaiya,* drive a little carefully, please. They say that politicians don't have a backbone but I don't want to prove it wrong by getting mine broken.' He nudged the driver as the car hit yet another jarring pothole at a speed of 100 kilometres per hour.

'Sorry, Chhote Sarkar. This bloody road is such a torture to drive.' He looked back at the young *kurta-pajama* clad passenger in the rear seat and grinned sheepishly. The last driver had lost his job within six months because Chhote Sarkar had complained. This one wanted a longer innings.

Chhote Sarkar sighed, 'This is unfortunately the story of the entire country. Going to the dogs, I tell you. These Orchid-wallahs will ruin the country one day. This state is also under their rule, isn't it?'

The aged gentleman sitting next to Chhote Sarkar slapped his head in disgust. 'Bablu, I have told you so many times. Try not to open your mouth, because invariably you end up speaking nonsense. This state is ours and we are driving through your mother's constituency. Didn't I ask you last night not to drink before trips?'

Chhote Sarkar pretended not to hear. He was busy looking out of the window, counting the number of sheep in the herd they were passing.

'Twenty-nine,' he announced.

The driver kept silent. The weirdo Panja had once broken the nose of a driver who smiled at one of Chhote Sarkar's gaffes. He knew very well that these 'trips', as Panja *sahab* called them, were serious business not to be trifled with.

'Concentrate, Bablu. Don't lose it now.' Panja kept a comforting

Day 2: The Great Leaders

arm on Chhote Sarkar's shoulder. Anger only made him more erratic. As Panja had once confided to his wife after checking all around, to make sure nobody was listening, every minute he spent with the stupid boy was torture, and he wondered if his offer to mentor some political sense into the boy had been a bad decision. Panja couldn't really complain, though. Badi Sarkar had rewarded him with the lucrative Ministry of Mobile Phones which, as everyone knew, was where all the action was these days. It was a fair bargain.

'Now listen,' he got Chhote Sarkar's attention with a cup of Blissful Blackberry ice-cream from the specially installed mini-refrigerator in the car and told him the plan. 'When we reach the village, we will find the most run-down house. You will then greet the people who live there, ask them how they are, what their problems are, find out their names and tell them that you will personally talk to the district collector to help them. Don't overdo it. Just stick to the questions listed on this sheet.' He handed him an A4 sheet of paper with a list of twenty questions.

'Memorize these. And don't goof up later. We have high expectations from you. You have to take care of this country. Don't disappoint us. Just do as I tell you.'

Chhote Sarkar took the list in his hand and started going over it, occasionally looking outside the window to check if there were any more sheep around.

A couple of hours later, he was done. On the back of the sheet he had scribbled a beautiful bird, ready to flutter its wings to fly away.

'What crap is this? Did you memorize the questions?' Panja suddenly woke up from his deep slumber, looked at him and took the paper from his hands.

'Yes, I am done. Don't worry.'

The driver announced that they were about to enter the village.

'Get ready, son. Your big test starts now.' Panja patted him on his back and spoke in a fatherly tone. The boy's failure was going to be his failure too. He didn't want to lose the mobile phone portfolio. The 7G auctions were coming up next year and were estimated to make the government a few lakh crores, of which a cool five per cent would make its way to his Swiss bank account. Thank God for technology. He had seen days when they used to come with suitcases full of cash. He had, at one point of time, a staff of twenty cash-counters, another five to watch them to make sure they weren't sneaking in a bundle or two and a couple more to keep an eye on the watchers. It was serious business.

The driver stopped his car in front of a small hut. There were a few television crew members milling around, their cameras setup in a semi-circle, the young journalists gossiping over cigarettes, some already interviewing locals about their thoughts at the prospect of such a big leader visiting their village, asking important questions such as *'Aapko kya lag raha hai, Chhote Sarkar ne apni stubble shave kari hogi ki nahi?'*

They noticed the SUV stop, recognized the familiar faces of the young leader and his elderly mentor sitting inside and everybody made a mad rush for the car and surrounded Chhote Sarkar as he stepped out onto the dusty ground.

Panja beckoned them to calm down and addressed the gathered journalists. 'What a surprise to see you all here. Chhote Sarkar wanted to keep this visit away from the media because he is not doing it for publicity. He is here because he genuinely cares for the welfare of our people.'

The gathered journalists, most of them fresh out of college, nodded attentively. Senior journalists didn't bother with assignments related to Chhote Sarkar anymore, even more so when they involved driving to the middle of nowhere. A cameraman sniggered, immediately covering it up with a bout of coughing. They all knew that the news of this event had 'leaked' from the party's office.

The questions started.

'Chhote Sarkar, what brings you here?'

'Chhote Sarkar, what will you do to bring this village out of poverty?'

'Chhote Sarkar, what whiskey were you drinking at that five-star hotel last night?'

The reporter who asked the last question was suddenly whisked away by an unknown shadow, to be maimed and thrown away in one of the ditches nearby.

Day 2: The Great Leaders

Chhote Sarkar looked uncomfortable in the glare of all the cameras. He took a deep look at the gathered crowd, hesitated and ran back inside his car. Panja followed him and spent the next 20 minutes cajoling him into coming outside.

As Chhote Sarkar gingerly got out of the car, his *kurta* caught in the door and there was the sound of a loud tear as a big chunk of the back of the *kurta* got ripped off. He hesitated but bravely stood in front of the mediapersons. One of the technicians quickly setup a microphone in front of him.

Chhote Sarkar cleared his throat and addressed the assembled people. 'You know, we all think that people are poor. People are rich. People are happy. Unhappy. It is all nonsense. There is no poverty or richness. It is all here.' He thumped his chest and his bracelet caught in the chain around his neck, resulting in a loud metallic clink.'

He laughed nervously while tucking his chain back under the collar of his *kurta*. 'No, no…I didn't mean gold chains.

'You see, our bodies are rich and our brains are a powerhouse with more energy than the biggest nuclear plant. Do you know of how rishi-munis of the past lived on for years without eating a single grain of rice?'

One of the journalists broke into a violent bout of coughing. Chhote Sarkar carried on. 'You don't have *dal-chawal*? Eat your thoughts. Imagine that you are sitting in Indraprastha's fanciest restaurant and eating *tandoori* chicken with the softest of *naans*. Even that's enough for the brain. You should try it. Ultimately, we are all mere souls. Souls don't need any food. They thrive on thoughts. Enrich your thoughts. That's all that matters.'

He coughed slightly, cleared his throat, and said. 'I need water.' His driver rushed to the car to grab a bottle of water but Chhote Sarkar gestured him to stop. He spoke to a teenage boy from the village standing nearby, listening keenly to what he was saying.

'Where do you get water in the village?'

The boy pondered over the question for a little while, and then pointed towards a well about 100 meters away from their location. Chhote Sarkar kept an arm around the boy's neck and said, 'Okay, today I'll drink the same water you drink.'

Panja looked like he had seen the ghost of Genghis Khan. He whispered something in Chhote Sarkar's ear but he just laughed and moved on, his arm still around the neck of the boy, who was smiling. Nobody drank from that well; they all had water filters at home.

People from the village and the group of journalists started following Chhote Sarkar, carefully stepping over piles of cow dung and avoiding the thorny bushes along the path. They reached the dilapidated well. The periphery was broken in parts and there were three stray dogs lazing right next to the undamaged part of the structure, the rest having crumbled under the ravages of Mother Nature.

Chhote Sarkar peeped inside the well. It was a good 100-feet drop to the surface of the water. There was a rope attached to the pulley and an iron bucket at its end. He would need to lower the bucket in the water, fill it up and then pull it back all the way up.

He peeped over his shoulder at the crowd intently watching him. The TV journalists were beaming live pictures, announcing to the world that this was a historic moment when the brave, new hope of the nation was going to drink water from a well – water that could infect people with jaundice, dysentery and God knows what else! The boy who had led Chhote Sarkar, winked at his buddies. The only purpose for which the villagers used the water from this well was to wash their animals and even *they* tried to resist that.

Chhote Sarkar loosened the rope and started lowering it down. He had never done this before. He had never even seen a well before. The iron bucket was surprisingly heavy. As he let the rope down, his hands lost their grip for a few seconds and the bucket plummeted down. Chhote Sarkar fumbled and managed to grab the rope tightly just as the bucket hit the water. By this time it had gathered momentum and the bucket had started to gain weight as water filled inside.

The crowd gasped as the bucket asserted its weight and Chhote Sarkar plunged into the well, landing with a loud splash.

*

Day 2: The Great Leaders

There was a knock on the door and the new girl with blue eyes entered his room. Baba looked up at the disturbance and asked the two girls massaging his legs to stop.

'Why in the name of the great neem tree must someone always come in with that stupid phone every time I am in the middle of important work,' he squinted his eyes, looked at the name tag on her chest and added, 'Girl 45?'

There were no names in the ashram. Only Baba and numbers. All 45 of them. All girls. Baba had transcended the boundaries imposed by names and assigned numbers to the girls when they joined the service of the neem tree. They came in for the love of God, neem supplements that promised to make their skins flawless and a salary of Rs five lakh per month as promised by the agency that screened candidates. The non-disclosure agreement they signed, had strict terms that forbade communication with the outside world. A girl had tried leaking a video of one of the sessions but Baba found out and she was never seen again. He had told the others that she had decided to move to a new land where there were no mobile phones, secret videos or YouTube.

Some of the girls stayed on after their two-year contracts ended for the love of Baba, who was a lover par excellence. 'Love is the supreme form of devotion to God,' he would tell them, before taking one or more of them to his chamber for a session of service to God. And also to the great neem tree.

'Baba, it is Badi Sarkar. She w…w…wants to talk to you.' Girl 45 had been at the ashram for a week now but still stammered while talking to him. She was an untamed animal waiting to be reined in by the master.

He smiled as he took the phone from her, patted her on the head, and answered the phone, gesturing to the three girls to stay silent.

'Badi Sarkar, how are you?' He spoke in that British accent, which endeared him to the girls. They loved it when he beckoned them with a finger and in Queen's English, asked, 'What's for supper, my lovely?' He had learnt to speak like the Brits from the naive Aggarwal who had lived in London for 20 years before returning to the country, to the good fortune of the Baba.

Badi Sarkar was not happy tonight. She never was. So clingy. So demanding. *I want this. I want that. My son, this. My son, that.* The Baba rolled his eyes, looked lovingly at Girl 45, 29, and 33 and asked them to leave him alone for a while. They quietly left the room.

'It's him, isn't it?'

'Oh, he is going to be on the show? I think we should double his dose of the neem juice. It will improve his energy levels and he will speak in a crisper accent. Neem is the truth.'

Her voice crackled over the phone receiver. She was sobbing now.

'Badi Sarkar, control yourself. There is no use worrying so much. Plenty of people wet their beds even at the age of forty or fifty. *Abhi toh* he is only thirty-five. Happens with a lot of people. Everything will be okay. You will win the election. He will become Prime Minister. It is his destiny. It is what he was made for. Let's do one thing. Let's put him on the super-winner formula, which I wanted to save for the last minute. It is very powerful but can have some side effects. Neem is the truth.'

She wanted to know the side effects. The Baba slapped his forehead in frustration. *Shouldn't have mentioned side effects. Now she will have a panic attack within minutes.*

'No, no, Badi Sarkar. It is nothing. Nothing that a good scoop of Belgian ice-cream cannot fix. Just make sure that you use the Naughty Nuts flavor, one scoop within ten minutes of a sip of the formula. Neem is the truth.'

She seemed satisfied.

He pressed the buzzer next to his bed asking for the girls to come in as he hung up the phone. The girls entered and he smiled lovingly as they walked towards him, in that carefully rehearsed walk that the agency had trained them for. They were wearing truncated versions of blouses barely covering the essentials and saris gracefully wrapped around their legs. He had seen the way the ladies dressed in old mythological serials on Doordarshan and commissioned a top Bollywood designer, one of his loyal followers, to create similar dresses for his girls. These exotic clothes, along with pearl necklaces and *payals* around the ankles, made up their uniform, as specified in the contract.

Day 2: The Great Leaders

The girls' tender skin was glowing from the neem revitalizer formula that he had found on the Internet, added some ingredients, and made his own. They used the neem shampoo that kept their hair light, bouncy and free of dandruff. The neem health drink they drank every day when they woke up, kept their digestion system working efficiently. Wasn't that the secret to a healthy body?

Baba Neemacharya was all about the neem tree. He had shared the great benefits of the tree of the gods with the world and was now one of the four thousand unofficial billionaires in the country. His income tax returns mentioned an income of Rs 50 lakhs last year, conveniently missing out on many zeros. He had gone from being a good-for-nothing driver in the dusty streets of Lucknow to being a billionaire in five years, and was one of the youngest members of the Unofficial Billionaires of India Association (UBIA), of which he was currently the General Secretary. He attributed his success to the great neem tree, grace of God and that stupid, childless, family-less Aggarwal, who had signed off his fortune to him on his deathbed. He gave away property worth Rs 12 crores to his driver, simply because he had made tea for him every morning and helped him to the bathroom when he had to pee. Who said dedication and loyalty *didn't pay*?!

As the girls started applying the neem revitalizer tonic on his legs, he gazed at the ceiling, covered entirely by a mirror that went from wall to wall. He had struggled to find any company that could provide a single piece of mirror for an uninterrupted, seamless view before German engineering came to his rescue. India had neem but for anything more than that, one had to look outside.

As the Baba lay on his bed, his hands rested behind his neck, he gazed at his reflection in the mirror. He had come a long way. The nights of sleeping hungry on the pavements of Lucknow was a remote but painful memory. He had enjoyed *tandoori* chicken for dinner a few hours ago, with a full bottle of wine. He struggled to recognize himself in that mirror. He didn't look like the Mangat Ram he used to be. Those ugly rashes all over the face were hidden behind that massive beard. It itched so much that he wanted to shave it off. But then people in the country would never accept a clean-shaven baba who gave a two-hour lecture on the benefits of a natural lifestyle every morning on TV. He had gone from having a single meagre meal in a day to this luxurious lifestyle. His wife would have never approved, but then she had never approved of anything he did. God bless her soul. And Aggarwal's too. He had struggled in his last few days. That slow poison in his daily *dal* over dinner really ate up his insides.

No, he didn't want to go back to that old self. It lay hidden beneath some deep crevices in his mind and it was best left there. He gestured to the three ladies to stop massaging his feet and move their attention a little northwards.

There are things money can't buy. For everything else, there is more money. *Neem is the truth*, he thought to himself, stroking his flowing beard as the women worked away on his neem tree.

*

Mohammad Panja turned on the television as his daughter-in-law laid out dinner. BB's show was going to start in a few minutes. There was a 60-second news recap going on, with an invisible voice reading the headlines as a globe turned on its axis on the TV screen and a stop-watch counted down on the top-right corner.

'Teenage boy kills girl for cropping him out of a picture from her birthday party posted on Facebook.'

'Girl alleges sexual harassment against classmate who pestered her to follow him back on Twitter.'

'Best-selling writer Feroz Daadiwala starts 'Find the PM' initiative on Twitter.'

'Minister who posted Facebook update saying *'Badi bhookh lagi hai'* dismissed from the party for causing hurt to Badi Sarkar. Party workers burn two buses and a McDammit outlet to protest the insult to Badi Sarkar.'

'Actress Loveena Kapoor found eating French Fries. Loses prestigious film assignment titled *Dirty Dentures*.'

'In fresh show of support to Chhote Sarkar, Union Minister Bhakt Lal gets 'Chhote Sarkar for PM' tattooed on his forehead.'

'Indian cricket team announces the decision to remove bowlers altogether and only play with 11 batsmen.'

Day 2: The Great Leaders

The channel's infamous 'crying baby' logo appeared, followed by an advertisement of Scream energy drink, the show's sponsors. Panja had already started eating his dinner of steamed rice and chicken curry with his bare hands. He had not had any vegetables for the last 20 years, which was when he gave up vegetarianism. He claimed that chicken was the reason he was as strong as some 40-year-olds, despite being over twice as old.

The standard daily video montage of crying people started playing – babies, politicians, film-stars, cricketers – all crying away live on camera, while the theme song from a James Bond movie played in the background. B for Buddhi was on.

BB's smiling face soon filled the screen of Panja's 60-inch ultra HD TV.

'Good evening, ladies and gentlemen. Social media has taken over our lives. Facebook and Twitter are where all the action is right now. We have politicians regularly quarrelling on Twitter. We recently had the CEO of the famous Come To Us Technologies Limited resign via Twitter. Teenagers are spending more time being social on Facebook as against actually going out with their friends to play in the park. There is no escaping social media anymore. The downside is that this is now redefining relationships as friendships get torn apart by an accidental unfollow or by someone not liking your latest profile picture on Facebook.'

BB looked up at the camera, held up his phone, an older model of the once-ubiquitous Jokia, for viewers to see, and said, 'I don't even own a smartphone. I am still to jump on to the bandwagon. Hopefully I will not get left behind in this age of technology.'

'You are watching B for Buddhi, brought to you tonight by Scream, the energy drink that will leave you screaming for more. I am your host Buddhiman Buddhiraja. Tonight, we have four distinguished guests on our show who will discuss the impact of social media on our lives. We have famous writer Feroz Daadiwala, Minister of Luxury Cars Bhakt Lal, CRO of the opposition Orchid party Dr Ravikant Girpade, and Twitter celebrity Patlii Kamar, who has revolutionized the world of advertising by using her body as a walking billboard. We'll come to that in a minute.' BB smiled for the cameras and turned his chair to look at the panelists, like a butcher about to get down to work.

'Mr Feroz Daadiwala, let's begin with you. How has social media changed things for you?'

The celebrated writer of eight bestsellers, the writer whose latest book launch had ended in a stampede of teenage girls going crazy at the sight of his stubbled face, scratched his chin as he answered, 'BB, social media is the future. The youth of the country is paying attention to what is happening around them and making their presence felt. It is…'

The minister Bhakt Lal coughed and cut off Feroz. 'BB, allow me to also present my viewpoint. First, I would like to thank Badi Sarkar and Chhote Sarkar, who are my biggest inspirations in life. Chhote Sarkar is especially incredibly smart and talented and only if he becomes the Prime Minister, can we get rid of corruption in our great nation.'

'What?' BB exclaimed.

'There he goes again,' Girpade said, following up with a mock applause. 'Lal *sahab*, you need to stop kissing Chhote Sarkar's ass so much. Did you see what he did today? I say he FELL pretty low this time.'

The nubile Patlii Kamar interrupted Girpade, saying 'I think Chhote Sarkar is cute. I literally stop breathing the moment I see him speaking on TV.'

'Come on, surely you don't,' Feroz Daadiwala said.

Panja looked fondly at his television and felt proud that he had played a big role in the party's success in the media. It was he who had suggested to Badi Sarkar that the party conduct training camps where its nominated spokesmen would learn how to shout over each other to make their mark on news channels. The camps had been a massive success. Everybody would be seated in a group as part of a moderated discussion and were instructed to talk while a loud Bollywood item number played in the background, making it even more difficult to be heard. Answering the question was immaterial. They just had to talk loudly. Panelists could always fall back to praising Badi Sarkar and Chhote Sarkar when they ran out

Day 2: The Great Leaders

of words. There were no rules. The party had conducted such sessions every fortnight for a period of six months and the clear winners had been himself, Bhakt Lal and Chamcha Das. The other leaders fizzled out towards the end. They had been gruelling sessions but nevertheless, a perfect blend of vocal, physical and mental strength. Despite his age, Panja had showed the young leaders that they still had much to learn.

Back on the show, BB addressed Bhakt Lal. 'Minister Sir, what you said has no bearing on today's discussion but I am still tempted to ask a question. Why did you need to get that tattoo on your forehead? Doesn't it bother you to go around bearing Chhote Sarkar's name on your body permanently?'

Bhakt Lal laughed, 'Not at all. The missus was a little bothered and has gone to her mother's house saying that she will never come back but I don't care. I owe it to Chhote Sarkar. We all owe it to Chhote Sarkar. He just has to become our PM.'

And then he started shouting slogans.

'East or west, Chhote Sarkar is the best.'

'We don't want *roti*, we don't want car. All we care about is Chhote Sarkar!'

Panja nearly gagged on his chicken curry. Bhakt was not the only one. Everybody in the party was trying to outdo each other in bending over to that SOB, Son of Badi Sarkar, which was what Panja called him in private. He was an utter nincompoop, currently lying in hospital after the disaster earlier that day. Media channels hadn't stopped playing the tape of the grown-up man falling in slow motion and then being pulled back clinging to that rope, shaken and stirred. Parody videos that made fun of the way he sobbed uncontrollably once back on the ground were propping up on the Internet rapidly. This had been a PR nightmare.

He knew nothing of the art of politics. He didn't even know the difference between a *khokha* and a *peti* (*khokha* = 1 crore and *peti* = 1 lakh), significant terms when it came to discussing what was now called Cooperation Charges with builders or investment bankers looking to invest their dollars in the country. How was he going to conduct any business?

Then there was the idiot, the Madrasi minister, who had somehow managed to get hold of Chhote Sarkar's freshly cut nails and put them up for auction on eBay. They had sold for Rs 10 lakh which the sycophantic minister had donated to the party fund. Panja was sure that he himself had bought them. Needless to say, Badi Sarkar had been impressed. But then, she was a cow.

Panja rolled his eyes. He was counting on Chhote Sarkar to keep doing something stupid and ruining his chances, which would leave Panja in the running for the top job. He had already started working on getting Badi Sarkar's affections, having taken on the important task of doing the weekly grocery shopping for her. He had tried to get the assignment to stay in line at the gas station to refuel her CNG cars but the bloody Bhakt Lal had beaten him to that one and Chamcha Das had cried and grovelled at her feet until she gave him the assignment to water the lawn twice a day and get milk for Chhote Sarkar every morning. *Losers*, Panja thought.

On BB's show, Bhakt Lal had now taken out the party manual Rock On and On and looked like he was going to read from it. Panja was shocked. Rock On and On had been personally written by Badi Sarkar and was a compilation of the rules by which party members needed to live. It was the Bible for party members, who were expected to know all the rules by heart and follow them religiously. It was supposed to be confidential and never leaked to the public. The bastard Bhakt was playing some new game.

Feroz Daadiwala cut him off, 'Bhakt ji, all of this is fine but where is the PM?' It has been such a long time since he retired to the Himalayas to pray for the long life of Badi Sarkar, leaving a pair of Chhote Sarkar's slippers on his chair like Bharat had done in *Ramayana*. When is he coming back?'

BB shouted at Feroz and Bhakt, 'Gentlemen, I have to ask you to come back to the point of our discussion. Let's focus on social media.'

Patli Kamar seemed frustrated at not getting the time to speak. She finally got up on the table and rolled up her shirt revealing her midriff. It had something beautiful painted on it. Panja squinted his eyes and realized that it was an ad for a popular brand of shampoo.

Day 2: The Great Leaders

'Just wanted to say thanks to my sponsors and the five lakh Twitter followers who have helped me along the journey. I am literally jumping with excitement right now,' she said as she sat down on her chair, satisfied.

Bhakt was not done yet. Panja listened in horror as Bhakt Lal, Minister of Luxury Cars, started reading from the manual.

'All party members must always wear kurta-pajama, which must never be worn with sneakers.'

BB interjected, 'Sir, I have to ask you to stop now.'

Bhakt continued talking, 'All party members must have pictures of the Great Liberator in their wallets. This will protect them from all evil. All party members must always accept cash donations in non-sequential notes. These are hard to track down in case of investigations. Opposition leaders must only be assassinated by the approved panel of ISI certified Politician Control Agencies.'

Bhakt Lal realized that he had made a mistake and immediately cupped his mouth in horror. BB's eyebrows were raised at this unexpected admission of wrongdoing. His nostrils were flaring and his breath was visibly laboured, with the atomic bomb of outrage building up inside him.

Panja watched on with an incredulous look. This could be the end of Bhakt Lal's career. Excited, he took a large bite and found himself choking on a chicken bone stuck in his throat. Hearing his muffled cries for help, his son came running from the adjoining room and thumped his back a few times, eventually managing to dislodge the bone, just in time for him to notice Bhakt Lal burst into tears and run away from the studio. Meanwhile, BB had gone from his wheatish shade to orange to red to crimson and was now purple. It looked like he was unable to breathe. The remaining panelists quickly ducked under the table to avoid the aftermath of the impending explosion.

Over in the studio, the chief doctor watched in horror as BB appeared in trouble. He started to lead his team on to the floor to check his vitals but BB gestured to him to stop.

The producer pressed the EVACUATE button and red lights started blinking in the studio, accompanied by a loud alarm. The cameras were left on and focused on BB as the recording crew quickly rushed into a secure room created just for such days, out of harm's reach behind ten-inch thick steel walls, strong enough to withstand ballistic missiles.

BB looked like he was possessed. He started banging on his desk with his hammer, before picking up his laptop and throwing it straight into Camera #5. The lights went off soon after.

DAY 3

COBWEBS OF THE MIND

AdarshBharatiya@AdarshBharatiya

Dear Chhote Sarkar, WELL done. Hahahaha

Chhichhora@Chhichhora

A small leap for Chhote Sarkar, a giant leap for man, kind-of.

TheOrchidParty@TheOrchidParty

The Great Leader hopes that the government will not allow Orchid prices to rise any further.

FerozWriter@FerozWriterIIMA

Who needs third degree torture when you can drive on Indian highways instead?

BowWowBreaking @BowWowBreaking

Breaking: South Indian actress Perky Padma to gain 100 kilos for her next movie.

1

'Adarsh, are you ready?' Madam called out to Adarsh from her room while getting dressed for work. Adarsh was going to drive her to school because he needed the car later in the day. One of her teachers would drop her back home in the afternoon.

'Sure, *ma*. I just need to put on a jacket and we can leave whenever you are ready.' He was sitting at the table reading the newspaper while his dad sipped tea.

'Okay, let's go in five minutes. At least wash your face and tidy up your hair?'

Adarsh wasn't listening anymore. He seemed lost in the newspaper. Suddenly he shouted out to his mother. 'Check this headline out – 'BB Destroys Studio in a Fit of Rage.' Apparently last night BB outdid himself. He got so angry that he smashed all the cameras and destroyed a lot of furniture. Looks like that idiot Bhakt Lal got him really angry. His panelists had to be rescued by security guards before he could strangle them in his outrage against the admission of corrupt practices. Just the day I had to miss the show!'

'Oh, here's another one. A minister from the south is building a temple for Chhote Sarkar. I guess this was the only thing left to do; a temple for that genius who can't even get water from a well without falling inside it.'

Madam was ready to leave. Adarsh folded up the paper and grabbed the car keys.

She called out to Preeti, Adarsh's sister, who was still in bed. 'Shut the door after we leave, Preeti. The new maid should come today. Show her around, make sure she cleans the utensils properly and waters the plants outside. Also keep an eye on her. We need to be extra careful with the maids these days.'

They were en-route. As the car sped away towards Madam's school, Adarsh started talking about his favorite topic – Politics.

'Do you know that the idiot Mohammad Panja is mentoring Chhote Sarkar these days? They say that Chhote Sarkar is such a flop that Badi Sarkar had to find someone to teach him some sense. And the corrupt Panja took up the offer. They rewarded him with the mobile phone portfolio in return.'

'*Acchha*? But he is just a kid, isn't he? I think there is too much pressure on him.'

'Come on, *ma*. You are so naive. He is already thirty-five years old. Anyway, my problem is not with him but with the so-called leaders in his party, all clamoring for him to become PM despite the fact that he is an idiot. What nonsense is this?'

Madam pondered over the question.

Adarsh pointed at a giant hoarding of Chhote Sarkar by the side of the road. 'Look at the fraud, hands folded and looking so innocent. After the elections, we will never get to see him again because he'll be busy counting the money. I hear he has some strange health problems that are never disclosed to the public. Apparently Badi Sarkar consults your Baba Neemacharya for his treatment.

'I tell you *ma*, they are all the same. Equally corrupt. The opposition is no less. People keep ranting about the Great Leader as the one who will set things right. I am sure even he will turn out to be a fraud eventually.'

Suddenly, a car tried to overtake him from the left, nearly crashing into them, and Adarsh let out a barrage of expletives before opening the window and showing the driver a middle finger.

Madam looked at him in disbelief, 'Adarsh, what is wrong with you? How can you lose your temper so easily? Some day you'll get into trouble if you keep behaving like this.'

Her phone rang just as Adarsh was about to argue his case. Madam answered the call.

'Hello?'

'*Arre*, good morning to you too. What a pleasant surprise. We have heard so much about you.'

'Yes I agree, the conditions are very bad. I, too, am trying to avoid eating potatoes these days because they are so expensive.'

'Sure, sir, sure. We will definitely vote for you.'

Day 3: Cobwebs of the Mind

'Thank you, sir. You also take care.'

Adarsh looked at his mother quizzically as she hung up, her face lit up.

'Adarsh, you will not believe it.'

'Who was it, *ma*?'

'The Great Leader. He personally called me to ask for my vote. I wonder where he got my number though.'

Adarsh burst out laughing, 'Aww, my sweet, innocent mother. Did he respond to any of your comments?'

'Not really. Seemed to be in a bit of hurry, not even letting me finish before moving on to the next sentence.'

Adarsh smiled, '*Ma*, that was a recorded call. It wasn't really the Great Leader talking to you. I can't believe you actually talked to the automated call. This is hilarious.'

Madam sank back into her seat, embarrassed, and murmured, 'I had no idea.'

Adarsh couldn't stop laughing, 'Wait till I tweet about this at the next traffic light. This is too funny!'

Meanwhile, a car behind them had been honking aggressively since the last few minutes. Madam stared at Adarsh and shook her head in disappointment, as he refused to change lanes to let the impatient driver pass. He finally relented but couldn't resist shaking a fist at the taxi driver as he drove past. They drove in silence until Adarsh reached the school.

He honked continuously until the guard opened the door, dropped off his mother and headed back home, still lost in his thoughts about the sad state of affairs in the country. He was disappointed that he didn't encounter a single red light and had to wait to tweet about his mother's 'conversation' with the Great Leader until he reached his destination.

*

'Come Ravi, my dear friend. Come on in. I have been waiting for you.' He looked up from his massive teakwood desk and ushered Ravikant Girpade in with a wave of his hand. As always, there were two sticks of purple orchids in a small vase on his desk. A similar vase was placed on a table by the sofa and there was one more on the reading table. A bigger vase on a side-table by the window had a massive arrangement of the expensive flowers.

Lying proudly on his desk was that beautiful cap, specially commissioned by him and put together over two months by half-a-dozen artists from Agra. It was rumored to be stitched out of real gold thread. Atop the cap were a number of feathers. Every time the Great Leader achieved something great, he added a feather to his cap. The first one was from when he got elected to the assembly at the age of 26. There was one added when he got SitarBucks to come to India and another one for achieving 100 per cent literacy in OrchidNagar.

'Good morning, Great Leader. How are you?' Girpade had never been at ease in this massive office of The Great Leader, feeling insignificant in this humungous room on the top floor of the secretariat, its floor-to-ceiling glass windows offering 360-degree views of this town that the Great Leader had taken great pains to develop. In one corner of the room was a fish tank in which about two-dozen imported fish were swimming around. The wall behind the Great Leader's desk displayed one of his charming portraits.

Girpade could spot the massive EyeMAX 3D theatre in the background. There were only a handful of these in the country but the Great Leader had gone out of the way to ensure that his city got one, just in time for the release of *Harry Potter and the Deathly Shallows*.

The Great Leader flashed a smile at Girpade. He was in a rare good mood today. 'I am good. Very good indeed. Look at what just came in the mail. A collector's edition special pack of all *Harry Potter* DVDs. And it came with this beautiful wand! They say it is made of buffalo and mosquito hair with a base of eucalyptus and *peepal* wood. Bah! I think it is all Hogwarts, err, hogwash'!

He lovingly brandished the wand in the air. It looked quite genuine. 'Now if only I could use it for some real magic spells.'

All of a sudden, he moved the wand in a gigantic arc going all around his head, pointed at Ravikant and screamed 'CRUCIO!,' his favorite *Harry Potter* spell.

Day 3: Cobwebs of the Mind

'I am happy Ravikant. Everything is going according to plan. Except for one thing. YOU!'

His wand was still pointing at Girpade's direction, who was gaping at the Great Leader in stunned silence. They said that he was capable of great things, so Girpade wouldn't have been surprised if the curse had actually worked and he had collapsed to the ground writhing in pain.

The Great Leader was sitting on his heavy, bespoke leather chair, imported from Burma, made with the most luxurious snake leather known to mankind. 'So what exactly ails you, my dear Ravikant? My loyal friend who has been my colleague and well-wisher for so many years? Do you want us to lose the elections?'

'Sir...' Ravikant Girpade, the double PhD from Pune University, was at a loss for words.

'Oh come on now, don't be so naive. You know I am referring to your WWF brawl with Mohammad Panja on television. I never knew your frail frame could deliver such a punch. Maybe we should move you from the party think-tank to the collection team and change your title to CCO – Chief Collection Officer. You should go from door-to-door collecting donations from people and beat up the ones who refuse to pay.'

The Great Leader had revolutionized politics in the country by structuring his party like a corporate organization. He ran it like a CEO, ably assisted by his management team. There was a Chief Outrage Officer, a Chief Sabotage Officer, a Chief Collection Officer, a Chief Flower Officer, a Chief Rally Officer – the title Girpade currently held – and several others. The party functioned like a well-greased war machine.

He got up and walked towards Girpade, who was standing frozen in front of his desk. The Great Leader was a massive man, standing tall at six feet and five inches, his bulky body resembling that of a wrestler more than a politician. His head was shaven clean and he was rubbing a hand over his head, as if trying to calm his temper. People who knew him knew that this gesture meant that he was angry. He had once beaten up one of the senior leaders in the party because he had dared to accept a call while the Great Leader was talking. The poor guy had suffered multiple fractures in his legs and six broken ribs simply because his wife had called to ask him to buy tomatoes on his way back home. Since that day, they all tread around him carefully.

Girpade fell to his knees. 'I am sorry, Great Leader. That fraud Panja is such a reckless jerk. He provoked me. I am sorry. I'll stay out of his traps from now on.'

'I really don't know, Ravikant. Going out in the open, getting some fresh air, meeting people, using a hockey stick to break someone's legs, it might help clear up your head. We need lots of funds to fight the elections anyway.

'Do you want to meet them?' The Great Leader asked, pointing at the fish-tank at the far end of the room. 'We can have you meet them. Maybe that will help you remember our vision at your fingertips?'

'No, sir. No, no, please forgive me. Please don't do that.' Girpade fell to the ground and lay prostate at the Great Leader's feet. 'I am truly sorry, sir. I swear on my mother that I will never again embarrass you.'

The Collection Department was a low-profile one and the Chief Collection Officer could at best expect the Fisheries Ministry, while the Chief Rally Officer was virtually assured of the lucrative Mining portfolio. Girpade didn't want to meet THE fish. They were vicious.

The Great Leader sighed as if beaten by a torpedo. 'Why must you bring your mother into this discussion? You know I hate it when people put their mothers at risk. Very well then, Ravikant Girpade. If you promise to behave, let's close the matter for now. Don't behave so irresponsibly again. You've been a great ambassador for the party so far. You get along well with that Buddhu…Buddhi… oh whatever the hell is that loudmouth's name. Use your relationships; you have a big role to play in the elections. Remember, if we win you will become the Minister of Mining.'

Girpade just sat there with his hands folded, begging forgiveness, like an errant schoolboy who had been caught painting dirty pictures inside the girls' washroom, waiting to be spanked by the headmaster.

The Great Leader lifted him by his shoulders. 'Come on, now,

Day 3: Cobwebs of the Mind 49

don't be so hard on yourself. Let's review my speech for the rally in Indraprastha next week. It is time to start addressing the muggles... err...people.'

Girpade hugged the Great Leader and sobbed on his broad chest. 'I promise you that I will never let you down. We will win this election, come what may.'

'Come, my friend, let's take a selfie.' The Great Leader kept a comforting arm on Girpade's shoulder and took out his mobile phone from his pocket. Girpade felt a huge sense of relief and his tentative smile now extended from ear-to-ear as he and the Great Leader gazed into the phone camera. This was a big honour. The Great Leader only took selfies with people important to him.

They walked to the couch by the window that overlooked the EyeMAX Theatre, and the Great Leader took out his gold-rimmed glasses to read from the hand-written draft of his speech on the notepad specially imported from Cameroon.

The Great Leader was a man of refined tastes, and the only country in the world to grow trees with the softest bark that made for an impeccable writing experience, was Cameroon. For the last few years, he had not as much as scribbled on any other paper. He had even managed to get his bank to issue cheque-books printed especially on reams of the same paper that he provided to them. They had been obstinate at first but an hour spent by a group of men ransacking their main branch in the Central Business District because the bank had 'disrespected the Great Goddess by using her name in a print advertisement' somehow seemed to make the bankers reconsider his proposal.

'Ready?' He asked Girpade, who was now wiping the sweat off his forehead using the red handkerchief his wife had gifted him on their anniversary. The Great Leader had not married. He had given up his personal life for the cause of the nation and promised to be celibate for the rest of his life. At 65, he still had enough verve left in him but he was neither keen on having someone in his life to control him, nor did he have time for the trivialities of familial duties. He had never been able to bring himself up to speed with the entire concept of parenthood and running after your child with a spoon of rice even when she wasn't keen on eating. Parenthood seemed to defy all laws of logic and science. Families were a concept created to keep common people occupied so they didn't have time to think for themselves. It was not for leaders with a mission to change the fortunes of a billion people.

Girpade nodded enthusiastically at the Great Leader, who started reading.

'My dear friends, you have come here from all over the country and I thank you for being a part of our movement. As you know, I have given up my life for the cause of the nation and will do my best to live up to your trust.'

He looked up at Girpade. 'Are we still on track to get 15 lakh muggles for the rally? I want to send out a strong message this time.' Girpade nodded. As Chief Rally Officer, he was responsible for managing the logistics. This year he was planning to bring in people via chartered flights and have them airdropped at the venue, to avoid people getting stuck in traffic.

'We all know what a tragedy the current government's term has been. Scam after scam. People wallowing in poverty. Frequent power cuts. No water. No highways. But how would they know? Do you know that Chhote Sarkar doesn't even drink water? He only drinks beer imported from America – Rs 2,000 for a small bottle. Does it befit the leader of such a poor nation to enjoy these western pleasures, in utter defiance of our great culture? My blood boils when I think of that. They have no sympathy for the people at all. Will you vote for such a party?'

The Great Leader had stood up and was speaking with full gusto, immersed in the moment. The hypocrisy of the ruling party always got him very excited. His life's mission was to ensure that they were voted out of power, never to return.

Ravi quietly mumbled, 'no', playing the role of an enraptured audience. The crowds loved the Great Leader for his oratorical style. The latest opinion polls had indicated that he was the clear favourite to win the elections. He was the darling of the middle class. In the eyes of the masses, he was the man who would set everything right.

'Friends, our country has a rich history. We have a culture, a heritage. What do the countries of the west that eat beef and drink diet Pepsi know? I see my brothers in other parts of the country asking for their own independent states and my heart cries out in pain. It hurts here, my friends,' he thumped his chest with an expression of deep hurt.

'When our government comes to power, we will listen to all such demands and take the number of states to 40. Why 40, you ask? My friends, I give you *Hanuman Chalisa. Durga Chalisa. Saat Chalis Ki Local. Chalis.* 40. It is the number the gods chose for us. I am just a mediator doing what he sent me to do.'

Ravi gave him a thumbs up. 'This is a great line, sir. Very powerful. The people will go crazy.'

The Great Leader extended his hand and shook Girpade's, while still looking at his notepad.

'One more thing, Ravi. We need some nice slogans for people to chant. Can you start working on this? I have some ideas already. Note these down.

'No Badi Sarkar. No Chhote Sarkar. Say no to their *parivaar*.

'Government has bribery rate. Orchid party has Leader Great.

'Whether a woman or a gent, vote for the Orchid government.'

'Sure, sir. These are great ideas. I will think of some more.' Girpade took out a notepad from his pocket and took down the slogans.

The Great Leader resumed his speech. 'Look at our government. What have they done for you? What did you eat for breakfast today? Bread? Nothing? Do you know what the Prime Minister eats? He eats the heart of a young lamb every day. The man is the devil himself. Do you know what he eats for lunch? Beef! Yes, my friends, our Prime Minister is a beef-eater. The cow is not just an animal, she is our mother. But the good Prime Minister *sahab* – he doesn't care for her. Would you eat your mother? Would you?'

Girpade whispered to him with a surprised look, 'Sir, the Prime Minister is vegetarian.'

The Great Leader placed a finger on his lips to signal silence and without so much as a glance at Girpade, continued reading, 'And

Chhote Sarkar. The great hope of the party. What has he done until now? Went to Bangladesh for his studies and was kicked out of college for burning down a classroom because he got drunk on just one beer. The future Prime Minister of this great nation can't tolerate a pint! Is this how leaders behave? Badi Sarkar should have beaten him up when he was still young so we wouldn't have to see this day. But then, I suspect even she wouldn't have had time for him because she was busy in the ashram of that fraud who wears a crown of neem leaves on his head. They have made a circus of the country. THEY MUST GO!'

He mumbled to Girpade, 'I just hate that Chhote Sarkar. Bloody kid who knows nothing and they want him to run the country. Let him try and run a small tea stall and then we will see if he can run the great nation where all civilization was born; the country that discovered water, fire and the Internet; the country that gave birth to all the great religions; the one where the Chinese first discovered martial arts and came up with their own hoo-haa. The country that gave the world *chicken tikka* and lamb *roganjosh*.'

Girpade nodded in agreement.

'Dear friends, do you know that the orchid is a flower that was created by our *rishi-munis* who prayed to the great lord Shiva for several decades asking for his blessings to make our nation the world's most beautiful country? Lord Shiva appeared after 40 years and gave them some seeds to plant. The sages went back, planted the seeds and were delighted to see the beautiful flowers emerging from them. Do you know where the dark blue color of the orchid comes from? It's the symbol of the Neelkanth. Do you know why most men in western countries love wearing blue shirts? Yes, it is our gift to them.

'During the Satyuga, orchids were grown in every house as a mark of respect to the great God. But then the ruling party took it all away. Ever since they came to power, no orchids grow in our homes. We import orchids from corrupt western countries at inflated rates and feel very happy paying Rs 30-40 per stick. This, my friends, is what the ruling party has done to the country. Show them the power of your vote. Vote for the Orchid.'

Day 3: Cobwebs of the Mind

Girpade clapped. 'Very good, sir. Very good. No doubt you are the best orator our country has ever seen.'

*

'*Oye* Rajnikant, what level?' Giani Seth asked the intern as he reached his desk outside his personal office on the 50th floor of the swankiest building in all of Indraprastha, the only one with mandatory finger, eardrum, toe and retina scans required to enter.

'Sir, my name is Sundar Varadarajan, not Rajnikant.'

'Shut up, you Madrasi. What level?'

'Sir, 156.'

'Get out. You're fired.'

'What, sir?'

'You are fired. *Po-da*.'

'Wh-wh-what happened, sir?'

'What happened *ke bachche*! That stupid Chaddha is already at 178 and you've only done 100 levels in the entire week. I hired you, just so that I can get ahead of Chaddha, and what have you done? Level 156? You think I have all the time to keep tracking you? As if my ten-lakh crore business will run itself?'

'Sir, I will try harder.'

'You bet your ass you will. You have two more hours. Chaddha is coming to my place for dinner tonight. Get to level 179 or pack your bags and don't show your face again, or I will beat you with my *chappal*.

'Now stop staring. Go, do your work.'

The intern got back to business. He was an engineering student and had been elated at landing a summer internship with the prestigious Giani group of industries, the largest industrial house in the country, with interests in mining, real estate, manufacturing, consumer goods, cars, electronics goods – the list was long. More importantly, he would be directly working with the Chairman Giani Seth, on a monthly stipend of a princely Rs 50,000, an all-time internship stipend record at his college. However, Sundar Varadarajan was no ordinary student. He had spent a semester at MIT on an exchange programme, one of his research papers was going to be published in an IEEE journal and both Stanford and MIT were competing to offer him a PhD. He was a genius at college, now playing Candy Crush for a fat billionaire.

Giani Seth walked into his 40,000 square feet office, reputedly the most expensive office suite anywhere in the country. The office offered 360-degree views of the Indraprastha skyline that looked even better from the infinity pool outside. There was a private helipad, a spa, a luxury suite, golf carts to take him around, an indoor waterfall by the sofas, and his pride – a washroom right behind his desk fitted with imported faucets and toilet seats that performed an instant analysis of his excretions and uploaded the reports to a central server monitored 24X7 by a dedicated team of seven doctors.

He approached the restroom as soon as he entered and said 'Khul Ja Sim Sim.' The door promptly opened. It was voice-controlled and only responded to Giani Seth. He had seen this in a movie and immediately told his secretary Alisha that he wanted just such a door for his bathroom. Nobody else was allowed access to his bathroom, except for the cleaning lady.

That enlarged prostate meant that he had to go every half an hour. The richest man in the entire country and doctors hadn't been able to fix his problem after years of treatment. The threats of getting their medical licenses revoked had also failed. Giani Seth had decided that his next step would be to get their wives kidnapped and hold them hostage until the doctors got him cured.

Giani Seth worked from an office that was five hundred feet above the ground and boasted of an infinity pool that opened up into the skies but the truth was that he was afraid of heights and water. He never looked out of the window and had never stepped into that exclusive pool, but when you're trying to make a statement, some things just need to be done. Who said being rich was easy?

Even the supercomputer was purchased only because he had read in a magazine that no individual owned a supercomputer in the world and only big scientific corporations could afford one. Among his many achievements was the fact that Giani Seth was the only man in the world who played Solitaire on a supercomputer.

Day 3: Cobwebs of the Mind

He pressed a button on the intercom and said, 'Alisha, come in.'

Five seconds later his secretary Alisha was standing in front of him.

He spoke to her without looking up, quickly going through the newspaper headlines on his desk. 'I have to buy a new car. A pigeon did potty on the lion *wali* car so I gave it to the maid's husband. I am thinking of buying that one, what do you call it, the one with the logo of a bird?'

Alisha scratched her chin and suddenly remembered having seen one recently. 'Bentley, sir?'

'I don't know. I just want the car with a bird outside. Get it for me.' He finally looked up from the paper at his secretary.

'*Oye*, what's going on?' He exclaimed.

'I am sorry, sir. What happened?' Alisha was a gorgeous 24-year-old girl. She stood tall at five feet eight inches, a few inches above her rich employer. She had the figure of a supermodel, with the right amount of fat in the right places. Alisha was the winner of last year's Miss India contest. She had done a few commercials for Giani Seth, who had offered her the position of his personal secretary for a salary of two crores per year and she had gladly accepted after being threatened that he would ensure she never got another modeling or film assignment ever again, if she said no.

'Go, get a pair of scissors.'

She was surprised but carried out the order and was soon back with the requested item.

Giani Seth took the scissors and moved towards Alisha, who watched as the richest man in all of India sat at her feet, his dhoti clad legs buckled under his rotund belly, his recently clean-shaven face bearing a serious look. He took a ruler and carefully measured the length of her skirt, before proceeding to cut off the hem of the expensive Prada skirt she had bought a day earlier such that it finished exactly six inches above her knees. Not an inch less, not an inch more, just like her stipulated contract.

He got up, satisfied, glancing at her glorious dusky legs. Giani Seth used to have a moustache until a week ago when he decided to shave it off on the suggestion of an astrologer who said that his wealth would double within two years if he chose to go clean-shaven. Alisha had barely managed to suppress her smile when she saw him walking into the office that day. It was like he was missing an essential item of clothing on his body.

'There. This looks much better now. Now go get that *chidiya wali* car for me. I want to see it in the garage by evening.'

'Sure, sir.' She turned to leave, remembered something, and stopped. 'Sir, one more thing. We got a call from the We Will We Will Rock You party campaign office asking for your support. What should I tell them?'

'Oh, the beggars want more money? Send them a check for five, no, ten crores. Also send them a note saying that I will surely vote for them and that I wish they form the government again. That should keep them happy for some time. Also send the same to the Orchid *wallahs*. God knows who will come to power but we need to plan ahead.'

'Sure, sir,' she noted it down in her diary. Giani Seth smiled at her as she was writing and said, 'that's a very nice nail-polish. It matches the soft skin of your hands perfectly. Is this the one I gave you?'

'Yes, sir, it is.' She blushed. 'I love it.'

'Good girl. We also need to get some new clothes for you. Let's go to Victoria's Secret some day.' He winked at her.

As Alisha walked back to her desk, Giani Seth got a call on his phone and answered it with his usual curt greeting, 'This is Giani Seth. What do you want?' while staring at her shapely behind.

The voice on the other end crackled and his tone changed instantly. 'Oh my rolly-polly, my candy crush, my lovely baby. What happened?' He spoke lovingly into his phone.

'You hit whom? How many people?'

'Five? Did anybody see you?'

'Okay, don't worry. Daddy will take care of it.'

*

'Good evening, ladies and gentlemen. The most talked about man in Indian politics today was chosen by Mother Nature to be the destiny of this nation of a billion men and women. While many people question his capabilities and readiness to play an active role in the country's politics, many in his party believe that the time is right for him. The one thing we know for sure is that history will remember this person for many years to come.

'You are watching B for Buddhi, brought to you tonight by Scream, the energy drink that will leave you screaming for more. I am your host Buddhiman Buddhiraja. Tonight we bring to you the man who will one day be the leader of our nation. Son of the venerated Badi Sarkar. The one and only, Chhote Sarkar.'

BB stared into Camera #2 as he raised his eyebrows and spoke in his usual impatient tone, the one he reserved for politicians, deserving as they were of all the contempt he could muster. After all, it was they who had pushed the nation into a giant manhole they had conveniently forgotten to cover.

He adjusted his glasses, lifted his hand and turned to look into Camera #5, the one with a wider angle that allowed viewers to see more of him than just the face, and continued. 'Of course there are questions about his readiness. Whether he has enough experience. Whether he...', and he coughed slightly, 'even deserves it.

'Let's listen from the horse's mouth directly.' He swiveled his chair in Chhote Sarkar's direction and shook his hand. 'Welcome to our show, Chhote Sarkar.'

Chhote Sarkar smiled back as he shook his hand, 'Thanks. So, 'listen from the horse's mouth' you said. Do you want me to, umm, talk like a horse now?'

BB looked taken aback as Chhote Sarkar cleared his throat, gripped his jaw and was about to emit sounds ostensibly in horse-tongue. 'Stop it,' he mumbled silently to his guest.

'You're too funny, sir. We never knew this side of you.' BB laughed loudly, looking into Camera #3. Even his laughter was perfect, carefully rehearsed to sound spontaneous.

Chhote Sarkar moved his hand away from his jaw and stared intently at BB. Yesterday had been a nightmare. He had been taken to the hospital for first-aid and some precautionary tests. He was lucky he had not sustained any serious injuries and had been promptly rescued by the villagers. His ankle was twisted and there was a band-aid on his chin. He had got a series of injections at the hospital to ward off the infections he had possibly received from the well and his stomach was emitting loud sounds, as he hadn't been allowed to eat anything all day. Apart from that, he was okay. As always, people on the internet had found humor in his humiliation but he had long stopped following the news. He had committed to this interview a few weeks ago so couldn't back out at the last minute.

Mom had been scared that he was going to squeal and run away scared. To be fair to her, that's what he had done at his last interview, resulting in some seriously bad press about the sissy boy leader who couldn't face tough questions. Badi Sarkar's office had to work overtime for damage control and a lot of 4-BHK apartments in Gurgone had to be gifted to shut blabbering mouths.

Then she had come over to his bedside at 1AM last night and made him drink that disgusting neem concoction. It had burnt his throat like poison, twice over. Once when it went down and the second time when it came back up and he threw it all up. Sometimes he wondered if she was a bit too paranoid. Maybe that paranoia was the problem. He wasn't a kid anymore. He too had feelings and thoughts. He had ideas about how to fix things. He didn't need to spend two hours every night memorizing those notes, in Arial font, size 16, printed on A3 paper. How about double-sided printing to save the environment, to start with?

His phone buzzed. It was a Whatsapp message from Chamcha Das. 'I am outside the studio with 200 men. We are with you, Chhote Sarkar. We will burn down the studio if he messes with you. Just give me a missed call and we will show them.'

'I want to keep this informal, sir. We have cookies and tea for you today. Do help yourself,' BB prompted his guest.

Chhote Sarkar didn't bat an eyelid. Cookies were a no-no. He was allergic to anything that had any sort of grain in it. He was allergic to most things with milk in them. There were only two things he could eat – french-fries and ice-cream. Anything else would make his face swell up like a balloon. This was his secret, hidden from the world, known only to his mother, the maid and their driver.

BB looked at him square in the eye, and shot off the first question. 'What happened the last time you were on a news show?'

Chhote Sarkar's answer was prompt, 'Pass.'

'I am sorry?'

'Pass. Let's move on.'

'Sure, sir. I understand if you don't want to answer questions that might indicate your mental health. I do realize it is a sensitive topic for you in your current state. Let's move on.'

Chhote Sarkar smiled. The trap was being laid. This was BB's signature style of interviewing guests. He would show some empathy for the guest being interviewed, lull the guest into a false sense of security and then, when least expected, tear into them with a series of biting and vicious questions. As a result, three of the last four interviewees had walked off while the fourth one had punched him in the face, before walking off.

Panja had come into Chhote Sarkar's room that morning, accompanied by his team of IIM-educated advisors. 'Let's practice for your interview, Bablu,' he had said. They had made him sit on a sofa and surrounded him from all sides, firing questions at him, evaluating his responses, correcting him, giving him more 'statistics' to play with, advising some generic answers that could work with any question to which he didn't have a clue. It was like being faced with an execution squad and Chhote Sarkar had come to this interview determined not to give any of the answers they had suggested.

'Remember two important tips Bablu,' Panja had said. 'One, always give people false hope. People are suckers for hope. Give them hope and they will give you their vote. Two, lie generously. Lie as much as you can. Lying is the greatest skill a politician can have. The more confident your lies, the more successful you will be.

'And if you ever get stuck, just say that we want to empower our women. That will work for most questions.'

BB took a cookie and held up the tray for Chhote Sarkar, insisting that he take one. He shook his head. Badi Sarkar had made several attempts to make him eat paranthas or bread sandwiches over the years. It was the same result every time. It took about six hours before his body returned to normal. No, he couldn't eat cookies tonight. Badi Sarkar had been giving him some concoction prepared by Baba Neemacharya every night but it clearly wasn't working. He had taken a small bite of a coconut cookie last week and instantly turned into a Halloween pumpkin.

'Okay. Who do you think will win the next election?'

'My party.'

'How are you so sure?'

'I am not but you asked so I answered.'

'So you think you will not win the election?'

Chhote Sarkar laughed. He had a disarming laugh, one that had allowed him the company of many pretty girls during college days. These days he hardly went out and nobody could get through his XXX security to talk to him, therefore leaving no room in his life for romantic liaisons. Only three people in the entire country enjoyed the highest level of security. Badi Sarkar, Chhote Sarkar and the statue of the Great Liberator near their bungalow.

'I never said that.'

BB opened his mouth to speak but Chhote Sarkar held up his hand. He had more.

'Let me tell you a story. When I was a child, I found it extremely difficult to comprehend that two plus two is four. You know what my mother did? Any guesses?'

'She beat you up?' BB smiled.

'Correct. She also made me take a broom and clean all the cobwebs in the house. And that, my dear friend, was the greatest lesson life ever taught me,' Chhote Sarkar sank back in his seat with the smug look of a boxer who had just dealt his opponent a knockout punch.

BB raised both hands in despair. 'This doesn't even make any sense. Where's the lesson in such a harsh punishment?'

Chhote Sarkar sighed like an exasperated professor trying to explain the concepts of fluid dynamics to a particularly slow child, 'Have you ever observed a cobweb carefully? Our minds should be like cobwebs.'

Day 3: Cobwebs of the Mind

BB sniggered, 'Are you serious?'

'Of course. I wish that every man and woman in this country trains their mind to be like a cobweb.'

'Wow that is pretty deep. I don't think I even understand but let's move on. What do you think of the tattoo on Bhakt Lal's forehead, the one asking you to become PM?'

Chhote Sarkar laughed again. 'Oh, that tattoo? I don't think it is a real one. I saw Bhakt today and his forehead seemed clean.'

'Are you sure?'

'No.'

BB gave a frustrated look into Camera #6. The telecast switched into a split screen mode, with BB on the left half and Chhote Sarkar's face covering the right half of viewers' TV screens. One looked confused with what was happening and the other bore the happy expression of a child playing with his favourite toy.

'Okay let's leave Bhakt Lal and his tattoo and talk of more pertinent matters. What do you think is India's biggest problem today?'

Chhote Sarkar pondered for a second before leaning forward in his chair, resting his elbows on the table and slowly pointing one finger at BB, followed by a courteous smile.

He laughed loudly. 'Me?'

Chhote Sarkar continued pointing in his direction for a few seconds as BB stared into Camera #4 and #5 that were now telecasting a split screen showing each side of his shocked face, and exclaimed. 'Ladies and gentlemen, this is preposterous. I cannot believe that the future leader of the nation wants to silence democracy in our country by curtailing media freedom. I cannot believe that this is happening. This is...'

Chhote Sarkar cut him off. 'You idiot. Look behind you at the view outside your window. Rows upon rows of slums. The filth in which those people live. Their lack of education or of avenues to grow out of their miserable lives. THAT is India's biggest problem!'

BB looked over his shoulder and grinned sheepishly. He was being trolled today, a most unexpected scenario.

'There's something on your face, BB,' Chhote Sarkar suddenly said, holding up a finger to his own face helping him locate the offending whatever-it-was.

BB fumbled for a handkerchief and wiped his face.

'No, no, a little up.'

He wiped his face again, flustered.

'Ah leave it. I suppose that's your nose.'

As the cameras turned off and everybody started packing up, Chhote Sarkar took out his phone, dialed Chamcha Das's number and hung up after one ring.

DAY 4

FIRE IN THE BELLY

AdarshBharatiya@AdarshBharatiya

You want food? The government will give you a smartphone.

BowWowBreaking@BowWowBreaking

Breaking: Man divorces his wife on Twitter by tweeting 'talaq talaq talaq'.

FerozWriter@FerozWriterIIMA

Between WWWWRY and the Orchid Party, the one that scores fewer self-goals will win the next election.

MeraKaamJoker@MeraKaamJoker

Minister says India has the lowest per capita rape incidence in the world. I knew there was a silver lining in all of this.

Swamy@Swamy1959

I have confirmed news that Chhote Sarkar eats only beef.

Ambika Madam parked her car and marched into her office. The day ahead would be hectic. The Minister of Mobile Phones, Mohammad Panja, had chosen her school for launching a pilot project under the *Badi Sarkar Smart Children Yojna* to provide a smartphone to all students who belonged to the 19-inch-TV line, and was going to visit in a few days for the distribution.

The instructions from the department had been strict. 'Put on your best behaviour, make sure that the children are in classrooms studying and no teacher is found forwarding Whatsapp jokes in the staffroom. If needed, hire private guards to ensure that there is no stampede while the phones are distributed.'

The government had launched a recent innovative plan to demarcate the middle class based on the size of their TV screens, as per the recommendations of the Justice Vyomkesh Bhakshi committee that had deliberated for the last eight years before submitting its path-breaking finding that the only consistent benchmark to accurately judge people's economic status was the size of their TV screens.

There were to be four categories – Below 19-inch TV line, Below 32-inch TV line, Below 40-inch TV line, and a fourth NTL, No TV Line, for people with no televisions in their homes, the poorest of the poor, the most wretched of the wretched, the ones left behind by the rapidly advancing Indian economy.

Media channels had shouted to the point of delirium when this was announced, saying that it was gross objectification of Indian people and just another ploy to create vote-banks, after last year's controversial decision to declare C++ developers a minority community. The opposition had walked out of Parliament every single day for the last six months in protest accusing the government of perpetrating a scam in alliance with Korean TV manufacturers, now that people were rushing to buy 19 and 32-inch TVs to procure their FREE cards. *Forever Remain Entirely Exempted*. Even residents of fancy golf-course facing villas in Indraprastha's posh suburb Gurgone were lining up outside electronic stores to buy 19-inch TVs and claim their FREE cards that entitled them to a lifetime of subsidized wheat, rice, sugar, on-demand Hollywood blockbusters and bottles of single-malt whiskey.

Of course, the classification based on TV sizes was tricky and came with its own challenges. The Left parties were already demanding that everybody be provided with equal access to paid channels like the newly launched *Saas-Bahu* TV which had grown to be the most popular channel in the country within a few weeks of its launch. Last week had seen the highest-ever TRP for a show on Indian television during an episode of the popular show *Tiger-Bahu*, when the daughter-in-law fed her mother-in-law to a python because she had put ginger in her cup of tea, when the daughter-in-law had asked for cardamom. Feminists all over India had been pleased with that episode, calling it payback for the ridiculous practice of arranged marriage rampant in many parts of the country.

With the elections approaching, this was a great time for the common man. Smart citizens aware of various ongoing schemes and possessing the right certificates, proclaiming their economic status, could easily furnish the entire house with fridges, food processors, induction cooking systems, nose-hair trimmers and coffee-makers. The minister of Mobile Phones couldn't afford to be left behind. He would come in with the Media Circus, with journalists jostling for vantage points and running over the precious plants of her school in pursuit of sound bites. This was not a PR opportunity to be missed. Madam had seen this circus the last time a minister came over, right before the previous elections, five years ago. They had come in to distribute textbooks but the order got mixed up and he had handed out an erotic novel titled *Jawani ka Jalwa* to students of class 5.

On this day, Madam had called a meeting with her staff to go over the plans for the distribution. There were lists that needed to be drawn up; certificates of relevant students to be checked; students with torn or untidy uniforms had to be provided with new sets; and

Day 4: Fire in the Belly

everybody had to be threatened with dire consequences, in case they slipped up in any way on the big day.

The meeting was to start in less than 20 minutes when she had a visitor. Sushil Kumar Yadav, the local ruling party leader, suddenly appeared at her door. He was dressed in his standard white kurta-pajama and was flanked by two security people, a girl, probably aged 14-15 and another middle-aged man whom Madam had never seen with the politician's entourage earlier. The girl had brown eyes, a pretty face and was wearing a clean, well-fitting school uniform with gold earrings, which meant that she was financially better off, compared to the typical students of Madam's school, some of them so poor that the free lunch provided at school was their biggest motivation for coming in everyday.

'Madam ji, how are you? It is always such a pleasure to meet you.' Yadav brought his hands together in a *namaste* as he walked into her office, his bearded face reflecting utter delight at meeting the principal Madam.

Madam was surprised at this sudden appearance. She had enough on her hands already for the politician to be walking in with another request. She stood up and welcomed her guest with an equally deceptive and pleasant smile. 'Yadav ji, how are you? Long time, no see. You don't love our school anymore. We hardly get to see you these days.'

'No, Madam ji. What are you saying? It is nothing of that sort. It is just that working for the welfare of the people takes so much of my time. I hardly have a proper meal in the day. All the time flies in just attending to the problems of someone or the other. Not that I am complaining. We are just selfless servants of the people. This is what gives us happiness.'

Madam noticed the expensive watch on his wrist and the heavy gold chain hanging from his neck and nodded. He cleared his throat and introduced the girl and the middle-aged man accompanying him.

'Madam ji, I need a personal favor from you. This is Nafisa, daughter of my good friend Rafi. She is a very bright child, Madam. Very bright. When we were coming here, I asked her who is the best school principal in the country and do you know whose name she said? She said it is Ambika Madam.'

The girl looked in Madam's direction and gave a faint smile. Rafi also looked on with his hands folded in Madam's direction, and a look on his face not too dissimilar from that of an *Indian Idol* contestant, who expectantly looks at the judges, after the audition performance, awaiting their verdict.

Madam raised her eyebrows. 'Yadav ji, I have a very important meeting starting in a few minutes. How can I help you?'

Yadav addressed the girl. 'Go child, touch Madam's feet.' The girl moved in Madam's direction but she asked her to stop.

He looked at Madam and said, 'Madam, if you could admit the girl to your school it will be a very big favor. She was in the Great Liberator Nagar School but the principal caught her outside the school with a boy and kicked her out. Imagine Madam ji, the two had just gone to a hotel to discuss homework but she wouldn't listen. Is this the way?'

Madam replied impatiently, still looking at the girl, who now seemed indifferent and lost in her thoughts. 'Yadav ji, you know this is December. The session ends in a few months. How can I admit a student in the middle of the session? You should go and apologize to her principal and ask her to take the girl back.'

'No Madam ji, now Nafisa says that she doesn't want to go back. The principal was very rude to her and she says that she cannot go back to that school anymore.'

'Very well, then. She can stay at home and discuss her homework with that boy. I can't admit her now. It is against department rules.'

The girl's father, who was standing until now with folded hands and an imploring look in his eyes, suddenly decided to change tactics. He took a few steps towards Madam's table and started shouting. 'Madam you cannot be so rude to us. We are the *aam aadmi*, the common man. You might be a big officer but you cannot insult us like that. You should apologize and admit Nafisa.'

Yadav kept a hand on his shoulder to calm him down but he wouldn't budge. He carried on ranting. 'We are requesting you but you won't even listen. I know some very senior people in the government. You have no idea. I can get you transfer…'

Day 4: Fire in the Belly

Madam had had enough. She impatiently rang her bell a few times in quick succession and the peon came running in. She asked him to call the guard and escort the gentleman and his daughter out of the school.

Yadav seemed a bit confused about what he should do next but the man went ballistic. 'We will not leave so easily Madam. We will wait outside the school for an hour. If you don't apologize to us and admit Nafisa to your school, I will burn her alive then and there.'

Nafisa looked at him with a quizzical expression as Madam gestured to them to get lost with a flick of her fingers. Yadav followed them without as much as a glance at Madam, who was seething in anger.

'If you want, I will ask the guard to lend you a matchbox,' she screamed at the retreating party.

*

'Thank you, sir. I can't have any more of the *tandoori*. It is so spicy that my insides are already burning.'

The Great Leader laughed and looked at young Buddhiman Buddhiraja with a wide smile on his face. BB was smartly dressed but then he had never been seen in public in an ill-fitting suit or with a single strand of hair out of place. His face was radiant with youth and success. His eyes had a tired look but again it was a well-known secret that he woke up every morning at 3AM to go through every single news report published anywhere in the world. Being at the top of the game meant that he only allowed himself three hours of sleep every night. BB's desk was rumored to have a printout that proclaimed in bold letters – 'No rest. No mercy. No pain.' An intern had been fired last year for appending 'No sense' to the poster.

As it is, he had a rough outing last night when the imbecile Chamcha Das had stormed his studio and tried to destroy all equipment for no clear reason. BB had personally wrestled Das to the ground and put him in the BB Jail until the police arrived to take him and his supporters away, though the goons had managed to damage many of the cameras by then. Thankfully, BB had managed to find replacement equipment in time or the next day's show would have been in danger. He didn't have any recording on Sundays, which had afforded him the time to visit OrchidNagar today, though he still planned to fly back immediately after the meeting. There was some other urgent work to be done tonight in a hotel suite that he had booked especially for the purpose.

It was the first time he had been invited to lunch with the Great Leader, the hope of the masses, the to-be-savior of the country. He had been flown to OrchidNagar in the Great Leader's private jet, driven over to his home in his Rolls Royce, and treated to some very fine food so far. The place was a sprawling bungalow in the posh part of town where the Great Leader lived along with just a single maid who cooked, cleaned and washed for him. The ruling party had started a campaign last year claiming that the maid was actually his wife. #OrchidBhabhi had trended on Twitter for two days before people got tired of it and moved on to #ReplaceAMovieNameWithVadaPao.

The Great Leader had spoken at length about the virtues of simple living over their meal comprising succulent butter chicken, *tandoori* shrimp, lamb chops and mutton *biryani*, paired with fine wine, specially imported from southern France. It was a biting winter afternoon, the sun shining bright, blessing OrchidNagar's inhabitants with generous warmth and ultraviolet rays. The Great Leader had asked for the food to be served on the balcony overlooking his pretty lawn, lined with rows of pretty orchids in colours of purple, blue, red and maroon. The last gardener had been naive enough to recommend some chrysanthemums and had been banished from OrchidNagar for five years for that show of disloyalty.

'Buddhi *sahab*, here try this *paan*. You will never have tasted one like this.' The Great Leader pushed the betel leaf *paan* filled with fragrant sweet stuffing in his direction and BB gratefully took it. His stomach could use some help to digest all that meat.

'Thank you, sir,' BB replied. He had turned his chair slightly to allow him a better view of the flower-beds without having to crane his neck. 'The flowers are lovely.'

The Great Leader got up from his chair and leaned by the ledge. BB followed suit and stood next to him. The Great Leader took out

Day 4: Fire in the Belly

his wand from the inner pocket of his coat, pointed it at the flowers, and shouted with a theatrical flair, AGUAMENTI, the *Harry Potter* spell that made water shoot out of the wand. No water came out of the Great Leader's wand but the maid turned on the sprinklers in the lawn at that moment. He turned to look at BB, his eyes full of pride.

'You see the flowers, Buddhi *sahab*. Orchids. The only flower in the world that has medicinal value, decorative value, great fragrance, and I'm not sure if you know this or not but they are a rich source of magnesium, radium and Vitamin B4.'

'Are you serious, sir? I have never heard of anyone eating orchids.'

'I am quite serious, Buddhi *sahab*. Did you enjoy that sweet and sour *chutney* with the *tandoori* chicken? What did you think it was made of?'

'Orchids?'

'Got you!' The Great Leader laughed aloud at his own joke. 'The *chutney* was made of coriander and mint but the *paan* has dried orchids in it. Quite tasty and it has aphrodisiac powers as well.' The Great Leader winked at his young guest.

'You must be wondering how a single flower can have so many great qualities?'

BB nodded, awaiting the revelation.

'It is a flower of the gods, Buddhi *sahab*. I tell you, one day orchids will make India the world's only superpower. We just need to harness the powers properly. There is so much wealth of knowledge in our country that we have ignored because we keep following the corrupt countries in the west.'

'Very impressive, sir. Quite an eye-opener, in fact.' Buddhi said, still looking at the pretty rows of flowers, savouring the rich taste of the *paan* in his mouth.

The Great Leader beckoned him to come inside. 'Buddhi sahab, let's move to the study for a while and talk over a cup of tea. I wanted to discuss some things with you that I am not sure we can do here in the open.'

They entered the study and the Great Leader shut the door from inside. BB looked around the spacious office, admiring the luxurious furnishings until his eyes rested on the portrait on the wall. It was a striking handsome young man with flowing hair, a passionate look in his eyes, sitting on a plush chair, his arms confidently placed on the side-rests, the right leg perched upon the left knee.

The Great Leader saw BB admiring the portrait and explained, 'That's me.'

BB's eyes had a look of shock. 'Sir, you look so...' he hesitated, 'different in the portrait.'

The Great Leader rubbed a hand on his bald head. 'You know Buddhi *sahab*, I used to love my hair. I would apply *dahi* and egg-white every Sunday. I ensured there was not one split-end in my hair. I used the best herbal shampoos in the world. My hair was the stuff everybody was jealous of. And I shaved it all off one day.'

'Why, sir?'

'Because Buddhi *sahab*, it was taking over me. My life is dedicated to the country. The time I wasted in tending to my hair could have been better used for the cause of the nation so I just shaved my head. I don't want any distractions in my life. Celibate for life. Hairless for life. All I care for is the nation.'

BB looked visibly surprised, 'Sir, I don't even know what to say...'

The Great Leader led him to the sofa and asked his young visitor to take a seat.

They sat on the sofa and BB spotted a large globe inside one of the cabinets. 'Sir, I have a question for you. We have heard a lot from you on internal matters but hardly anything on foreign policy. If you become the Prime Minister, what will your foreign policy be?'

The Great Leader let out a loud laugh. 'Not *if*, Buddhi *sahab*, but *when*. There is no question that the ruling party is going to bite the dust this time. As for foreign policy, does it really matter? Generally, I just spin the globe and pick the country where my finger lands. Buy fighter aircrafts from the first country. Talk to the second one to export Alphonso mangoes. Request the third country for nuclear fuel. Send delegation of industrialists to the fourth one and so on. It doesn't really merit any more effort than that. My Chief Foreign Officer tells me this is how America also picks countries to bomb.

Day 4: Fire in the Belly

There are so many countries in the world that you can never fall short of options. What is more important is to revive Indian culture and spread the message of the orchid.'

BB nodded, a little unsure about how to react to this unique and random approach to foreign policy.

'Buddhi *sahab*, tell me one thing. What drives you? What do you want to do in life?'

'Excuse me, sir?'

'I just want to know what your ambition is. What are your plans for your future?'

BB rubbed a hand on his chin, pondering over the question, before responding with, 'I want to be the most effective journalist in India. I want to be the man who every Indian listens to carefully because they trust him. I want to root out corruption and make all Indian leaders accountable for their actions. I want to...'

The Great Leader interrupted with a wave of his hand. 'Come on, *yaar*. Surely you have material needs, too? You'd be no use to the country if you didn't have money to eat.'

'What do you mean, sir?'

'Nothing. Just that you should also start building that cozy nest that lets you continue your pursuit of corruption.'

The Great Leader waved his wand at the door saying 'ACHIO tea,' and immediately there was a knock on the door. It was the maid.

The Great Leader asked her to come in. She entered with a tray and served tea to the two men. After stirring in a spoonful of sugar in the Great Leader's cup, she turned to BB and smiled.

'Sugar, sir?' She asked BB.

'One spoon. Thanks.' BB had never used the word please in his life. His parents had tried their best to get him to say it when he was younger but they had never been successful. 'Nobody is doing me a favour, mom. If they don't do it, I will do it myself,' he used to tell his mother. His vanity just didn't allow him to lower his guard.

'Sorry sir, I am not sure I follow,' BB said.

The Great Leader leaned towards BB and said, 'I agree with you Buddhi *sahab*. This country is in a very bad shape and the ruling party has worked hard to fill their own pockets instead of helping reduce poverty and providing our people a quality life. It is my life's great vision that no man in India will ever sleep on a hungry stomach. The RIGHT to a SitarBucks coffee every day. *AVADA KEDAVRA* to poverty. We have it in our manifesto.'

He continued. 'Today, they have taken over the media with false propaganda disguised as news. Surely you know how the Galaxy TV channel only airs news that benefits the government. Or how *Khabardaar News* is effectively the party's mouthpiece. Last week, they reported that the Defense Minister has gone to Siachen, when he was actually locked inside his house by his wife because he hadn't washed the clothes properly.'

BB smiled. He was wondering where this conversation was heading to.

'I saw what Chamcha Das did to your studio last night. That was just uncalled for. I don't know what is wrong with these people.'

BB clenched his fists at the mention of Das. The recording with Chhote Sarkar had ended on time and had gone well but a few minutes after Chhote Sarkar left, Chamcha Das had stormed the studio with his men shouting loud slogans against BB. It had been a tough battle between the two sides but ultimately BB had saved the day. It helped that he was a blackbelt in Karate, Jujitsu, Jeet Kune Do, Taekwondo and a master of the Indian martial art Kalaripayattu. Das and his men had been no match.

'That is why I was wondering if we could get some like-minded people to join hands and take this great nation out of the hole these people have dug up.'

BB raised his eyebrows at this suggestion but didn't say anything. He adjusted his tie as if it was suffocating him, took out the pen from his coat's pocket and kept it on the table.

'Sir, I am not sure what you are getting at.'

The Great Leader smiled. 'Come on Buddhi *sahab*, you are a smart man. I want your help to counter this bias against us from the other channels that Badi Sarkar has bought off.'

'And how will this work, sir?'

The Great Leader held up a small bag that was lying by the side of the sofa they were seated on, and offered it to BB. BB opened it to find bundles of thousand rupee notes.

'Five crores. For more, just give us your Swiss bank account number and tell me how much more you want transferred and in which currency.'

BB took the bag and shook The Great Leader's hand. 'Thank you, sir. Give me a few days to think this over and I will get back to you.'

The Great Leader patted his back. 'Thanks, Buddhi *sahab*. Together we can surely achieve many great things and give the people of our nation what they rightly deserve.'

He picked up BB's pen from the table and handed it to him. 'You have the most interesting-looking pen, Buddhi *sahab*. Imported?' BB smiled nervously and kept the pen back in the pocket of his jacket.

'Oh, one more thing. Before you leave, there's one very important thing to do,' he said as Buddhi got ready to leave.

'Let's take a selfie.' He pulled out his phone from his pocket.

*

Baba Neemacharya completed his daily sermon and headed back to his chambers from the prayer hall, where an audience of about five-thousand had just heard him live, each of them paying Rs 100 for their ticket but would be *urged* to drop more into the collection boxes on their way out. His sermon was also telecast live on TNN, The Neem Network, which was his own TV channel that beamed his daily lectures on the principles of good living to his millions of fans who obediently lapped up all of his new offerings. All he had to do was tell them to wash their hair daily with his new Neem shampoo fortified with the essence of Hydrocarboblabla that the marketing people made up for him and they would line up at stores to buy his products.

Girl 4 joined him as he walked back and handed him his mobile phone. It was made of solid gold and encrusted with diamonds – a custom-made device gifted to him by the owner of Motaphone, the largest mobile operator in the country, another of his fans.

'Giani Seth called, Baba. He is coming to meet you over lunch.'

Baba kissed Girl 4 on the cheek. She was one of his most loyal girls, having stayed on after completing her two-year contract. In fact, she was the only one who also had a name by which she was addressed in the ashram, while everybody else was a number. Padmini. She was the only one who knew almost all the details of his business empire. Almost.

'This is good news. He must be coming to discuss the port he wants to setup. The richest man in the country needs Baba's support to get his most ambitious project through,' Baba stroked his beard and mumbled, 'The neem is the truth.'

'Which reminds me, how is Girl 45 doing? We did the Neem Yoga last night and she seemed surprisingly uptight. Maybe it was because it was her first time. Can you check on her? By the grace of Neem, I would like to meet her again tonight,' he winked at her.

Padmini did not look happy. Now that she was more like a partner in his business, he didn't summon her for these nightly sessions anymore but she wished he would stop altogether. The girls talked about the things he did with them and it was ugly. Girl 45 had been crying in her room all morning and had refused to come for any of the meditation sessions.

'I will check on her, Baba. I think I saw her in the morning.'

'Very good. The neem is the truth.'

'One more thing, Padmini, how much was the collection yesterday?'

'Just over 24 lakhs, Baba.'

'Only 24? Last week we had touched 30!' He looked at her with raised eyebrows. 'What is going on? I will have to personally watch the CCTV tapes from the cash counting at this rate. You need to keep a strict eye on the staff, okay?'

'Yes, Baba. I will look into it myself,' she mumbled.

He walked off to his room. The beard was getting itchy and needed some of that neem shampoo.

A couple of hours later Giani Seth arrived and was received at the VIP gate by Padmini who escorted him to Baba's chambers, where a royal lunch spread awaited.

'Giani, my loyal follower. How are you? Everything okay, by the grace of the great neem tree?'

Day 4: Fire in the Belly

'Baba ji, just give me a minute. I have to use the bathroom.' Giani Seth rushed into Baba Neemacharya's attached bathroom for his half-hourly trip. He emerged a couple of minutes later, wiping his wet hands on the sleeve of his *kurta*, a contented look on his moustache-free face.

'Baba ji, how are you? It is always so great to meet you. The business is doing well, thanks to your blessings. I am very close to formalizing a deal to buy a small refinery in Mexico. Now I was thinking of buying Hairbus, that aircraft manufacturer. Let me know if you have any contacts there.'

'I am happy to hear that, Giani. We can send out an email to the UBIA mailing list and see if anybody responds. Are you standing for President this year? By the grace of the great neem tree, you will buy Hairbus, too.'

'Thanks, Baba ji. No, I don't think I will stand for elections. I am just so caught up in the Gian Port project that there is no time left.'

'*Accha* leave it, we will discuss work later. Come help yourself to some food. I am starving.'

Baba picked up a plate and started piling on the lobster cake and crab legs. He handed a plate to Giani and offered some lobster. He refused. 'Today is Tuesday, Baba ji. I don't eat non-veg on Tuesdays.'

'Oh,' Baba sounded muffled through a mouthful.

Giani Seth got chowmein and some dal and the two walked to the dining table. Baba's chamber was a picture of opulence. All furniture was specially handcrafted and imported from Brazil. The lamps were pieces of art originally smuggled from the palaces of the Nawabs of Lucknow and purchased by the Baba from an auction at Sotheby's. The curtains were made from the gold *zari* saris of the erstwhile Rajmata of the state of Jai Jai Pradesh.

The two billionaires started chatting between mouthfuls from their heavy silver plates. One of the girls served champagne. Baba was rumored to have among the largest wine cellars in all of India. He did surprise Giani Seth with a new wine every time he came over. As responsible billionaires, the two had attended wine-appreciation sessions in France last year together and returned with a list of the most expensive wines money could buy. Giani Seth still enjoyed a bottle of *desi* more than any of the imported wines but couldn't say that in public. Being a billionaire was a big social responsibility.

'Baba ji, this port project is getting stalled. I have paid all the cooperation charge they asked for but still they are not approving the project. Can you please work your magic? I have already paid a total of Rs 5,000 crores as per the going rate of ten per cent of the project cost, which is Rs 50,000 crores.'

'What are they saying?'

'Nothing, Baba ji. I spoke to Panja and he said that the file is pending with Badi Sarkar. Can you please talk to her?'

'Sure, your work will be done. Neem is the truth.'

'Thank you, Baba ji. I have the board meeting next week and we have our quarterly result announcement coming up then. If the project approval doesn't come by that time, the stock price of Giani Enterprises will crash and they will surely kick me out of my own company.'

Giani Seth, the most powerful man in India, was jittery. He had invested far too much in this ambitious project. If it went through, he would double his wealth in a few years. If it didn't, he might not be able to play Solitaire on that supercomputer anymore. Worse, the board members would go after him like a pack of dogs chasing a young girl carying a box of sausages.

'Have faith in the power of the great Neem tree. Everything will be all right. Just relax. And transfer my *dakshina* to my Swiss account.'

'The standard rate, Baba ji? Can I get *thoda* discount?'

The Baba flicked a piece of lobster that had dropped onto his beard and smiled benevolently at Giani Seth. 'Giani, my dear, the industry is tight these days. Giving a discount will be difficult. I am afraid the facilitation fees would be two per cent. If you want, I can give you an EMI scheme.

'*Aur batao*, Giani? What's the buzz these days?'

'Nothing much, Baba ji. Same old problems that come with being rich. My voice-activated lift broke down yesterday and I was stuck in it for ten minutes. I kept saying, go to 50th floor, go to 50th floor but the stupid thing went to the basement. It is like there is no

Day 4: Fire in the Belly

quality left in anything any more. At this rate, I'll need to get a normal button-operated lift, like a poor common man.' He sighed.

The Baba patted his shoulder in sympathy. He suddenly remembered another important topic he wanted to discuss.

'Did you read the newspaper? They all declared their assets as part of the election nominations. Did you know how much Badi Sarkar declared?'

'No I haven't seen the news. Isn't she ranked 10th on the UBIA billionaires' list? I remember she had to open a new Swiss account last year because the bank didn't let a single account have so much money.'

Baba laughed loudly. 'Yes, I remember. She has declared a total net worth of three lakhs – 60,000 in cash, one Maruti car and a pearl necklace.' He slapped his knees in glee. 'Three lakh crore would be more like it.'

Giani Seth smiled woefully. A lot of that money was his but then it had all been a worthy investment, allowing him to expand his businesses faster than his competitors.

'Oh and you haven't even heard about Great Leader. He has declared a Vespa scooter, two cows and a brain worth two crores. I remember he bought his personal jet on a cash-down payment just last month.'

The two giggled like schoolboys for the next few minutes.

'Did you like the wine, Giani Seth? Only twenty bottles of this wine were made. It cost me ten thousand for a bottle.'

'Rupees? That's very cheap.'

Baba laughed. 'No, silly. Dollars.'

'Neem is the truth, Giani Seth. Neem is the truth,' Baba Neemacharya said, as he let out a loud burp.

*

Adarsh kept the tray at his favorite table by the window and sat down. His colleague Samarth soon joined in, carrying his tray laden with the free company-provided food in the office cafeteria. The two of them always had lunch together. This was their hour to vent their frustrations, whether related to work, family or the all-round state of the world around them.

This had been a busy week for Adarsh so far. First the high of appearing on BB's show and gaining all those Twitter followers, followed by the embarrassment of dozing off during the new director's strategy meeting. He had been lucky that the director had seen BB's episode and believed that he would have gone to bed late after the TV appearance. Nevertheless, the eccentric man had given Adarsh a handful of A4 sheets and told him to fill them up with 'I will not sleep during a meeting again.'

Adarsh took a bite of the *matar paneer* and opened the conversation. 'Chhote Sarkar has a rally tomorrow. I wonder how that will go. The guy is a clown. Did you see what happened during his visit to that village? And ministers in his party are going around getting his name tattooed on their foreheads. Such a joke. Going by his performance so far, he will probably say 'My mom cried when she heard my last speech', at his next speech.'

Samarth grinned. 'You really dislike him, don't you? I saw his interview with BB yesterday. I thought he was okay. He is probably on drugs most of the time which is why he does weird things, though he seemed pretty normal last night. You had to see BB's face when he pointed his finger in his direction and poor BB thought HE was being called the biggest problem in India! Not that I would object to that. His show should be shown to people with low blood pressure to keep their blood pumping. All he does is make funny faces and stare into the camera.'

'Come on, *yaar*. I think he should just get lost and give some worthy leader a chance. Being born to Badi Sarkar doesn't mean that he becomes heir to the throne.'

'Oh by the way, Galaxy TV just gave him the Person of the Year award. Don't know about person of the year but he sure is the son of the year.'

Samarth laughed, as Adarsh got down to tweeting this latest one-liner. This should get him a good number of RTs. People lapped up Chhote Sarkar jokes.

The two ate in silence for a few minutes, mulling over their thoughts. Adarsh disliked and distrusted all politicians. Samarth was a few years older than him and slightly more pragmatic.

Day 4: Fire in the Belly

Adarsh broke the silence, 'I am losing hope now. Nothing good can come out of all this. The ruling party is messed up but the Orchid *wallahs* are no better. If they get elected, they will just spend time filling their own pockets. There is no alternative. This democracy is failing us. People are dying on the roads. Software engineers are committing suicides for being on the bench for too long. We are the country with the most number of poor people in the world and at the same time we have so many billionaires who drive cars that cost nothing less than a crore. We need to start afresh. The only option is either a dictatorship or for someone to press a reboot button on India that cleans up everything once and for all. It is becoming maddening. I have started looking at job opportunities in Singapore or America now. Will need to convince mom and dad, though.'

'Good luck with that.'

Adarsh's phone buzzed from a Twitter notification. The son of the year joke had reached two hundred RTs already and a popular Bollywood actress had just followed him. The frustration was swept aside with this new victory as the two got up from their table to reluctantly head back to work.

*

The peon came running, his breath heavy from the exertion, 'Madam, it is getting crazy outside. He has gathered a small crowd and is now raising slogans about how you abused him. He has got a can of kerosene and is threatening that he will burn his daughter and himself in 15 minutes.

Madam picked up the telephone and dialed 100. She explained the situation to the police control room and asked them to send a team to help.

She then called up Big Boss and apprised him of the situation. As per department rules she was supposed to keep senior people in the loop, especially in situations when somebody was threatening to kill themselves in front of the school. This could become a major scandal for the news channels and for the opposition party leaders, who awaited such opportunities to present no-confidence motions against the government.

The police arrived within five minutes. They came with ten constables and an anti-riot vehicle equipped with a water cannon, lovingly referred to as the poor man's free shower. A few *lathis* came in direct contact with a few bottoms and the crowd was dispersed in a couple of minutes.

The offending prospective self-immolator was brought to Madam's office for a peaceful settlement. The girl was told to wait outside the office while the adults talked about her case.

Madam was less strict with him this time. A man who threatens to burn himself and his daughter deserves some respect.

'Rafi ji, you should really tell your daughter that she should go back to her school. As per department rules, we cannot admit her in the middle of the session. If you want, I will talk to the principal and request her to take her back.'

Rafi was looking scared. His face had a red tint after being slapped by the policemen as they dragged him off his supposedly peaceful form of protest. He had been threatened that he would be put in jail and beaten up like a dog if he even dreamt of troubling Madam again. The local police inspector's son had been Madam's student.

The inspector who had come in to Madam's office to negotiate the settlement spoke to Rafi. 'Come on speak up. *Jaldi kar*. Listen to Madam and tell your stupid girl to behave properly. Did you even ask her what she was doing with that boy in a hotel? Is this Indian culture?'

Madam raised a hand to calm down the eager policeman and offered Rafi a glass of water. Her voice was calm and composed, from her years of experience counseling troubled teens.

'Rafi ji, you are a reasonable adult. Think logically. How does burning yourself or your daughter help anyone? She is a child. Just talk to her and tell her that the only solution is to resume education in the same school. Maybe we can consider her for next session, when admissions are open. Okay?'

He gave a nervous nod.

'Very good, then. Let's get this in writing and we can all go back.' The policeman took out his notepad and quickly scribbled a short report.

'Sign this,' he handed it to Rafi who signed the paper without even looking at it.

The policeman got up from the chair. 'Madam ji, I am sorry for the trouble this has caused you. I hope the matter is now closed. We will send you a copy of this settlement and close the report on our end. You have a good day!'

Rafi walked off, not looking in Madam's direction. The girl followed him with a sullen look on her face.

*

The doorbell rang.

'Room service.'

He got up, quickly put on his satin pajamas and opened the door, while she slunk under the comforter.

The waiter kept the tray on the table and left, trying hard not to look at the clothes strewn all over the floor while BB signed the delivery slip.

He pulled the comforter off her and threw it off the bed. She squealed in delight, her naked body writhing with excitement. She pulled him down to her and whispered something in her ear. He laughed. 'You want me to be Buddhiman Buddhiraja from B for Buddhi? You crazy, weird woman!'

She insisted. 'Please, baby. Be a sport. I want a private performance of BB, the great interrogator. I will do anything for you in return. Anything!'

'Ooh. Ok, baby. Anything for you.' He went to the work desk and took the chair, facing her. He sat straight and soon got into character, his face rigid and cold, though a smile was threatening to leak through any minute.

'Gosh, it is hard to get into the mood without my regular preparatory material. Do they show *Saas-Bahu* TV here by any chance? I always watch an episode before my recordings as it gets my blood boiling and the adrenalin going.'

'Shut up. Do it. Do it. BB. BB. BB. We want BB. East or west, BB is the best,' she started chanting encouragements.

He leaned forward in his chair, and started. 'You are watching B for Buddhi, brought to you tonight by Scream, the energy drink that will leave you screaming for more. I am your host Buddhiman Buddhiraja. Tonight we have on our show, the idiotic Badi Sarkar and her stupid son, the one we all hate. All politicians are stupid idiots and only BB deserves to be the Prime Minister.'

She applauded loudly, clapping her hands. 'Bravo! Bravo! My Buddhi is the best. My cuddly puddly monkey. Come here you.' She beckoned him with a seductive flick of her finger.

'Get the chocolate sauce also,' she said, her voice a hoarse whisper.

'Anything for the prettiest woman in the world, my pumpkin, the queen of Bollywood, my sweetie pie.'

He took off his pajamas and threw them towards her, grabbed the bowl of chocolate sauce they had requested from room service and turned off the light as he pounced on his latest prey.

'You're going to BB Jail tonight, baby.'

'Ooh I love it! Will you also handcuff me, you angry man?'

DAY 5

RIGHT TO METRO SEATS

AdarshBharatiya @AdarshBharatiya

Maybe Chhote Sarkar should just play to his strengths and threaten people that he will give a speech if they don't vote for his party.

Chhicchora@ Chhicchora

Roses are red, violets are blue. Dear Chhote Sarkar, I am gay for you.

FerozWriter@FerozWriterIIMA

The Lord of the Rings: The Return of the Chhote Sarkar
#ReplaceAMovieNameWithChhoteSarkar

MeraKaamJoker@MeraKaamJoker

BB treats Girpade and Panja so badly every other night, yet they return episode after episode. This is called true love.

'Dear friends, do you know why India will be a superpower very soon?'

Chhote Sarkar waited a few seconds, smiled at the crowd, and answered his own question with another question. 'Okay, tell me this. What is it that India has in abundance that the world does not?'

Another generous flash of his teeth before he spoke again. 'People. Yes, my friends. We have lots of people. People who waste their time being unproductive. People who spend their time playing cricket, chatting with friends, chasing girls, watching TV, playing *Temple Run* on their phones, doing everything except contributing to the nation's growth.'

The assembled crowd looked on, slightly confused about the point being made by the heir to India's throne. Chhote Sarkar had been speaking at this rally for 15 minutes now, and the 10,000-strong crowd, brought in from various corners of the city in specially chartered buses on promises of Rs 500 and a free bottle of IMFL, was getting restless.

Earlier in the morning, Badi Sarkar had stopped him right before he stepped out of the door to drive to the venue and slapped him hard before kissing him on the forehead. 'There, this should act as a lucky charm and ensure that nobody else slaps you or tries to cause you any harm.' She had read reports of how an angry farmer nearly slapped another of the party's leaders at a rally and decided that this was the best way to protect her son from bad luck. After all, lightning doesn't strike at the same spot twice.

His mentor Mohammad Panja looked on at the crowd from the stage, sitting right next to the podium from where Chhote Sarkar was delivering his fifth speech of the season. The volunteers would soon get into action, reminding the crowd that they won't get anything if they left before an hour elapsed. That was the deal. People had got so business-minded these days. For the better orators in the party, they were happy with Rs 200 but Chhote Sarkar went for a premium. Nobody came for less than 500!

This was a record crowd for Chhote Sarkar. Badi Sarkar would be happy with Panja's performance. It was always a challenge managing rallies for Chhote Sarkar, who seemed to show an utter disinterest in the art of election campaigning. There were some other leaders also helping out but ultimately it was Panja running the election campaign for the party. He would ensure that they won the elections. This was his *agnipariksha*. He would get the lucrative Home Ministry if they won. At the next elections, he would bring in his son and get him into Parliament. God willing, he might even have a shot at becoming a Prime Minister one day as a compromise candidate.

Chhote Sarkar was speaking extempore, which also meant that no TV crews could be allowed at the rally. Print media could always report the speech the party wanted them to report. Live coverage was a problem.

For some reason, Chhote Sarkar had been refusing to use the speeches specially prepared by his 12-member team of IIT/IIM graduates; his own 'commando' unit setup by Badi Sarkar to provide creative inputs. The Engineers-turned-MBAs were camped in 5-star hotels, each earning Rs 5 lakhs per month for doing nothing. Why should Panja complain? A few crores was small change in the scheme of things, if it kept Badi Sarkar happy.

Chhote Sarkar helped himself to a glass of water and finally answered his question. 'The only way for India to become a superpower is to use its people efficiently. We cannot waste our time doing unproductive work. Our party is talking to consultants to build a power plant where people can walk-in during their free time. You pedal away on a cycle and it harnesses your energy to produce electricity. Our people become fitter. The nation gets much needed power.'

The crowd suddenly seemed to get very excited. Not for the ingenious suggestion but because a group of workers were done installing a giant promotional hoarding of the latest Bollywood movie outside the ground, just behind the stage from where Chhote

Day 5: Right to Metro Seats

Sarkar was speaking. The giant cleavage of Perky Padma, the latest voluptuous sensation from the south, stared at the crowd.

Chhote Sarkar felt encouraged by the response, unaware of what was happening behind the stage. He had another suggestion.

'Friends, do you know Kirchhoff's law of electricity? It is the most fascinating principle. Basically, when you complete an electrical circuit, current flows from a point of high potential to low potential.'

He gave the crowd a moment to let this sink in, before continuing. 'You must be wondering – what is this guy blabbering about? You want food. You want freedom from poverty. You don't care about dead scientists. Friends, there is a lesson here. This principle also applies to the weather. Air always flows in from high pressure to low pressure. You know how this applies to you? You want power? You want food? Create a low-pressure area around you.'

Panja felt relief at the decision to keep the news channels away. This might have ended up becoming another disaster but he had learnt after the first speech. That day, Chhote Sarkar had spent ten minutes talking about how human beings were like onions, with layer upon layer that they needed to peel off to discover their true potential and then gone on to announce that his party was full of corrupt people who deserved to be beaten up by the public. Badi Sarkar had been furious that night and Chhote Sarkar had made it worse by switching to channel MTV and turning up the volume while she ranted on about the hardship she had endured in raising him.

The bravest of tigresses finds it hard to give up on her own offspring. They eventually patched up. Panja took Chhote Sarkar under his wings and assured Badi Sarkar that he would make the boy well-versed in the fine art of politics.

'Friends, do you know why I enjoy talking to you people?' Chhote Sarkar took another sip of water and wiped the perspiration from his brow. The sun was now directly overhead and he was feeling stifled in the four layers of warm clothing Badi Sarkar had insisted he wear, lest he catch an infection at this busy time before the elections.

A section of the crowd suddenly started chanting slogans against

Chhote Sarkar. Panja looked at his event-coordinator who was responsible for paying out the promised amount to everybody upfront and he shook his head. This section had not been paid as they had fallen short of cash as well as liquor.

'We will just say that they were planted by the opposition to disrupt the rally. Call a few of your men and shoo them off,' Panja instructed him.

'We just have to change the system, my dear friends. We have to empower our women.' He flashed that dazzling smile, and rambled on. 'You know what happens every time I discuss politics with my mother?' Someone in the crowd shouted 'she cries' and everybody laughed. The voice carried to Chhote Sarkar, who looked at the fellow who was now being dragged away by security and said 'No, no, she doesn't cry. She says Chhote you are too naive. You think too much about people.'

Suddenly his phone rang. He looked at it and said, 'It's my mother. Hold on one second,' and turned off the mike.

'Hello, *ma*?

'Yes it is going well. I am still giving the speech. There are so many people here. I was so nervous earlier that I think my pants are wet but now I am okay.'

'Yes, yes. Don't worry. I am fine.'

'I love you, too.'

The crowd broke into applause as he hung up. The mike hadn't been off after all.

Oblivious, he took a sip of water and continued. 'I say what is wrong in thinking about people? Without people, what would our country be? Nothing.' The crowd applauded. Perky Padma's left eye had just fallen off, as a section of the hoarding came loose.

'I say if we have a shortage of wheat, why not look at alternatives. We have been eating *dal-roti* for many years now, let's find something else. Let's eat pizza maybe. What do you think? Have you ever eaten a nice cheesy pizza, hot off the oven?

'My dear friends, we all need to circumcise otherwise nothing will change. Yes, circumcise.' One of his MBAs ran up to him and whispered in his ear, prompting a correction. 'Oh sorry, circumspect. We all need to circumspect.'

Day 5: Right to Metro Seats

A fight seemed to have broken out among the crowd as the party volunteers started roughing up the people shouting slogans for their payment. Panja got up from his seat. He came by Chhote Sarkar's side and whispered in his ear. 'Bablu, let's go. Enough for today.'

Chhote Sarkar nodded and spoke into the microphone. 'Our honorable Minister of Mobile Phones, ladies and gentlemen. Please clap for the learned Panja ji.' The crowd responded with a polite applause, mainly coming from the party volunteers strategically blended into the audience.

'Okay then friends, I have enjoyed talking to you all today. Take care. Remember, create that low pressure around you and things will start flowing to you.'

Chhote Sarkar bowed to the crowd and started to move to the back of the stage. The audience was already getting up and rushing for the exits before the long lines formed, when Chhote Sarkar remembered one last thing and came back onto the microphone.

'Oh yes, I forgot. Vote for We Will We Will Rock You party. My mother will be very angry if you don't do that.'

*

As the maid ushered Giani Seth into the Great Leader's office, a man ran out howling in pain. Giani Seth noticed that the *kurta-pajama* clad person had blood oozing out of his hand and seemed to have a few fingers missing. He hesitatingly entered the Great Leader's plush office.

'Giani Seth, my good friend. I have heard so much about you. I always wanted to personally thank you for your generous contributions to our party fund and looks like today is the day. Thank you very much and I am so happy that we have you on our side.' The Great Leader was wiping his hands on a towel and it was stained red.

'He has blood on his hands,' Giani Seth mumbled as he looked at him quizzically.

'Oh this? Come with me.' The Great Leader noticed Giani Seth staring, and took him to the far end of the room where the fish tank was located. The fish seemed agitated and the water was bloody.

'The man you saw running outside was Chawla, my accounts manager. I just discovered that he had committed a fraud of Rs 5,200 – a donation that he kept for himself. So I gave him a small punishment.'

Giani Seth was staring at the fish with amazement. 'These don't look like the fish people normally have in their fish tanks.'

'Piranha, Giani Seth. The fiercest species of fish found in the world. Dip your foot in the water and they will strip the bone clean in seconds. I just made Chawla immerse his hand and count to five. They took away two fingers.'

Giani Seth was still looking at him in shock.

'You look surprised, Giani Seth. In my party, I have zero tolerance for cheating. Such people just make me go crazy. That fellow learnt an important lesson today. He will never commit a fraud again in his life.'

The Great Leader lovingly held Giani Seth by his shoulders. 'Giani Seth, I cannot tell you how happy I am that you could find time to visit OrchidNagar.' Giani Seth looked around the office impressed especially with the view outside the window, suddenly feeling the urge to go to the toilet. The Great Leader saw him staring and led him to the window.

'Giani Seth, look around. As far as your eyes can see, this is all OrchidNagar, the picture of prosperity not found anywhere else in India. In this city, nobody goes to bed hungry, nobody sleeps on pavements because we don't build any and there is always a SitarBucks within ten minutes of wherever you are.

The Great Leader walked to his desk, beckoned Giani Seth to take a seat, and asked, 'Please make yourself comfortable. How was your trip?'

Giani Seth made himself comfortable by folding his legs under him as he took the chair, and inserted a finger inside his left ear as he answered. 'It was very good, Great Leader. Thank God for technology. All I have to do is call up my pilot who keeps Rocky ready to fly at ten minutes' notice. He just has to check the tire pressure, fill up petrol, and I can go anywhere in India.'

'Rocky?'

Day 5: Right to Metro Seats

'Oh,' Giani Seth laughed. 'Rocky is my Hairbus jet, which I got for 425 crores recently. They gave a three-year onsite warranty and threw in free foot-mats. The mileage is terrible though.' He shrugged his shoulders. 'And the government just keeps raising petrol prices. Inflation is killing us poor people.'

The Great Leader was impressed. 'You should take me on a ride on Rocky some time. My jet has just ten seats and it becomes such a pain. Last week two dozen of us senior leaders had to go for a rally, and we decided to go together in my plane. The pilot was complaining about overloading but we managed to fit everyone, with the junior members going standing. Maybe I'll also buy a bigger one from Hairbus.'

The Great Leader looked at Giani Seth, who had now taken out a packet of *pan masala* from his shirt pocket and was opening it up. The Seth offered some to him but he refused.

'So Giani Seth, what brings you here?'

Giani Seth emptied the *pan masala* pack in his mouth as he answered. 'Sir ji, you know I want to build the world's largest port in India but the government is just not providing approval for the project. We have already paid 5,000 crores but still there is no sign of action. I came to see if you could help. It is a Rs 50,000 crore project. There is a lot at stake for me.'

The Great Leader pondered on his sentence, got up from his seat, and walked to the window. Giani Seth followed him.

'Do you see the EyeMAX Theater, Giani Seth? This one is the largest screen in the world. Who brought it to India? The Great Leader.'

'Who brought Juicy Donuts to...'

Giani Seth felt that his bladder was about to burst and immediately held up his little finger at the Great Leader – the same gesture that he used, to convey his need to go to the washroom during his school days. The Great Leader looked surprised at this juvenile expression but pointed towards the door of his bathroom. Giani Seth hurried to relieve himself while the Great Leader stared into the distance.

A few minutes later, Giani Seth exited the bathroom wiping his hands on the sleeve of his *kurta*, and the Great Leader asked him, 'Giani Seth, do you know which flower is Harry Potter's favorite?'

Giani Seth walked up to him by the window, shrugging his shoulders. 'Sorry sir, Harry who? The cement guy?'

The Great leader sighed in disbelief. 'Never mind, Giani Seth. I was saying, you should have come to me earlier. We could have walked out of the Parliament to put pressure on the government. We could have put one of my people on a fast-unto-death to get them to agree. We could have...' he stopped, as another thought came into his mind.

'Why do you need MY help?'

Giani Seth looked at the Great Leader and said, 'Because I believe in you, Great Leader. I think you are the Lord Krishna if I am Arjun. I think you will take India into a glorious future. This government is all corrupt.' His eyes welled up. 'They took 5,000 crores and didn't even give a receipt. Bloody *chors*.'

The Great Leader looked satisfied with the answer. 'Well, then, my dear Arjun. I will do what I can. You just take care of our election fund.'

Giani Seth smiled. 'Not to worry, sir. There are ten bags of *prasad* that I brought along in Rocky, a little gift from me, according to the standard market rate of two percent. I hope that is okay?'

'Of course it is, Giani Seth. I am always there to help the needy.'

*

Adarsh's blood was boiling. He had reached home after a two-hour drive from work, stuck again in traffic jams. To make it worse, a car had been tailing him half of that time with the driver honking like his life depended on it. Road rage had got the better of Adarsh and after the first ten minutes, he had ended up opening the window and showing him a finger, which just made it worse. The dude tailgated him continuously after that and his persistent honking had driven Adarsh insane.

Madam was supervising the maid cleaning the kitchen while Adarsh went through the day's newspaper. The front page had a picture of Bhakt Lal, proudly displaying that tattoo on his forehead,

Day 5: Right to Metro Seats 95

now surrounded by about two dozen youngsters with shaven heads bearing 'Chhote Sarkar for PM' tattoos. He claimed that he was building an army of loyal followers who would do whatever they could to ensure that Chhote Sarkar became the Prime Minister of India.

Meanwhile, Madam was shouting at the domestic help in the kitchen, 'What are you doing? Didn't I tell you not to use the metal scrub on the ceramic plates? Do you know how much each one of them costs? You will ruin them all. Make sure you clean the sink after you are done. It was so dirty yesterday and I had to clean it myself.'

He turned the page to find news of an Indian diplomat attending the UN session in New York who had confused the American president for a security guard, commenting that they must pay him really well for him to afford the nice suit he was wearing. The president apparently took it in good humor, not realizing the insult until the Foreign Minister called him up to apologize for the 'terrible mistake that one of our representatives committed today.' Bow Wow news channel was already speculating that a US aircraft carrier was headed towards India as a retaliatory measure.

'Mom, check out this piece of news. There is going to be a war between India and America!'

'Where are you going? The floor is still wet! Do you want me to slip and break my legs?' Mom was busy with the maid.

'Never mind,' he called out.

'Bunch of idiots,' he mumbled as Madam brought tea five minutes later, sat down next to him and switched on the TV.

'What did you say?'

'No, nothing *ma*. Let's have tea.'

'Once you are done, can you go to the Mother Dairy and get milk?'

'Sure, *ma*.'

Madam asked him. 'Why do you look so upset? Is something wrong?'

'No, not really. The newspaper is full of depressing news.' For this very reason, newspapers had been ordered to carry a statutory warning about potential loss of sanity by the Supreme Court five years ago. The warning featured a man pulling the trigger on a gun held to his head, a newspaper in his other hand, accompanied by the text 'Newspaper Reading Can Be Injurious To Mental Health.'

He took out his phone to register his outrage on Twitter. Madam took the phone from his hands. 'You and your stupid phone. I will throw it away one day.' Adarsh made a wry face as he sipped tea, holding his mug with both hands, soaking in the warmth.

Madam said, 'Look at your hair. Your dad still has a head full of thick hair and you have already lost half of it. Baba says that this is all because of phones and computer and stress. You should go for a walk in the morning and try not to stare at the phone all the time.'

Madam was a fan of Baba Neemacharya and listened to his sermons regularly. 'He suggested some sure-shot remedies today. Hold a neem leaf under your armpit when you go to the toilet. It helps improve your memory. For hair loss, he said that a juice made of the root of a neem tree mixed with *karela* and *tulsi* leaves is guaranteed to increase your hair growth within a few days.'

She caught Adarsh make a gagging gesture and asked, 'Don't make that face, Adarsh. Can you find some neem roots for me?' She switched to *Saas-Bahu* TV and continued, 'By the way, Mohammad Panja is coming to my school tomorrow to give free phones to the poor children. I hope he doesn't bring pornographic books again like the last time.' She smiled, though she was nervous about the visit. Panja was a powerful man and would be accompanied by all the senior people in the department, including Big Boss.

'Please give Panja a tight slap on my behalf,' Adarsh said. 'You know he is accused of having embezzled many thousands of crores during his term already. Let us also not forget the story of the girl who had accused him of molesting her when she had gone for an interview to his office. He is apparently tutoring that imbecile Chhote Sarkar these days. As if tutoring would help.'

The maid called out to Madam. She was finally done. 'Give me a missed call tomorrow when you are ready so that I don't have to waste any time waiting,' she said as she left.

'Okay, Meena,' Madam shouted back over the sound of the ladies quarrelling on TV.

Day 5: Right to Metro Seats

Adarsh wasn't done yet. 'They are all the bloody same. And people keep harping on about the Great Leader like he is some sort of miracle. I read an article in a magazine where they said that once he had to go to a meeting and got stuck in a traffic jam because a tree had fallen on the road. Apparently, he looked at the tree and it suddenly gave way. Are we supposed to believe this?' He could hear his heartbeat get louder again.

Madam reminded him to get the milk as she got up to make some phone calls to her staff about the next day's visit.

The Mother Dairy depot was a ten-minute walk. Adarsh wore a jacket and headed outside.

He was halfway there, mulling over the US aircraft-carrier crisis for the Indian government when he reached a traffic intersection. He duly stepped to the zebra crossing and was about to cross the road when a Honda City car came towards him speeding at what must be over 60kmph in the residential area and Adarsh hurriedly stepped back onto the pavement. He wasn't surprised at the rash driving but annoyed nevertheless. He started moving when he noticed another jeep coming by so he stopped again. The road was finally clear. There was a Scorpio in the distance but it was slow and there should have been sufficient time for Adarsh to cross. He started moving but the car gathered speed instead of slowing down. Adarsh was barely a few metres away from the other side of the road and the car was almost upon him. He expected it to stop now but the driver had other ideas. He sped up and tried to squeeze past the little space between Adarsh and the pavement. He missed Adarsh by a few inches and that too because Adarsh pulled back at the last second to avoid getting run over. He was shocked. People needed to start showing some courtesy to others.

As the car passed by, Adarsh noticed four young boys sitting inside. The driver didn't seem to be of legal age. There was loud music playing inside and the four were sitting with smug expressions, their spiked hair standing like they had been subjected to electrical shocks.

In his rage, Adarsh hit the car with his hand as it passed him. He did it fairly strongly and his hand stung from the impact. The car slowed down and the driver took his head out of the window to stare at Adarsh, who shouted 'Are you fucking blind?'

The car stopped. One by one the four alighted with annoyed expressions on their faces. One of them looked at his watch and said 'Guys we are getting late. Let's leave him.' The others clearly didn't agree as they moved towards Adarsh. One of them rolled up his sleeves and shouted a profanity at Adarsh. Another opened the trunk of the car and handed out cricket bats.

Adarsh looked around. There weren't too many people visible, though cars were regularly passing by. He decided to stand his ground. These guys were wrong to cut across him. They could have run him over. He could have died. Surely he was the aggrieved party and had the right to complain.

The guy with the rolled up sleeves swung his hand and landed a blow on his chin.

*

'Good evening, ladies and gentlemen. The nation is in the midst of an election fever. Nobody knows which party will win, but isn't this the great joy of the democratic process? The people of the nation will want to keep their cards close and make an informed decision about whom they want to bring into power. This was the vision of the forefathers of the nation. This was the dream they saw.'

BB stared long and hard into Camera #5, did an almost imperceptible roll of his eyes and continued. 'Whether that vision of clean democracy came alive or not, our viewers are well-aware. The nation is in the midst of crisis. Our esteemed government has managed to annoy the masters of the universe, no less. As we speak, a 200,000 ton aircraft carrier is coming in our direction at full speed. As per unverified reports, this is a vessel capable of launching nuclear missiles deep into India's interiors.'

He sighed into Camera #2 and shook his head in disgust. 'We can just hope that good sense prevails and our capable,' he coughed ever so slightly, 'leaders are able to diffuse this crisis.

'That, of course, is a topic for another discussion. You are watching B for Buddhi, brought to you tonight by Scream, the energy drink

Day 5: Right to Metro Seats

that will leave you screaming for more. I am your host Buddhiman Buddhiraja. Tonight we have on our show Dr Mohammad Panja from the ruling We Will We Will Rock You party and Dr Girpade from the Orchid party. The two gentlemen will briefly outline the key features of their election manifestos for the benefit of our audience so that the people of India can decide which party they want to vote for.'

BB gestured towards Panja and said, 'First, let me welcome Dr Panja, a regular participant on our show. Sir, if you could take five minutes to tell us what your party wants to do differently if voted to power again.'

Panja smiled into Camera #7 and began. 'My dear BB ji, it is always an honour to be on your show. Thanks for allowing me this opportunity to represent the party to your millions of viewers.

'You see, BB ji, our party believes that India's biggest problem is poverty and we will do our best to remove poverty. Within thirty days you will see results, I promise you.'

BB smirked, 'Sir, you've had many years already. What will you do differently this time?'

Panja answered.'BB ji, you know when I was a child, we used to get a kilo of *jalebis* for two paise. Steaming hot *jalebis* made in fresh *desi* ghee. Go to the market today and they will cost you Rs 600! Too expensive. I have stopped eating *jalebis* completely.'

Girpade had been listening on, a wide smile on his face. He couldn't control it any longer and burst out laughing. 'Panja ji, if *you* can't afford *jalebi*, what will the poor people do? The hyenas of a jungle where the lion is a member of PETA don't eat meat.'

Panja ignored him. 'BB ji, there is a popular saying in my village that goes like this – those who cannot eat *jalebi* eat sugarcane jaggery. Those who can't eat jaggery drown their sorrow in alcohol. We will make sure alcohol is readily available and affordable to everybody.'

BB sniggered, 'THAT's your solution, sir?'

'BB ji, when our government comes to power we will ensure that there's a smartphone in every house. In fact I am visiting one of our schools tomorrow to hand out touch-screen phones to the poorest of the poor, the below-19 inch line students. We will even give them free 3G data packages for two years.'

Girpade interrupted him. 'Panja ji, how will people charge their phones if there is no power anywhere in the city?'

'No problem. We will send charging vans to their colonies so that people can charge their phones. Girpade ji, we are not fools. We have thought of everything.'

'But sir, what about food? People want food, not 3G packages,' BB asked him.

'BB ji, we are a spiritual nation. Food for thought is more important than food. Look at me. I have been gaining so much weight eating stupid food,' Panja let out a timely burp and Girpade turned away his face in disgust, as the air was filled with the smell of chicken *tikka* and mint chutney.

Panja looked at BB and asked him, 'BB ji, you tell me have you ever seen a fat poor man? No, right? See it works out well for them. At least people in India won't suffer from obesity and heart problems like in the west. This is our culture BB ji. We don't run after material gains but are content with whatever we have.'

'That's a fascinating insight, sir. I am happy we don't have too many politicians who can think out of the box like you do,' BB's tone was sarcastic and his eyes now had a murderous look.

He switched his attention to Girpade, sitting next to Panja with a smug look on his face. 'Dr Girpade, the latest surveys are reaffirming that there is a strong buzz in favor of the Great Leader. People have a sense of optimism that he will be able to improve the state of affairs in the country. Can you talk us through some of the prominent features of your manifesto? What will you do differently if people bring you to power?'

'Certainly, Mr BB. It is easy to see that there is going to be a lot for us to do under the watchful leadership of the visionary Great Leader, whose dynamism has enthused the nation like never before.' He took out his reading glasses and a piece of paper from the pocket of his jacket, wore the glasses and started reading from the notes he had scribbled.

'If the Orchid party comes to power, the first thing we will do is to reduce the price of orchids all over the nation. This is the flower of knowledge, of medicinal and spiritual importance, and a stick lasts in a vase for up to a week if you keep changing water. Then we will start our war against poverty. We will kill every poor person in the country...'

'Excuse me!' BB interjected, incredulous.

'Ah! I am sorry, Mr BB. I meant that we will kill poverty and everybody will have food to eat, a roof over their heads and at least a 100cc motorcycle to drive to work. A bee cannot produce honey if it doesn't have wings to fly.'

'You will give free motorcycles to people?' Panja exclaimed, at the same time wondering how he didn't think of that earlier.

Girpade continued reading. 'We will change the way our defence forces work by reviving the lost science of archery, the most potent weapon used in ancient times. We will immediately start research into state-of-the-art bows and arrows that will strike terror deep into the hearts of the enemies. Guns and fighter jets are too expensive and not a part of Indian culture.'

'We will give people the right to a metro seat so that everybody gets a seat for at least ten minutes every time they ride the metro for more than 15 kilometers. Because we believe that tired people are unproductive people and standing in the metro tires them.'

'We will build schools that lay emphasis on practical education and do away with exams of all sorts. That way, children can focus on learning and not worry about failing in exams. This will also make India the most educated nation in the world because the pass percentages will always be 100 per cent!' Girpade looked up and smiled at Panja and BB. BB didn't look too excited.

'We will give call-centre training to students starting from class 10. There will be specializations available for credit cards, IT helpdesks and mobile phone customer support.'

'We will start helicopter services between Indraprastha and Gurgone so that our office workers don't have to spend time stuck in traffic.'

'In our ancient texts, there are references to how the orchid can be used to produce a petrol-like substance if burnt at a temperature of exactly 344.5 degree Celsius in a container made of a special compound of gold, silver and resin extracted from a four-year-old mango tree. We will set up labs to research Orchetrol,' he looked up and smiled at the ingenuity of the name that was his personal suggestion to the party high command and continued, 'which will be the cheapest fuel known to mankind. Soon, we won't just have enough fuel for ourselves but could become the largest exporter in the world and be able to recover India's lost pride.'

He kept the paper down, got up, raised his hands and proclaimed, 'This, dear people, is the vision of the Great Leader. India is headed for greatness. Not only will we become the most powerful nation in the world but we will actually save humanity from destruction once the current petrol deposits finish. That will be the day India reclaims its rightful place in the world!'

'But...' Panja tried to interject but Girpade kept going.

'Mr BB, do you know that when the Great Leader was five years old, he heard an *aakashvaani* – a proclamation – from the skies. He was playing cricket with his friends when he took a break to urinate under an old *peepal* tree when suddenly a voice from one of the branches high in the tree rang out and said, in clear words, 'you who answers the call of nature at the roots of this tree, will one day see the gods urinate on you.' After that, all the knowledge of our ancient scriptures got immediately transferred into the Great Leader's mind.'

'BB ji, all this is nonsense,' Panja was getting fidgety and his hands were wrapped around a paper-weight kept on the table. BB raised a hand to shut him up.

Girpade folded his hands together, looked up towards the skies, and said a silent prayer. The Great Leader would save the nation from all evil one day. He was THE one.

Panja picked up the paper-weight and threw it in Girpade's direction. There was a scream as it hit the cameraman instead.

DAY 6

BADI SARKAR SMART CHILDREN YOJNA

AdarshBharatiya@AdarshBharatiya

There's something fishy about BB tonight.

BowWowBreaking@BowWowBreaking

Breaking: Actor Veerkhan Bhai redefines 'fashionably late'. Arrives at gym inauguration a day late.

RightToTroll@RightToTroll

Yes Chhote Sarkar, you should circumcise every day. Oh, sorry I meant circumspect.

Chhicchora@Chhicchora

Maybe Badi Sarkar named him Chhote Sarkar due to the size of his small brain.

BhaktLal@BhaktLalMP

Our movement now has 100 volunteers with tattooed heads asking Chhote Sarkar to become PM.

TheOrchidParty@TheOrchidParty

When he was 15 years old, the Great Leader saved two cows from starvation by giving them his school lunch for a month. #GreatLeaderFacts

Madam was sobbing as she draped the magenta chiffon sari she used to reserve for special occasions. Today was the big day when the Minister of Mobile Phones, Mohammad Panja, was visiting her school to hand out free smartphones to students. All preparations had been completed. The designated students had been instructed to come to school on time and leave immediately after getting their phones to avoid them being snatched away by those who weren't getting one. The teachers had been warned not to be late by even a minute. The school had been thoroughly cleaned. The trees had been watered. The grass in the lawns had been mowed. A sweeper had been hired to clean the toilets. Everything was in order.

Except that Madam had lost all enthusiasm. Some people had beaten up Adarsh last evening when he was on his way to Mother Dairy. From what he told her, they had almost run him over when he was crossing the road and his protest had provoked violence. Thankfully they had left him the moment he crumpled to the ground after a few blows and kicks. He had ended up with a bruised lip, a grazed ankle, severe pain in the stomach and a fractured ego.

Adarsh had returned home without milk and was trying to clean his wounds with Dettol when Madam saw him and cried for an hour after dressing him up. Adarsh's short temper was a major cause of worry. He needed to get a grip on his anger.

'You better do some *Pranayaam* today if you want to live a peaceful life. We can't keep dressing your wounds if you get into fights with goons over petty matters. You were lucky they didn't break your legs, or worse, shoot...' She stopped herself from completing the sentence and broke into tears again.

Adarsh was too emotionally scarred to speak. He had vented his outrage on Twitter after the incident and hundreds of retweets and messages of support had reinforced his belief that he did the right thing. What if freedom fighters like Bhagat Singh, Subhash Chandra Bose and many others had also shied away from getting hurt by the British? India might have never won her independence. But tell that to his mother who was sobbing away like one of those melodramatic ladies on *Saas-Bahu* TV!

He had memorized the registration number of the car and gone to the police station to register a complaint. The cops promised to help him initially but went cold when he started giving details of the car. No sooner did he say that on the hood of the car there was a flag bearing the image of a cricket bat, the symbol of BAAP, Bhartiya Akhand Ahinsa Party, that they told him to go back home.

'I can just pray to God that he gives you some good sense to not get so angry over the smallest of issues. The rest is up to you. You are an adult now. How long are we going to be around to take care of you?'

Adarsh rolled his eyes. Emotional blackmail had always been her most effective weapon.

'Okay *ma*, you're getting late for school. Please go.'

Madam sighed as she headed out of the door.

Adarsh picked up the newspaper and noticed the front page headline:

'GOVERNMENT WANTS TO PAY *YOU* FOR POWER'

The ruling party had announced that if they won the elections, they would start paying people for consuming electricity and water. This was a new day in populist politics, a big step up on the days of discounts and subsidies. So far they had just promised as much as 50 per cent subsidies on water and electricity, but this was a whole new level altogether. Now the government was not only not charging people to use basic amenities but they were actually going to pay them for it!

The Orchid party had been outdone this time.

*

'Hurry up, Chutki, it is your turn.'

'Wait, *mama*. I am trying to calculate what number I need.'

Day 6: Badi Sarkar Smart Children Yojna

'Okay, *jaldi kar*. I'll go to the kitchen to look for some Cheeky Chocolate ice-cream.'

'No, *mama*, I want cookies.'

'No, no. We will eat chocolate ice-cream today. Wait till you taste it. I'll be back in a minute.'

As Chhote Sarkar lifted his six-year-old niece from his lap and headed towards the kitchen, the phone in his *kurta* pocket buzzed. It was a text message from Panja, his mentor.

'Chhote Sarkar, I hope you are en route to inaugurate the Badi Sarkar museum in Great Liberator Nagar. It is right off Badi Sarkar Road, next to the Great Liberator metro station, a stone's throw away from the Badi Sarkar super-specialty hospital.'

He deleted the message and headed into the kitchen.

This new museum had been created by demolishing a 30-year-old school for 1200 under-privileged students. The announcement of the project two years ago, on Badi Sarkar's 60th birthday as a token of appreciation for her untiring love and dedication, had been followed by a mad scramble among party leaders desperate to take credit for the idea. A particularly stormy Working Group meeting had ended in a fist-fight that left Panja with a dislocated shoulder, Chamcha Das needing 12 stitches on the gash to his forehead and Bhakt Lal temporarily blinded with red chilli powder in his eyes. Finally, it was decided that the credit be split among the leaders, and the museum be called a gift from the entire Working Group to Badi Sarkar.

The museum was going to house paintings, statues and other assorted craftwork – all dedicated to Badi Sarkar. There was a solid gold statue of Badi Sarkar as Goddess Lakshmi, a very life-like statue of Badi Sarkar as Mother Teresa, and some two hundred portraits of Badi Sarkar. She had been featured in various poses such as standing, reading a newspaper, washing her dirty laundry, addressing a crowd, sipping tea, eating a momo, sitting astride a horse, jabbing at a punching bag, praying in a mosque and brushing her teeth.

'*Mama*, come soon. I got a four. One of your reds is going to get out!' Chutki squealed from the living room, delighted.

He found the ice-cream tub and headed out triumphantly when Michael Jackson's 'All I wanna say is that they don't really care about us' started playing on his phone. This was the ring-tone he had set for calls from Panja and his mother. Chhote Sarkar ignored it, letting the song play out until the call got disconnected.

Chutki killed one of his red players from the board and ran around the room holding it like a trophy. '*Mama* is going to lose today. *Mama* is going to lose today,' she sang in her adorable voice.

Chhote Sarkar's phone rang again. He ignored the call yet again. That museum could wait. He wasn't going anywhere. There were plenty of museums in the country anyway. Who cared about one more?

His phone buzzed. A text message from Panja. 'Bablu, the governor and Badi Sarkar are waiting for you at the inauguration. Come soon or I will teach you a lesson you will never forget.'

'Teach me a lesson?' He mumbled to himself, turned on his laptop and logged on to a Classifieds site. Five minutes later, he was done. He giggled as he kept the laptop aside.

He took Chutki in his lap and they dug into the ice-cream tub with spoons. 'Chutki, what do you want to become when you grow up?'

Chutki licked the ice-cream off her spoon and started tapping on her forehead, a serious expression on her angelic face. She had learnt this from one of her favorite cartoon characters. It took her five taps to arrive at her answer.

'I want to be a mummy when I grow older.'

Chhote Sarkar laughed loudly and kissed her on her cheek. 'Sure you will become a mummy one day.'

'What do you want to become, *mama*?'

Chhote Sarkar started tapping on his forehead, his eyes narrowed and his lips drawn out into a pout. 'I don't know Chutki. Growing up is so tough.'

As Chutki happily ate her ice-cream and took the dice in her tiny hands for the next roll, Chhote Sarkar's thoughts went back to when he was young and wanted to become an artist when he grew up.

The phone rang again. It was Badi Sarkar this time. She was the

Day 6: Badi Sarkar Smart Children Yojna

one who had refused to let him go for that art history course at Stanford. 'You can become anything you want when you grow up Chhote, as long as it is a politician.'

Chhote Sarkar frowned. When he was younger, she used to make him play the harmonium every time she had guests. There was the one time when he kept begging for an ice-cream but she didn't give him one until he told her the names of all districts in the country, their demographic composition, the prominent castes in that region and who they voted for. He was ten years old then.

As a child, he had gone to bed hungry quite a few nights because he gave the wrong answers to her surprise questions on how to create vote-banks or how to influence poor people to vote for your party. People his age used to play cricket and football but he was forced to play Badi Sarkar's favorite game – Monopoly.

Other children in his class had posters of actors and rock-stars in their rooms. He had pictures of past Prime Ministers and the people from the current lot expected to be his competitors when his 'time to take the throne' neared, which was how she put it. Panja and other party leaders had even insisted that his room be named the Great Liberator Room of Studies.

He pressed the 'Reject Call' button on his phone.

*

The minister's cavalcade reached the school compound and Panja got out of his bullet-proof Ambassador. Madam and her welcome committee of four teachers were waiting for him at the entrance. Some of the senior officers of the department were already present. The Big Boss had come an hour ago and personally inspected everything to make sure nothing was left to chance. He even sniffed the flowers to make sure they were fresh. If Panja became Home Minister, he was in with a chance of a plum bureaucratic post.

Madam garlanded Panja and his secretary, followed by Big Boss and some lesser bosses, taking care to follow due protocol. The principal before her had lost her job because she invited all the bosses for an annual day and then called upon one of the lesser bosses to address the school before Big Boss, who had suspended her on his way out of the school an hour later.

Madam invited Panja to take a tour of the school before addressing the students at a special assembly that would be followed by the phone distribution ceremony.

She showed him the computer lab where students were taught basic skills in word-processing and programming. She showed him the home science labs, the chemistry lab, the physics lab, the multipurpose hall, the classrooms, the teacher's staff room, the toilets. Panja didn't speak a word. He just seemed to be calling somebody repeatedly while walking through the school corridors absent-mindedly. Madam heard him tell his secretary, 'Get in touch with that SOB urgently.'

His phone rang as they reached the library. He answered it with a gruff 'hello' and frowned. 'No I don't want to sell my microwave.' He gazed at the phone for a few seconds and kept it back in his pocket. They entered the library and he exclaimed, '*The Hindu*? Madam, how can you make your students read such a non-secular newspaper?'

Before Madam could respond, his phone rang. He answered it impatiently, heard the person on the other end, and got infuriated. 'How big is my microwave? You will know when I push it up your butt, you stupid idiot.'

He didn't eat any of the snacks offered by Madam. 'What is this? *Dhokla*? *Samosa*?' he said with a disgusted look on his face. He refused the glass of water as well. 'Just get me some mineral water. Do you want to kill me by giving me tap water? You must be agents of that stupid Orchid party.'

His secretary whispered in the ear of the arts teacher who was overlooking the catering. 'Sir is pure non-vegetarian. He sticks to it very religiously.'

They headed to the school assembly where he was due to address the students before handing out their smartphones. His phone rang just as he was starting his speech. He took the call, heard the person on the other end and shouted, 'YOU MOTHERFUCKER, I WILL NOT SELL YOU MY MICROWAVE. I WILL BURN YOU ALIVE IN A TANDOOR IF YOU CALL ME AGAIN.' He then proceeded to hurl the phone against the wall of the stage, smashing it to bits.

Day 6: Badi Sarkar Smart Children Yojna

He turned to the students, smiled benevolently and started his address.

'Good morning, brothers and sisters,' the octagenerian started with great aplomb as the children, aged four to sixteen, sat on the sprawling school ground in front of him.

He spoke for 30 minutes, during which he talked about the many evils of the opposition. He spoke ill about the Great Leader, promised the young students a life free of poverty and freedom from the grips of evil money-lenders, offered them counseling support in case of marital problems, promised he would regularize their unauthorized colonies, offered their children reservation in call-center jobs. All while the students looked on, amused. Panja had no idea that he was reading the speech to be given at the election rally later that day, not the one prepared for these students.

Panja completed his speech with a flourish asking them to give their votes to the We Will We Will Rock You party and secure a joyous future for their children. The students clapped loudly, in part because it was over and more so because it was time to get their mobile phones.

Panja asked Madam for the list of students who were getting the phones, took a look at the list, and his face went red with anger. He asked Madam to break it into three lists – students belonging to the religion-that-must-not-be-named, those from the other-religion-that-must-not-be-named, and all others. Madam asked her staff to breakdown the lists as requested.

This process took fifteen minutes, and to the dismay of the assembled students, Panja ji spent the time describing to them the great virtues of Badi Sarkar and Chhote Sarkar.

'When Chhote Sarkar was born, he already knew a, b, c. At the age of two he knew tables until 20. By the time he was five, Chhote Sarkar knew the capitals of all countries and could solve algebra equations involving three variables. By the age of ten he could calculate differential equations and knew all laws of fluid-mechanics and thermo-chemistry. Chhote Sarkar is a genius. You should take inspiration from him. One day we will ask him to talk to you so that you can learn from him and put in more effort to become smart like him.

'Badi Sarkar is a goddess. So kind. So empathetic. Even if she finds a cow outside on the road, she will go and give it a grilled cheese sandwich. Last week she organized a *langar* for the stray dogs in the neighborhood. She is a very kind soul and it is our honour that she is around us. I feel blessed that I get to interact with her every day. May God give a long life to Badi Sarkar.'

'*Bolo Badi Sarkar ki…*'

His secretary got up and prompted the students. '*Jai.*' The students followed.

'*Badi Sarkar ki…jai.*'

'*Chhote Sarkar ki…jai.*'

The arts teacher was back with the three lists and handed them to Madam who passed them onto the secretary, who finally handed the lists to Panja ji. Protocol.

'Good,' said Panja.

He handed over imported Chinese phones to students from list 1, latest overpriced imported phones to students from list 2, and cheap, locally assembled phones to the ones in list 3.

The ones who didn't get the phones looked on as their classmates happily received the phones, got off the stage and were escorted outside the school gates to avoid any conflict. The students were to find out that the phones came with galleries of images of Badi Sarkar and Chhote Sarkar, Badi Sarkar wallpapers, and their password was 'BadiSarkarRocks123'. They were given strict warnings not to change these settings, or the phones would get blocked immediately and they would be sent to jail for treason.

The ceremony was over. Panja headed back to Madam's office where he asked the others to wait outside while he had a private conversation with her.

*

Girl 15 offered a glass of *lassi* to Baba Neemacharya, who was in the media centre for a rare visit.

'Thanks, baby,' he said as he took the drink and gave her a kiss on the cheek. 'How are you? It has been a while since we watered the bushes together. I just love getting you wet.'

Day 6: Badi Sarkar Smart Children Yojna

Baba turned to Girl 45 and gave her a peck on her cheek. She had been assigned the media centre for her first rotation and was supposed to manage all CCTV recordings. 'Aah! Girl 45 is here – the wild, untamed beast who can't wait for the Baba to rein her in.' He laughed and smacked her behind. She smarted from his touch, clenched her jaw and looked at Padmini, who was staring at the ground.

He ignored her defiance. They all behaved a little stiff initially but got comfortable after a few weeks. 'Okay, let's take a look at the counting after the morning session.'

She turned on the giant TV screen and set it to play the recording. Baba looked intently, observing the counting process, which had been outsourced to a firm that handled all of their cash. They would come in every morning, empty the collection boxes, count the cash, fill it up in duly labeled gunny sacks, hand over a receipt for the collection and take the cash to be deposited into a safe-house. None of the girls knew too many details of this operation, including the location of the final destination of all that cash.

They watched carefully, rewinding and pausing, trying to find anything that seemed off. The counting men were almost done and were labeling and keeping the gunny bags in their van. Baba suddenly spotted something and shouted at Girl 45 to stop the tape. 'There...did you see that!' His voice sounded triumphant.

'What, Baba?'

'Look carefully. That person just...'

His phone rang in the hands of Padmini, who managed all of his calls. Baba looked annoyed at the sudden interruption.

She looked at the display. 'It is Badi Sarkar, Baba.'

He took the phone from her and answered it.

'Badi Sarkar, how are you, by the grace of the neem tree?'

'What happened? What did he do now?' Baba was scratching his beard as he spoke.

'Oho, he didn't turn up for the inauguration? That must have been awkward. I think we need to double his medication. He will be alright. We just need to get over his allergies and that will fix the other problem as well.'

'Don't cry, Badi Sarkar. He will be fine. The neem is the truth.'

'That's much better. One more thing. One of my disciples Giani Seth is trying to open a new port for the benefit of the nation but looks like he is not getting approval for it. Can you help him please?'

'Oh Panja ji is already talking to him? Thanks Badi Sarkar. He is a good guy. Please look after him. He can be very useful to everybody. I am sure you need funds for running the elections also.'

'Take care, Badi Sarkar. The neem is the truth.'

He handed the phone back to Padmini and asked Girl 45 to rewind the recording by ten seconds.

The TV again started displaying visuals of the bags being sealed and labeled. 'Pause!' he shouted. 'Did you see it?' He asked the two girls. The visual was frozen on a sealed bag going into the van. Only it wasn't one but two. One labeled and the other unlabeled.

'There, the man with the long gun just put it in the backdoor.' He jumped up on his chair, excited.

'You were right, Baba ji. These people are cheating us by sneaking away such unaccounted bags.'

Baba stroked his beard. 'The neem is the truth, Girl 22. I didn't become a billionaire just like that. I am successful because I love being on top,' He winked at the girls.

Padmini and Girl 45 shared a nervous glance at each other. Padmini gave her a quick nod before leaving with the Baba.

*

'Ladies and Gentlemen, here on Bow Wow channel it is our endeavour to provide accurate, unbiased coverage to viewers. It is your trust in us that keeps us on our feet in the face of temptations. We believe that we are a mere medium between the people of this great nation and the leaders in whom the people put their trust.'

'You are watching B for Buddhi, brought to you tonight by Scream, the energy drink that will leave you screaming for more. I am your host Buddhiman Buddhiraja and tonight I am sad. Heartbroken.'

BB stared into Camera #5, a glum look on his handsome face.

Day 6: Badi Sarkar Smart Children Yojna

'Who broke the sugar scam? Who broke the cinema-ticket scam? Who supported the agitation against SitarBucks when they raised the prices of their cold-coffee? Who risked their lives doing a sting operation to expose the evil restaurants who serve their customers undercooked *paneer tikka*?

'We did!' he said proudly.

'What happens when the nation's leaders try to break your trust and influence the democratic process through unfair means? What happens when they try to break us down with offers of bags full of currency notes, until now used to trade elected representatives?'

'Today we will show you a video that will shatter your belief and perception of how the leaders of our nation do not shy from using unfair means to deceive you, the trusting *junta* of the nation.'

His face was still morose, cold enough to freeze a human soul who might dare to stare in those deep brown eyes.

The channel cut to a low-resolution grainy video. Soon a voice could be heard. There was no face. The camera was focused on someone's crotch.

'I agree with you Buddhi *sahab*. This country is in a very bad shape and the ruling party has worked hard to fill their own pockets instead of helping reduce poverty and providing our people a quality life. It is my life's great vision that no man in India ever sleeps on a hungry stomach. The Right to a SitarBucks coffee every day. *AVADA KEDAVRA* to poverty. We have it in our manifesto.'

The voice belonged to none other than the Great Leader.

The producer brought on the split screen, with the Great Leader's crotch on the right half and BB with a hand on his forehead on the left.

Adarsh shouted to Madam. '*Ma*, you have to watch this. BB has done some sort of sting on the Great Leader. Come quickly.' His leg still hurt, and he had taken sick-leave from work. The time had been spent watching TV and posting Twitter updates every few minutes.

The crotch continued talking, 'That is why I was wondering if we could get some like-minded people to join hands and take this great nation out of the hole these people have dug up.'

There was a shuffling sound and the view on the right half of the

TV screen changed, now focused on a giant wall-mounted portrait of a striking handsome man.

'Sir, I am not sure what you are getting at.' This was BB's voice.

'Come on Buddhi *sahab*, you are a smart man. I want your help to counter this bias against us from the other channels that Badi Sarkar has bought off.'

'And how will this work, sir?' BB's voice came on the video, and he stared through Camera #5 straight into Adarsh's eyes.

The screen was suddenly very shaky and there was the rustling of a plastic bag being held up.

'Five crores. For more, just give us your Swiss bank account number and tell me how much you want transferred, and in which currency.'

The video stopped, and it was BB's morose face covering the entire screen again.

'Ladies and gentlemen, this happened yesterday. Now, to everybody watching this show, let me make one thing very clear. Buddhiman Buddhiraja is not for sale. No sir, BB is not cattle that you can buy with money. NOT FOR SALE. NEVER!' he shouted. He was nearly sobbing by now.

There was the loud sound of a motor being turned on and all of a sudden, it started raining in the studio. Thousand rupee notes, ostensibly the five crore paid to him by Great Leader, floating in the air created by giant fans procured from a movie studio just for this day.

BB stood up as Camera #6 took over, someone came and set up a mike in front of his desk and the good BB, favorite news anchor of millions of people, broke into song, a first on national television. He was wearing a white and blue striped pajama under his designer coat. Those rumors were true afterall!

'Not for sale. Not for sale.
Buddhi is not for sale.

Tell your neighbour. Tell your friend.
Tell the corrupt politician who is a Twitter trend
Buddhi is not for sale.

Day 6: Badi Sarkar Smart Children Yojna

Unbiased media is the name. I am not one after fame.
If you want to win the elections, then play by the game.
Buddhi is not for sale. Buddhi is not for sale.'

Adarsh watched in disbelief as BB completed his song and threw the mike headlong into the camera, shattering it. He then collapsed on the ground sobbing hysterically.

'Such drama,' Adarsh thought, as Cameras #2, #3, #4, and #6 closed in on a BB writhing on the floor like a tuna gasping without water.

'There's something fishy about BB tonight. LOL!' he tweeted.

*

The massive aircraft carrier sailed through the waters of the Arabian Sea, cutting smoothly across the waters at a speed of 40knots, flanked on its sides by two of the biggest destroyer ships ever built in the world. The ships entered the waters outside Mumbai and launched a deadly strike as a series of missiles flew towards their destination leaving a trail of fire and smoke behind. The target was a small town in the heart of the country – small enough to be destroyed, yet big enough to send a potent message.

Residents of Mumbai out for a post-dinner stroll along Marine Drive watched agape as the messengers of destruction headed towards a city of a few million people, many of whom were probably already asleep.

Adarsh watched the TV in disbelief at the visuals immediately following B for Buddhi. This couldn't be. Surely America wasn't raining missiles at India over a petty incident.

A news anchor came on the screen. 'The Americans are on an offensive. The insult to their President has not been taken well and our nation is under a serious threat. We have received unconfirmed reports that it is not just an aircraft carrier but a whole navy formation with destroyers and nuclear submarines that have been sent towards India.'

She continued, 'What you just saw was a representation of what could happen. At Bow Wow, we don't believe in any rumour-mongering. Please don't panic. We just hope that the two governments are going to get this issue resolved amicably.'

Adarsh heaved a sigh of relief. No missiles had been fired. Yet.

The anchor repeated, 'Please don't panic. We are sure the issue will get resolved,' just as the ticker at the bottom of the TV screen changed to, 'World War III is HERE.'

'Coming up next,' she announced. 'Ten things you can do to prepare your home for nuclear war.'

DAY 7

THE MEDIA CIRCUS

AdarshBharatiya@AdarshBharatiya

Vote for Change. Because I am tired of shopkeepers giving me eclairs.

Chhicchora@Chhicchora

Badi Sarkar is sweet. Badi Sarkar is great. If you say her name while working out, you will lose weight.

Swamy@Swamy1959

I have got proof that Badi Sarkar got married to Baba Neemacharya last year in Scotland.

TheOrchidParty@TheOrchidParty

'The only thing I am guilty of, is my love for my motherland' – Great Leader

RightToTroll@RightToTroll

BB probably got offended that the Great Leader priced him at only 5 crores.

BowWowBreaking @BowWowBreaking

It is confirmed. Three aircraft carriers and 25 destroyers. #GodBlessIndia #WW3IsHere

'Madam ji, I have bad news today. Very bad news.' The politician Sushil Kumar Yadav said, as soon as he entered Madam's office accompanied by his regular security escort.

She asked him to take a seat, rang a bell for the peon to get some water and tea, and asked Yadav. 'What happened, Yadav ji? You seem to be sweating.'

'Madam ji, forget the *chai*. This is serious. Do you remember the girl Nafisa who had come for admission earlier this week?'

Madam leaned forward in her table and answered. 'What about her, Yadav ji?'

'She is gone, Madam. Gone. Rafi called me in the morning and said that she has been missing since yesterday. He said that she had already been very upset since the Great Liberator School principal suspended her and your refusal to take her only made it worse. She had gone out yesterday morning telling him that she was going to visit a friend and hasn't returned since.'

'Oh my god, Yadav ji. Have they reported to the police?' She got up from her seat.

'Yes, Madam. The police filed a report. Rafi has gone with them to look for her in the area. I should get a call from him soon.'

Madam felt sweat forming on her forehead. This could become a career-threatening scandal.

Yadav's phone rang. 'Hello,' he answered.

'You found her? Oh, you found what? Where? Oh my God, this is terrible. Control yourself, Rafi. I will come by right away. You stay there.'

'Madam, I have bad news. They found her clothes near the Great Liberator lake behind the bus station. Looks like she committed suicide. God bless her soul. I have to go.'

Madam gasped as the politician rushed out of her office.

*

'The Great Leader will be here shortly. Please be ready with your questions and enjoy the snacks until then,' Girpade addressed the assembled crowd of journalists falling over each other in the mad scramble for samosas at the snack counter. The biggest hall in the party's office in Indraprastha was still not big enough for the Media Circus – all of them anxious to be the first to break the news of the Great Leader's response to BB's sting against him.

Girpade felt a deep sense of gratitude for Jagriti and the Indian Association of Paid Media for coming up with the brilliant idea of the Media Circus many years ago. Earlier it was a pain sending out notifications to all media agencies, rounding up TV channels, newspaper reporters and International news agencies but thanks to the masterstroke, getting the Media Circus at your doorstep was as simple as a single SMS sent to a central number and they would be there within minutes. Even the ubiquitous DeMello's Pizza took longer to deliver and they were supposed to be the fastest possible delivery of happiness.

Jagriti Jha, the Media Circus coordinator, came over to Girpade and asked if he would like them to perform on stage while everybody waited for the Great Leader. Girpade smiled at the efficiency of their operation. This was part of the value-added proposition. The Media Circus didn't just provide extensive news coverage but could actually perform trapeze acts, jugglery, card tricks, tight-rope walking, vanishing acts and a lot more, though they had stopped performing animal tricks since last year after the PETA animal activists got all top models and actresses from popular TV serials to pose naked in protest against animal cruelty.

Girpade politely refused the offer saying, 'When the main course is a steaming hot *aloo-parantha* with fresh butter, who needs a plate of boiled rice?'

He excused himself from Jagriti, beckoned a waiter and asked him to get cold drinks for a group of journalists from the *Crimes of India* group who had just arrived and pushed another one carrying *tandoori chicken* in the direction of a section that had not been attended to.

All the party top brass was present. The Chief Snacks Officer was personally supervising the kitchen to ensure that everything was being deep-fried in the best quality saturated fatty oils. His added responsibility was to get the cold drinks spiked with just a little vodka to make the guests feel 'relaxed', as the Great Leader called it. The Chief Motivation Officer was at the dais doing a standup act to keep the journalists in a good mood. The Chief Media Officer was talking to the senior journalists to 'urge' them to make sure the coverage of this news was fair and free, with a wink. The ones on the party payroll were not a problem and the ones on the ruling party's payroll had not been invited but the fence-sitters were the most problematic. Invariably they had demands, ranging from a Bangkok trip to a gas cylinder dealership.

Girpade was the overall coordinator, responsible for ensuring a successful event. Last night's BB broadcast had been devastating to the party's image and the ruling party had already started calling for the Great Leader's resignation. After watching the BB telecast, the Great Leader had called Girpade with a heavy heart and a disappointed voice and said, 'he made a video!'. He had been especially disappointed because he thought there was a spark between him and BB and was already looking forward to a healthy collaboration with him. He had always insisted that BB had the right skills to help the party achieve success and ensure that the nation attained the greatness it deserved. The Great Leader had deliberated for months before deciding to talk to him but BB had ruthlessly stabbed him in the back.

'He is here!' someone shouted. Everybody dropped their *samosas*, wiped their oily hands on the chairs and the cameras started clicking and whirring as the Great Leader entered the hall and took a seat on the stage. Girpade joined him, touching his feet before sitting down next to him.

The Chief Media Officer announced that there would be a statement from the Great Leader, following which journalists could ask questions. The Great Leader took out a folded sheet from his pocket and read from it.

'My dear friends. You all know that I have dedicated my life to the service of this great nation. My only dream in life is to make sure that India attains a great stature in the world and we are able to restore the glory of ancient Indian culture.

'However, there are biased elements who want to stop us from being able to achieve that. I was informed this morning that there was a telecast on a news channel that showed a clip that was suggested to be my voice. Let me reassure all of you that this is in no way true. I never talked to the person, let alone offer a bribe to him. WE have truth on our side. Why would we need to bribe anyone?'

He looked skywards, pointed towards the heavens, and thundered, 'The gods are watching. They know who is right. I work not for any personal benefit but for the benefit of the nation, as compared to the ruling party that just wants to silence every dissenting voice and continue with their corrupt ways. Today they have tried to silence me. Tomorrow they will try to silence you. The video is a doctored tape and a conspiracy to defame me. I demand an investigation by the Central Agency of Clean Chits into this tape to reveal the party behind this fraud.'

He folded the paper and kept it back in his pocket. Immediately a clamour ensued in the audience and there were two dozen hands raised to ask questions.

Girpade pointed in the direction of an old party faithful, 'Go ahead, sir.'

'Thank you Great Leader, sir. We have no doubt in our minds that you could never try to bribe an independent media organization. Do you think this is a new trick of Chhote Sarkar, who has earlier also implied that you are in the habit of buying out journalists?'

The Great Leader looked at him with love in his eyes and said, 'I have no doubt in my mind that it is a conspiracy of the ruling party to derail our campaign. They are afraid that we are going to win so they are getting desperate. Make sure you let them know that their Ministry of Dirty Tricks will not be able to stop us.'

'Next one please.' Girpade pointed at Jagriti who was a senior journalist from Hyper News, in addition to being the coordinator for the non-profit Media Circus. She wasn't on the party payroll but had agreed to go light today in exchange for her niece's admission to the recently opened IIT Greater Noida.

Day 7: The Media Circus

'Dear Great Leader, the tape looks pretty convincing. How can we believe that it wasn't you?'

Girpade gritted his teeth. Was she going to betray his trust at this crucial juncture?

She continued. 'Of course, unless you have a valid alibi, which you do. I just thought that I would put it on record that you were recording an interview with me on the purported day of the OrchidGate tape recording, as it is being called.'

Girpade heaved a sigh of relief and marveled at the woman's genius. She had scored an interview with the Great Leader in exchange for giving him a clean chit.

The Great Leader laughed nervously. 'My dear Jagriti, of course I was. Thank you for your kind support. I hope this clears it up for everybody. Thank you for coming. Let's wrap up the press-conference.'

As he stood up to exit via the side door, another journalist frantically started waving sheets of paper. 'It is all a lie. You were not recording anything with Jagriti. You invited BB to OrchidNagar and offered him a bribe.' This was Vajra Singh, a particularly hyperventilating journalist from *Khabardaar TV* famous for his columns against the Great Leader. In his last column he had claimed that the Great Leader had a harem of 50 wives whom he kept hidden in his massive house and used as slaves to stitch his clothes.

'Vajra, didn't you just hear from Jagriti? How can you claim it is me in the tape when I was with Jagriti that day?'

'Because Jagriti is one of your wives,' he shouted back and spat on the ground.

Everybody gasped.

'How dare you, Vajra?' Jagriti pounced on him and they were soon on the floor, hitting each other.

'STOP IT!' Girpade shouted at the top of his voice. Jagriti and Vajra got up and brushed their clothes. The Great leader also looked a bit stunned at the sudden outburst.

Girpade addressed the audience. 'The Great Leader is like God to me. He is the only man who can show India its destiny. He is a kind, noble soul and the government is out to malign him.'

'We have had enough,' he continued. 'We will not tolerate this anymore. I hereby announce that I will sit on a fast unto death in defense of the Great Leader and will only break the fast when the government apologizes for this cheap attack on such a noble soul.'

As he said this, the lights went off immersing the room in darkness. The Ministry of Dirty Tricks had cut off electricity to the party office over non-payment of dues.

In the silence that ensued, there was a loud sound as Vajra cried out in pain. Jagriti had bitten off a part of his left earlobe.

*

Giani Seth entered his office, picked up the large flower vase and threw it straight into the 100-inch Super Extra-HiDef BLEEDTV mounted on the wall. He then picked up a cricket bat he had kept as a safety measure just in case an enemy managed to get through the retina scan, full-body pat-down and the finger-print validation against the national database at the building entrance, the sniffer dogs in the lift, and the cavity search on his executive floor, and proceeded to destroy any glass surface he could spot in the office. All flower vases were gone, all table lamps were demolished, the center table lay shattered and by the time he was done, his office looked like a scene out of a Steven Spielberg World War movie.

Alisha opened the door and gasped, 'Sir?' A few minutes ago she had seen him slap the intern when he told him that he had been stuck on level 225 of Candy Crush for the last one week, drag him to the lift and tell him to get lost. She had seen Giani Seth angry before but never this much.

Giani Seth sat on his chair and started weeping, his head held in his hands, sobbing uncontrollably like a toddler who has just been told by an astrologer that he will never make it to IIT. Alisha came over to him, balanced herself on the armrest of his chair and ran her freshly manicured hands through his hair, trying to soothe him.

She called up the pantry on the intercom and asked them to send over some *lassi* for Giani Seth.

He cried for the next half an hour before he looked up at his pretty assistant who was still running her fingers through his hair, trying to cheer him up.

Day 7: The Media Circus

'The board. Those bastards.' He finally spoke. She looked at him intently, a puzzled look in her eyes.

'The deal to buy that Australian bank got cancelled today after their government announced that there was too much outrage against an Indian acquiring one of their banks. Those slimy bastards. I had paid off every single one of their MPs. Two million dollars each, a crystal replica of the Tajmahal and a box of Alphonso mangoes as a special token of appreciation. After spending so much money, they backed off at the last minute. And now the board is after me. They want to know how we will recoup the money spent in this failed acquisition. Bloody scoundrels. I built this company and they are threatening to throw me out? I'll kill each one of them if they even dare try!

'And then my stupid daughter had to run her car over five labourers. How many times have I told her to take the chopper but she won't listen. She just has to drive and now I need to fix it.'

She handed him the *lassi* glass and he gulped it down gratefully.

'They had already been after me about the approval for the Gian Port project which the government has stalled, again despite my having paid them so much money. It's like there is no honesty in the world anymore. People take money and still don't want to work.'

'Relax Giani Seth, it will be alright. I have full trust in you.'

'You bet your pretty ass it will be alright. I will make sure the Gian Port goes through. Thanks for your support. Now go. GO!' He got up, a determined look on his face.

He ushered her out of the office, wiped his face with his *kurta*, and took out his mobile.

'Call police commissioner,' he told his voice-activated phone.

'Calling Polish mission,' the phone responded.

'*Abe gadhe*, I said police commissioner.'

'Unrecognized contact.'

Giani Seth gritted his teeth and tried again, in a calmer voice, just like the customer support lady had asked him the last time he had complained about the voice command feature not working on his phone. The phone accepted it and dialed the Commissioner's private number.

'Giani Seth, what a pleasant surprise,' the Commissioner's voice was echoing, for some reason.

'Arora, how are you, you *taklu*?'

There was the sound of a zipper on the other end followed by a flush going off and a door being opened. The Commissioner answered, his voice loud and clear, with no echo this time, 'Sirji, you will never stop pulling my leg. How can I help you?'

'*Yaar* my daughter had a small accident today. She says her car ran over five labourers sleeping on the road. The poor girl has just gone into trauma after this horrible incident and says that she feels terrible that those evil labourers just had to choose her car under which to die. You know how she has always been very responsible. Now the silly girl is saying that she will pay to repair the scratches on the Land Cruiser. I think she must have suffered a head injury to talk like that. Can you get this sorted? She is just a child. *Galti ho jaati hai bachchon se*. Probably must have got a text message that she had to answer while driving and those *kameene* labourers chose just that moment to sleep. So irresponsible of them.'

'*Arre sirjee*, that is such a small thing. I thought you were calling about a serious problem. No problem, Giani Seth. This is what the police is for, after all. Our job is to help kind people like you. I'll ask one of my constables to say that he did it. We will see if anyone grumbles. When will our *lathis* come in handy?' He laughed.

'Thanks *bhai*. I'll transfer your fees to your Swiss account.'

The Commissioner gave his useful cheerful laugh. 'Remember Giani Seth, five labourers means five times the *prasad*. After all I don't eat the *prasad* alone. It gets shared with a lot of people.'

'Don't worry, Arora,' Giani Seth said, and hung up.

This matter taken care of, there was the other important business.

'Call the *kameena* Panja,' he told his phone.

'Unrecognized contact,' the phone responded, in that droll, mechanical voice. Giani Seth almost threw the phone into the window but controlled himself.

'Call Panja,' he tried again.

The phone rang. And it rang for the next few minutes. There was no response. Giani Seth tried again ten times. Each time the phone rang before getting cut off. Panja wasn't taking his call.

Day 7: The Media Circus

Giani Seth was furious. He decided it was time to shake things up.

*

The Media Circus gathered in the press room at the Minister for Mobile Phone's office. Dr Mohammad Panja was going to address them in a few minutes. Most of them had been at the Great Leader's press conference earlier in the day and received Media Circus SMSes that Panja was also going to hold a press conference a few hours after they got out of the Orchid party event.

The door opened and Dr Panja walked in, looking distressed.

'My dear friends,' he looked into empty space as he read from a written statement, his sound weak and feeble unlike the usual high-pitch dramatic voice, 'thank you for coming in at short notice. Our nation is under threat and the communal forces that want to puncture the secular fabric of our nation must be stopped at any cost.'

He seemed to get lost in distant thoughts for a few seconds before resuming, 'I am sure that you all saw on Bow Wow channel how the Great Leader thinks that he can buy anything, including all of you. So shameful. That too for a meagre five crores? Is that all the power of the pen and the camera is worth?'

He smirked. Khabardaar TV's Vajra had cost them two hundred crores. The Galaxy TV star Tez Talwar had only agreed after getting confirmation of the four hundred crores transferred to his Swiss account. And the Great Leader wanted to buy the stalwart BB for just five crores? He suppressed a chuckle before resuming. Someone had no idea of market rates.

'The We Will We Will Rock You party is fully committed to secularism and independence of the media but we fear that the communal powers are trying hard to gain strength and use unfair means to win the elections.' He raised his hand like a general leading his unit into war and said, 'THE GREAT LEADER MUST APOLOGIZE. We will not let him get away this time. He must answer to the people of India and tell them why he should not be put behind bars immediately.'

He continued, 'We were surprised to hear Dr Girpade's

announcement of going on a fast-unto-death in support of the Great Leader. The gimmicks of the communal forces must be stopped immediately. As the country's beacon of secularism, I take this challenge personally.'

He paused for effect, before coming up with the big announcement. 'I will sit on a fast-unto-death from tomorrow to protest against Girpade's fast-unto-death. I will not break my fast until he breaks his and apologizes for the Great Leader's actions.'

There was the loud clap of thunder as the PR team played a recorded sound from a National Geographic show, turned down the lights and projected lightning strikes on the projector behind Panja, for dramatic effect. All assembled journalists clapped as Panja stood frozen, his hand high in the air, a determined finger pointing skywards, as if challenging the forces of communalism to dare strike him.

'Dr Panja will now take questions,' the media coordinator announced. Jagriti raised her hand. She had changed into a bright purple sari and managed to shampoo her hair after the morning's scuffle.

'Dr Panja, we have received news that Nafisa, a young 14-year-old girl, is suspected to have committed suicide because she was denied admission by an arrogant school principal. Incidentally, you went to the same school a few days ago to distribute smartphones under the Badi Sarkar Smart Children Yojna.'

Panja gritted his teeth. 'Nafisa, did you say? It clearly looks to be another example of crimes against minority communities. I think that principal should be given such a strict punishment that she learns not to push a student to kill herself again. We should create an example out of her or our girls will continue to suffer at the hands of such communal people. We should...,' he brought his hands in front as if strangling someone.

He threw the mike on the ground and walked off.

*

Madam returned to her office from her round of the school and pressed a buzzer for the peon. She had found two teachers loitering

Day 7: The Media Circus

in the staffroom, one busy on Whatsapp and the other playing Subway Surfer on her phone. Both teachers had been given memos and told to submit an explanation in two days.

She asked the peon to get a cup of tea and turned on the CCTV monitor. All the common areas of the school – the playground, the staffroom, the lobby, the main gate, were covered under CCTV surveillance and she could check what was happening at the flick of a button in her office.

The peon brought the tea and she started shuffling across the various cameras. The school day would end in half-an-hour and she always switched the CCTV to the main gate around this time to make sure that the children were getting dispersed in an orderly fashion.

She noticed a couple of minivans turn up at the gate. They had the big logo of Hyper News prominently painted on them. The vans parked outside the gate and within a few minutes there were about ten such vans from all prominent channels outside her school's gate.

The Media Circus was at her doorstep! Her worst fears were coming true. She called up the Big Boss but he didn't take her call. She called up the local police inspector but he too declined the call. She called up Adarsh and he didn't answer either. His day was spent in meetings, so perhaps busy in one, she thought. He always called back as soon as his meetings ended.

Soon the main gate was blocked with all the vans parked outside. She noticed the journalists setting up their cameras, like a battalion of soldiers preparing for an ambush on an enemy position. They checked their equipment, some of them relieved themselves under the massive *peepal* tree right outside the gate, cigarettes were handed out and puffs of smoke filled the air. Madam watched the guard Ram Prasad look on helplessly as the crowd of media people forced the gate open and ran inside, cameras perched on the shoulders of cameramen, mikes in the hands of the journalists, everybody sprinting to be the first inside her office and be the one who 'broke' the news.

Madam adjusted the *pallu* of her sari, took a sip of water, wiped the sweat off her face, checked herself in her portable mirror and sat back in her executive chair to face the incoming onslaught of questions. She had done nothing wrong. She was confident that they would go back satisfied that she was nowhere at fault in the issue over Nafisa's disappearance.

She heard them many seconds before they appeared, huffing and puffing their way through the long corridor leading to her office. Madam braced herself for impact as the army entered her fortress through the open door. They were face-to-face.

Their faces lit up as they entered her well-equipped office. The cool air from the air-conditioner was a refreshing change from the heat that they had been braving outside. They were all sweating, panting and tired. Climate change had turned out to be a game-changer. Earlier this year, it had snowed for the first time in 100 years in Indraprastha in June and now there was an oppressive heat wave in December.

'Let me get some water and tea for all of you,' she smiled graciously at the journalists.

'Thank you, Madam,' about half of them said in chorus. The others were too parched to even speak, panting from the exertion.

'Let's start after tea, okay?'

The battalion nodded.

Madam's office was a spacious room where she occasionally conducted meetings with her entire staff. There were about a dozen chairs and a big carpet right next to Madam's desk. The media persons made themselves comfortable in the room, happily enjoying their tea with Parle-G biscuits, sitting down wherever there was an opportunity.

Ten minutes later they were done and ready for battle. Madam observed the journalists get in the mood for questioning. Some were doing push-ups to get the adrenalin flowing, a few of the lady reporters tore at their hair and some others got their cameramen to slap them to get the blood pumping. A particularly enthusiastic young man actually started beating his head against a wall.

The students and staff started gathering outside the office, curious to know what was going on in Madam's office.

'Alright Madam, ENOUGH. DON'T WASTE ANY MORE OF

Day 7: The Media Circus

OUR TIME.' The one who had been beating his head against the wall slammed his teacup into the floor and shouted. Everybody else also looked ready. The cameras were rolling like tanks about to crush enemy positions, while the mikes were all pointed in Madam's direction like light machine guns, ready for fire.

'Madam, are you not ashamed of yourself?' He shouted at her.

'What?'

'A young girl, her entire life in front of her, came to you begging, pleading, asking that you admit her to your school, and you kicked her out? Are you a human or the devil?'

'But, I never kicked...' she was taken aback by the intensity of the onslaught.

A lady clad in a purple sari suddenly shouted, 'You are a teacher. How could you do this to a budding life? It is women like you who are the real reason why India sees so many cases of rape, dowry deaths and cancer. You are the bane of humanity!'

The first journalist, the head-banger, spoke again. There was a small streak of blood running across his forehead but he didn't seem to notice. 'Madam, it just shames me to stand in this same office where you killed that young girl. My head already feels dizzy and it's like my life is gradually getting sucked out of me.'

She pointed a finger at his head. 'What nonsense are you saying? You need to go see a doctor.'

The journalist standing next to him took offense and shouted at Madam. 'Madam, I will not allow you to insult one of my colleagues like this. You are the one who should see a doctor, you psychopathic killer of young girls. You are the reason why our daughters can't go out to clubs in mini-skirts.'

'*Madam hai hai. Madam hai hai,*' she started shouting. The others also joined in.

Madam was now beginning to lose her patience. 'Why did you people even come here if you didn't want to listen to me? I am not feeling well. I need to go now.'

One of the lady journalists turned to her camera and said, 'Dear viewers, as you can see this is the face of a killer. This is the face of a woman who forced a young innocent girl to commit suicide. Look at her closely. Look how she is trying to avoid our questions and run away, in a clear admission of her guilt. We just wonder how many more lives she has taken sitting in this plush air-conditioned office while the students of her school don't even have water to drink.'

Madam slapped her head in frustration as the assembled journalists blocked the door of her office.

'Okay, okay I am not going anywhere. You guys can ask whatever you want.'

As they referred to their cheat-sheets for more questions, she got up from her chair and moved towards the attached bathroom in her room. 'You people keep your questions ready. I will be back in a minute.'

The attached bathroom opened up into the ground through a small window. Madam turned on the tap to drown out the sound and started pushing herself through the tiny opening. She had outgrown it long ago but after a lot of strenuous effort she was through, out in the ground, looking at two students staring at her curiously.

'Why are you not in your class?' She shouted at them and ran towards her car.

Her escape took about five minutes. She reached the car, got in, turned on the ignition and drove towards the gate. Thankfully the minivan drivers had cleared the gate in preparation to leave the school. Madam drove off.

Meanwhile in the office, the journalists got curious after she had been gone for a few minutes and discovered the CCTV video playing on her computer screen, just in time to notice her get in her car.

'SHE IS ESCAPING!' There was a collective gasp as the Media Circus rushed outside, in pursuit of the killer principal. A few heads got trampled in the mad scramble. The head-banger dude had already collapsed to the ground after asking the last question.

They ran back towards the gate, cursing the government for making schools with such long corridors. 'They should at least make the principal's office right by the main gate,' someone said.

Madam's car was out of the gate and speeding away towards the traffic intersection as the minivans started moving. 'Oh God, they found out,' she said with trepidation, noticing them in her rear-view mirror. Her legs felt weak now and her arms were bruised from the crawl through that window.

There were five seconds to go for the light to turn to green as the media vans closed in. She could see a cameraman hanging out the passenger side of his van, holding on to his camera with one hand and clinging on to the door with the other. Behind him, another van appeared. This one had the purple sari speaking from the roof, pointing at her with disgust in her eyes as the cameraman followed her excited gestures.

The light turned green and Madam was off, the media people in pursuit, shouting at her, chanting slogans against her and capturing every moment of the chase of this evil killer of an innocent girl on their cameras.

*

Baba came out of the changing room and all the girls cheered.

'Baba, you look like Michael Jackson,' one of the girls said.

'Baba, that belt is just rocking,' said another.

Baba smiled proudly. He was wearing a tight leather jacket, jeans that were torn at the knees and held on his waist by a belt that had a chrome buckle shaped like a handgun. His long hair was left open which, combined with his freshly shampooed beard and the blue aviator shades, didn't leave much of his face visible.

He pressed a few keys on the electric guitar slung around his neck and rehearsed a line. 'My gun is very long, this is a happiness song.'

The producer came to Baba and asked if he was ready. The cameras and recording equipment were ready to roll, as was his band of girls manning the keyboards, drums, trumpets and an acoustic guitar.

Baba was recording a rap song for his album, 'Neem Is The Truth.' He had already recorded two songs last week and the album was due to be released next month.

A few months ago some of the girls had expressed a desire to start a music hobby group in the ashram. Baba had discovered their talents with the instruments and decided that they needed to record an album, with him as the lead singer.

Baba took position, holding the mike close to his mouth as the girls started playing the music. The cameras were rolling and all the girls were watching the proceedings. It was time for Baba to rock and roll.

'My gun is very long, this is a happiness song,' he started but immediately stopped and stared at the girls on the trumpets. 'Come on girls, you are not blowing hard enough.

'Ok, let's resume.'

'Don't wear a thong, don't wear a sarong, because this is a happiness song.' He sang to the loud music, banging his head, his long hair all over his face, jumping from one girl to the next, pretending to play the electronic guitar in his hands, fully enjoying performing in this new avatar.

Padmini came running into the room and blurted out as soon as she entered, 'Baba, she is not here!'

'Padmini!' He shouted at her. 'You ruined the entire flow.'

'I am sorry, Baba,' she said. 'Girl 45 is missing from the ashram.'

A loud gasp went around the room. Baba shouted to Padmini above the din. 'What? I think I saw her at the morning sermon.'

'Yes, Baba she was here but she is gone now. I've checked every corner of the ashram.'

Baba put down his guitar, a serious look on his face. 'You checked everywhere?'

'Yes, Baba. I have also checked the storeroom. She is nowhere to be found.'

One of the girls spoke up. 'I remember talking to her during breakfast. She seemed very upset.'

'Yes her eyes seemed red but she said that everything was going to be okay soon,' another one added.

'Oh God, what is going on?' Baba scratched his beard.

Padmini's phone rang. She took the call, gasped, and looked at Baba. 'Baba, it was the security officer. I had asked him to check where she could have gone. He found out where she is.'

'Oh great! Thank God.' Baba heaved a sigh of relief.

Day 7: The Media Circus

'Baba, she went to the police. She has filed a complaint against you.'

'WHAT!' Baba exclaimed.

'How could she? What did I do to her?'

Padmini stared at her feet, wondering whether to tell him the complete truth. She realized it was best to come out with the full truth. 'Baba, she has filed a rape complaint against you.'

Baba kept his hands on his ears. 'Nooooooo! Don't use that disgusting word.' He seemed stunned. 'This is not possible.'

She continued looking at him, her eyes cold. She had never approved of him taking liberties with the girls but he hadn't listened. Girl 45 had been the last straw. She had helped the girl escape after Baba's sermon in the morning and sent her off in one of the grocery supply trucks, hidden amidst sacks of potatoes and onions. She felt guilty of cheating the Baba after so many years of togetherness but the girl's tears had broken her heart.

As it turned out, the girl had ended up breaking her promise. She had given Padmini her word that she just wanted to get away from Baba and wouldn't go to the police. This was not the outcome Padmini had expected.

Baba sat on the ground, silent. He then started crying loudly. 'How could she do this to me? I was so nice to her.'

He wailed and wailed for the next few hours as the girls watched the Baba lying on the ground, his long hair a mess, dressed in a Metallica t-shirt and distressed jeans revealing his hairy legs.

*

Adarsh sat down for lunch in the cafeteria and glanced at his phone. It had been a long day sitting in a training session on how to extract the maximum productivity out of your team and he had been unable to look at his phone even once. There were three missed calls from mom, 200 Twitter notifications, 12 emails and a few Facebook updates.

'I'll call up mom after eating,' he thought to himself. Normally she never called during the day, so it was a bit odd that she had called thrice. He rushed through his food as the training session was restarting in 30 minutes and he was starving. He had very little time to eat, call her up and check his Twitter notifications within that short break.

He noticed the people at the next table staring intently at the television and turned to look. It was Bow Wow news channel. The headline screamed 'She Killed a 14-Year-Old Girl!'

Adarsh felt dizzy when he realized what was going on. They were showing a clip of a woman sitting in her office surrounded by a roomful of journalists, as the three rows of tickers at the bottom corner of the screen ran the following in bold letters.

> 'A 14-Year-Old Girl Had Gone To Seek admission But She Told Her To Burn Herself.'
>
> 'Girl's Clothes Found Near Great Liberator Lake. The Devil Principal Dumped Her Body There.'
>
> 'Coward Principal Escaped Through Bathroom When We Tried to Question Her.'

He felt his head spinning. It was his mother!

The same clip was being repeated over and over again. There was no voice but it showed Madam walking towards the ensuite washroom and then it zoomed on the handle of the washroom door.

The anchor came on the screen. 'You are watching Bow Wow news. Today is another day of shame for everybody in our country. An innocent 14-year-old girl went to seek admission to this school but the principal refused point blank, instead asking her to immolate herself.'

She rolled her eyes and said in an angry tone. 'Watch carefully. This is the face of a principal who could be murdering your child at the moment. Watch her nails. Watch her teeth. Watch the chain around her neck. Watch the arrogance with which she is casually going to the bathroom after killing that young girl.'

Her male counterpart came on. 'Bow Wow channel was the first to break news of this tragedy for our viewers because at Bow Wow, our constant endeavor is to make sure that you are informed with the latest, unbiased, unadulterated news coverage.'

Day 7: The Media Circus

The lady continued her report, transitioning seamlessly from the male anchor. 'When we went to this school to find the devil principal, we found her eating snacks and tea, completely oblivious of the crime she had committed. She even had the courage to offer our staff tea and biscuits. But when we insisted on asking why she killed that girl, she had no answer. NO ANSWER, ladies and gentlemen. She had no answer.'

The ticker on the screen changed to, 'SHE HAD NO ANSWER.'

She continued. 'When the hateful principal realized that she was not going to be able to bribe our crew with tea, she decided to run.'

The male anchor came on. 'Ladies and Gentlemen, we have live feeds coming in. Our crew has been following her as she tries to escape from the school. Little does she know that Bow Wow will not spare any criminal. We will find out everything about her. We will make sure such a disgusting crime never happens again.'

Adarsh was startled as the video changed to a live feed. It was his mother. She was driving frantically through the roads of Great Liberator Nagar, surrounded by media vans on both sides and a couple of vans ahead. The Bow Wow team pursuing her was shouting at her to stop. 'Stop or we will continue the live telecast. The world is going to see how a criminal drives her car, oblivious to the safety of other vehicles around her.'

They showed the face of the Bow Wow journalist, sitting on top of her van, hair flying in the air, her forehead sweaty from the afternoon sun, and what seemed like froth coming out of her mouth. Another reporter jumped on top of Madam's car and started jabbing the roof of the car with his mike.

Adarsh dropped his food and ran to Samarth to borrow his car. He had to go to his mum's aid.

*

'Here, have something to eat,' Adarsh turned on the light in her room, woke up Madam, and asked her to have some dinner. His dad and sister also came in the room and dad kept a comforting hand on her shoulder. It had been a harrowing day for her. First the news of that girl committing suicide, then that horrible chase through the city's streets by the hungry wolves of the media.

Adarsh had rushed to help Madam as soon as he watched the live telecast in his office cafeteria. Unknown to him at the time, the telecast had ended within ten minutes and the chasing vans had been called back to report on another breaking news. One of the girls from Neemacharya's ashram had filed a rape complaint against him.

The vans had pulled off the chase while Madam was battling her way through the vegetable vendors of the Badi Sarkar fruit market. It was a jam-packed street and in her nervousness she had ended up hitting a rickshaw. There had been no major damage to it though. She had heaved a sigh of relief as she saw the Media Circus get off her back but noticed a group of rickshaw drivers running towards her and sped off. By the time Adarsh managed to get through on her phone, she had reached home, so he too came home directly.

As Madam ate her dinner, sobbing and wiping her eyes, shaken from the traumatic experience, Adarsh walked into his room and turned on the TV. Galaxy TV was showing an animated video featuring Madam scolding the girl and hitting her with a broom until she burst into flames and died. Another channel had a reporter standing outside the school gates and saying, 'the next time you send your child to this school, kiss him goodbye. You never know...'

Thankfully Hyper News was the one news channel not focusing on Madam but instead doing a story on Baba Neemacharya. As Adarsh listened on, some interesting facts were being revealed in the news report. While the rest of the world thought of him as a spiritual guru, Baba Neemacharya was being portrayed as a sex maniac. Hyper News was showing clips of an interview with a girl who had apparently worked in the ashram before. Her face was blurred out but she was talking about how the Baba was a sex-addict and regularly had threesomes with his girls.

Adarsh checked his phone. Twitter had been ablaze today with feminists having a field day. The top trends had been #MartyrNafisa, #PrincipalFromHell, #RapistNeemacharya, #BieberIsGod, and #SaveOurWomen. Adarsh had been appalled to find people posting hateful tweets about his mother without even being aware of the facts of the case. He battled valiantly but the loudest people on

Day 7: The Media Circus

Twitter were also the most misinformed. The place was overflowing with venom against #DevilPrincipal.

He wondered what would happen next. While there had been no formal complaint against her, there was a big outcry for action against Madam. He was worried that the police would give in to the social media pressure and take some action against Madam, even if she had done nothing wrong and only followed the rule-book in this case.

'The Media Circus takes down another innocent victim. Madam did nothing wrong.' he posted another tweet and immediately got 35 replies admonishing him for being such an irresponsible citizen by defending a school principal who was clearly guilty of murder. He hadn't yet posted that Madam was his mother.

B for Buddhi started and Buddhi's worried face appeared on the TV screen.

He spoke in a depressed voice. 'Ladies and Gentlemen, today is a sad day for all Indians. We have completely and utterly failed in our duty to protect our women. On the same day, we've had not one but two absolutely heart-rending stories of how our faith is betrayed by the people from whom we least expect it. One is a teacher, someone whom we trust to educate our children and make them responsible adults. The other, a man of God, someone millions look up to for advice on how to lead better lives.

'Tonight we look at two individuals that our country is ashamed to have given birth to – Ambika Pandey and Baba Neemacharya. You are watching B for Buddhi, brought to you tonight by Scream, the energy drink that will leave you screaming for more. I am your host Buddhiman Buddhiraja.'

He stared into Camera #2 for five minutes without blinking, his eyes full of disappointment and anguish. The producers eventually started playing the most melancholic song from the saddest Bollywood movie ever made, *Doom 6*, a love quadrilateral between a 10,000cc motorbike, a gay policeman played by Bollywood sensation Veerkhan Bhai and playboy robber Mooch Pratap Singh, all of who die of heartbreak in the end when their common love interest Loverr Khan declares that he is straight and in love with Veerkhan's sister.

Adarsh wondered if BB had dozed off but he soon got back into action as he introduced his panel. 'Tonight we have some of the most distinguished women's rights activists on our show. We have famous writer Aparajita Sharma, chairperson of the Badi Sarkar Commission for Women's Empowerment Ms Kusum, the youngest air-hostess from the Where India airline 65-year-old Peena Kumari, and Twitter activist Raveena whose handle is @AllMenMustDie.

'Before we get their views, we have another special guest on our show – Mrs Tarla Sahni, our specialist psychic who helped predict the results of the last elections and who also provides us the weather forecast, an area where she has consistently performed better than the Met department.'

A woman suddenly emerged in the centre of the studio. She was surrounded by candles and was sitting on a table looking into a crystal ball. BB looked at her and said, 'Welcome Mrs Sahni. Nafisa is reported missing. All evidence seems to point that she has committed suicide but the divers have not been able to find her body yet. God bless her soul and I wish she is found alive. Can you look into your ball and tell us if you can locate her?'

She took out a bottle of perfume and sprayed it around her. Then she lit a dozen more candles and asked for the studio lights to be dimmed. The mood having been created, she gazed into her crystal ball which suddenly opened up and she took out her iPad from the open cavity.

After a few minutes of playing around with various applications, she announced. 'I see her running amidst vast mustard fields...the air is clean and unpolluted...people around her seem happy...there are no cars in sight...she seems to be dancing in the rain...'

'Oh my god, SHE IS DEAD!' BB exclaimed, and pressed a button on his desk that made Tarla disappear.

The ticker on the viewer's televisions changed to 'BREAKING: NAFISA IS DEAD. RIP #DaughterNafisa.'

BB was already sobbing uncontrollably, his tears running down the sleeves of his expensive jacket as he tried to control them by wiping his eyes.

He turned to the ladies in the panel. Aparajita broke into tears as

Day 7: The Media Circus

soon as BB looked in her direction and the picture of a random girl picked from Google search was displayed on the giant screen in the studio. 'Look at that girl,' she said. 'Poor Nafisa looks like she can't wait to complete her homework and look what the devil principal did to her.'

BB looked at all women crying in remembrance of the brave martyr who had given her life for the benefit of mankind and suggested a five-minute break to get done with the tears and then resume the discussion on Nafisa and Neemacharya. The panelists readily agreed. The studio floor had been flooded by about an inch of accumulated tears that needed to be mopped up.

When the break was over, BB looked at Kusum while Aparajita took out a pocket mirror to make sure that the tears hadn't spoiled her makeup. Kusum put on her glasses and was about to start speaking when @AllMenMustDie started shouting slogans.

'Neemacharya is a bastard!'

'Neemacharya is a BC!'

'Neemacharya is an MC!'

BB glared at her and said in a calm voice, 'Lady, say another filthy word and I will throw you into BB Jail.' She mumbled something about all men being dogs but promptly shut up. Kusum looked at her through her glasses and smiled benevolently. 'Ah, the young people today are so brash. Of course, all men are not dogs. We have gentlemen like Chhote Sarkar who are beacons of kindness. Yes, most others are dogs.'

BB seemed incredulous. His weeping had finally stopped.

He looked in the direction of Where India's Peena Kumari, who was happily knitting a sweater while listening to the other ladies. She looked at him, suddenly realized that she was on TV and put her knitting down, 'Sorry, old habits. I am just so used to doing this on flights that my fingers move of their own volition.'

She saw the other ladies staring at her with disgust. Kusum spoke first. 'You know Peena ji, knitting was invented by men just to subvert all women and make them their slaves. And look at you, so happy in your submissiveness. You are the reason men think they can get away with treating us like animals.'

Peena Kumari looked hurt at this accusation but made her comeback with, 'I agree with you. All men are dogs.'

And then they all started chanting 'All men are dogs. All men are dogs. All men are dogs.'

Unable to hear this any longer, BB stood up and cupped his palms on his ears.

'You know ladies, today I feel ashamed. Ashamed of my existence. Ashamed of being a man in this society that treats women so badly.'

He walked off into a dark corner of the studio and returned with a can and a lighter. He stood in front of the cameras, his dark black jacket and red tie sharply contrasted by his pajamas bearing pictures of Superman and Spiderman, his childhood heroes.

'Tonight, I shall end my miserable existence. Enough of living this horrible life as a MAN who seeks to subjugate the kind women of the world. I am sorry.' He wiped his eyes on the sleeve of his jacket and flicked his hair into place. Even in his misery, BB made for a strikingly handsome man.

All cameras were focused on him. Adarsh watched the TV screen split into five different sections, one showing the anguish in his eyes, one focused on his sad face from a long shot camera, one on the lighter in his hand, one on the can and for some strange reason, the last one seemed pointed at his crotch, bearing a scene of Superman about to take flight.

BB emptied the contents of the can on his body and proceeded to light his lighter.

'This is it, ladies and gentlemen. This is Buddhiman Buddhiraja signing off forever. My apologies to all the women out there who have ever been caused harm by one of my species. May the Devil Principal rot in jail for killing that innocent girl. May Baba Neemacharya go to hell for his misdeeds. Goodbye, my friends. Goodbye. Please forgive me for being a man. I am sorry. Very sorry.'

As he brought the lighter flame close to his arm, Aparajita Sharma got off her chair and tackled him like a rugby player, knocking him onto the ground and sending the burning lighter flying.

DAY 8

HIMALAYAN PROBLEMS

MeraKaamJoker@MeraKaamJoker

Madam walks into a bar and sets it on fire.

PatliiKamar@PatliiKamar

I am just appalled at this Madam. So disgusting. How did she just set a girl on fire?

RightToTroll@RightToTroll

Girpade goes on fast. Panja goes on counter-fast. It's like a buy-one-get-one offer.

Chhicchora@Chhicchora

Madam sounds like my mother, though my mom hasn't killed me yet.

FerozWriter@FerozWriterIIMA

A progressive society like ours has no place for vile creatures like Madam. Shame shame.

TheOrchidParty@TheOrchidParty

Shri Girpade is a brave soldier of the party. I wish him best of luck for his fast – Great Leader

BowWowBreaking @BowWowBreaking

BREAKING: HE IS BACK!

With great trepidation, Madam approached her school. The newspaper *wallah* had just delivered the paper as she was heading out. She had shuddered when she noticed that she was on the front page along with Neemacharya, sharing news space with the man whose sermons she used to follow so religiously. She would have smiled at the irony of the situation, if she hadn't been terrified. All her calls to Big Boss had gone unanswered since the previous day's turn of events. She would have called in sick but there was a Sports Day event planned for today. Adarsh and his dad had convinced her that she shouldn't worry and must go about her normal life. Media speculation meant nothing in the eyes of the law and she had truth on her side. There was no reason to fear.

As she approached the gate of her school, a waiting crowd of young men and women noticed the car and came into action. They started shouting slogans and pelting eggs at her car. The placards in their hands had slogans ranging from absurd comments to downright filthy abuses. She honked at Ram Prasad who promptly opened the gate and she drove inside. Luckily, the group of protestors didn't chase her inside. NGOs these days just didn't have the efficiency and vigour of the Media Circus.

The staff didn't dare say anything to her but she could see it in their eyes. Everybody was looking at her differently, including her trusted teachers. When she went on her morning round, she heard murmurs behind her back as soon as she went around the corner. Even the students seemed to be whispering as she walked past.

The Sports Day celebration was to start at 10AM and the Assistant Commissioner of Police had been invited to be the chief guest. Last morning his office had called to confirm that he would be in on time. Big Boss and some other officers were also going to be present but the secretary to Big Boss called up and informed her that due to an urgent meeting, nobody from the department would be able to attend the function.

It was 10:30AM and the ACP hadn't arrived. She asked the teachers to get the event started when she noticed a couple of police cars enter the school gate. It was the ACP. She walked to the car along with her student guard of honor who were to garland the chief guest and escort him to the stage.

As the students took the flower garlands in their hands, he hesitated and looked at Madam with a guilty expression in his eyes, 'Let's go to your office, Madam.'

Madam nodded and walked the officer to her office.

Ten minutes later, she walked out of the office with the ACP by her side and two constables behind. She had been arrested for her suspected involvement in the suicide case of Nafisa, daughter of Rafi Mohammad. The officer was sympathetic and said that because of her seniority he would not handcuff her but the public sentiment was too strong against her and there was pressure from the government and media to take some action in the case.

*

'Dear friends, they may try their hardest to keep me down but they will fail. The one sitting upstairs is watching everything, and will never let the evil powers have their way. NEVER, my friends.' The Great Leader roared to the crowd of 45,000 listening on with interest. 'Never!'

Girpade nodded in agreement as he listened to the Great Leader with a faint smile on his face. Until yesterday, all had seemed lost. The Great Leader was going to be trapped in the media bribery allegations, their image would take a beating and the whole plot would be lost. The happenings that day had ended up changing everything. The Neemacharya scandal was a God-send, given Badi Sarkar's proximity to him. News of the Baba being a rapist could have alone been enough for the Great Leader to go on a massive offensive against Badi Sarkar, but as a bonus they had a government school principal responsible for the death of an innocent teen, a Muslim no less. This was a victory waiting to be gift-wrapped and delivered to the so-called secular government.

Day 8: Himalayan Problems

'Did you see the news about Baba Neemacharya? The man who claims to teach people how to live a simple life actually rapes women every day? This is what they are doing to Indian culture? Do you people know why Neemacharya felt that he could commit such a depraved crime and still get away with it? Tell me, do you?' He exhorted the gathered crowd.

Suddenly a man in a blue safari suit climbed on the stage, approached the Great Leader and took off the orchid garland around his neck. 'I am from the Election Commission and this is against the code of conduct.' He threw the garland off the stage and walked off, as the Great Leader watched, astonished. Girpade was about to instruct the party-men to teach the man a lesson for his temerity by hanging him from a nearby tree using the same garland but the Great Leader stopped him and continued speaking.

'Look at this, friends. The ruling party does not even allow us to wear our orchid garlands anymore. The flower of the gods, the symbol of Indian culture but we can't use it. Is this democracy?' He thundered, his massive frame seething from the insult.

'Neemacharya feels he can do anything because he has the support of Badi Sarkar. Do you know she spends half her time at the ashram of the fraud Baba? Do you know she calls him for advice about her son's bed-wetting problem? She is the one who is breeding all these devils. Dear friends, Badi Sarkar is the biggest problem affecting India. It is only up to you to make her go away, and take all these crooks with her.' He thumped the dais loudly. The crowds applauded.

His phone rang. He squinted at the screen. The number seemed an unknown one but he took the call nevertheless. Only a few important people had his direct number so he couldn't risk missing a call. Who knew maybe Badi Sarkar was calling for a deal?

'Hello?' he said.

He listened to the person at the other end and frowned, before erupting in anger. 'I DON'T WANT A HOME-LOAN. STOP CALLING ME!' He hung up, kept the phone back in his pocket, smiled as if nothing had happened and continued speaking.

'And they call themselves secular? Did you see what happened in that school? A poor Muslim girl went to seek admission and the principal forced her to commit suicide! Is this what happens in schools run by this government? Is this their idea of secularism?' He shouted in anger, causing the birds sitting on a nearby electric wire to fly away.

Girpade watched the crowd as the Great Leader spoke with the enthusiasm of a Greek emperor preparing his troops for battle and his mind went back to a great plan that he had come up with. He had suggested that ten of the party's volunteers get pressed into action to throw eggs at the Great Leader. Obviously they'd aim carefully to ensure that none of the eggs made contact but the party would blame it on the opposition party and its Ministry of Dirty Tricks. They had in the past tried to disrupt the campaigns of powerful leaders through similar means. The eggs being fired at the Great Leader would be turned into ammunition against the ruling party. It was a genius plan.

However, they received news that the ruling party was already planning to send a group of egg-throwers to the rally, so Girpade asked his team to hold off and let the ruling party do the job they were going to be blamed for anyway. Apparently, the ruling party got wind that Girpade's men had been buying eggs in preparation and they told their men to back off, given that the opposition was going to do the job for them. As luck would have it, both sides pre-empted and pre-pre-empted each other and no eggs got thrown. Girpade sighed at how complicated politics had become.

He came back to the rally with a start, when the Great Leader suddenly screamed loudly and jumped atop his chair. Girpade heard a squeaking sound nearby. There was a rat nibbling on the Great Leader's *kurta*. There was one crawling down his back. There were rats all over the stage. The government's Ministry of Dirty Tricks had found out about the Great Leader's fear of rats. 'Those dirty scoundrels,' he muttered under his breath.

The Great Leader screamed at the top of his lungs for the next ten minutes as the party volunteers chased away every single rat from the stage. Needless to say, the Media Circus had a field day, and images of the Great Leader howling from his chair would be turned into many parody videos and memes on Twitter and Facebook. The rats dispensed with, the Great Leader drank a glass of water, took a few deep breaths, sobbed into Girpade's shoulder for a few minutes and proceeded with his speech. Girpade watched in amazement as he resumed his speech with full gusto showing no trace of his dishevelled state a few minutes ago. This was the genius of the Great Leader. He was a natural.

'They called me a liar. They called me someone who would try to buy the media. Now see who the real criminal is. I have done nothing. Nothing at all. All I want is to restore India to its greatness. All I want is that India should become a superpower that can at least get the latest model of iPhone as soon as it is launched in America.'

He stepped away from the dais and came to the edge of the stage, in full view of the audience. 'I throw an open challenge to anyone who can prove that I have done any wrong. Because I know in my heart what the truth is.' He then looked skywards and said with a loud dramatic flourish. 'I ask the gods to help prove my innocence. If I have done any wrong, may the earth open up right at this moment and may I sink in it, straight to hell.'

He stood with his hands outstretched, awaiting divine justice. Prompted by the party volunteers, the crowds broke into a thunderous applause.

The earth did not shatter but the Great Leader felt something light and gooey on his forehead. He touched it and looked at his fingers. A bird had pooped on his bald head. It was a divine symbol of his innocence.

Girpade got up and broke into applause before touching the leader's feet. He then shouted into the mike. 'This is it, people of India. This is a symbol of the Great Leader's innocence from the gods. I hope the ruling party is happy now.'

'*Great Leader ki...jai.*'

'*Great Leader ki...jai.*'

'*Jab tak sooraj chand rahega, Great Leader tera naam rahega.*'

The Great Leader hugged his Chief Rally Officer and together they chanted into the mike. 'Vote for the Orchid. Vote for Indian culture.'

The Great Leader took out his phone, turned on the front-facing camera and clicked a selfie with Girpade, with the massive crowd applauding in the background. This picture was going to be posted on the party's Facebook page and would go on to get a million likes in the next few hours.

*

Adarsh felt his legs shaking and his vision getting blurred. Madam had just called to tell him that she had been arrested and was being taken to the police station. He could not believe his ears. She had nothing to do with the girl's disappearance. She had done nothing wrong. Where was the justice in arresting her?

Things had gone unbelievably wrong. Madam was being punished for going by the book, for being honest and loyal to her job. This was just symbolic of the state of affairs in the country.

Adarsh punched the wall of his office cubicle. He had to rush home. They would need to find a lawyer. He was going to leverage the social media to secure her freedom. He had to get his mother out of jail.

As he left office for home, he tweeted, 'My mother did nothing wrong. She is being made a scapegoat in the Nafisa case. Please RT.'

*

Girpade changed from his suit into a comfortable pair of *kurta-pajamas*, wore a heavy sweater, wrapped a muffler around his neck, meditated for an hour and he was ready. 'Let's go,' he told his deputy, the Vice-President of Rally Planning and Coordination.

The two took an auto to travel to the Ram-Leela ground, hundred acres of barren mud, the place where every year the epic battle of Ramayana was enacted to show the victory of good over evil, and walked up onto the stage created in one corner of the massive ground. It was a cold December day, the temperature was in the single digits, a big change from the sweltering heat of the day before and Girpade was freezing despite the layers of protection. The weather had gone to the dogs – another sign of the ineptitude of the government.

Day 8: Himalayan Problems

As soon as he reached the stage, the assembled crowd of about 200 cheered him. There were carpets laid out on the stage and a couple of mattresses on which he was supposed to sit. The Media Circus was also there and dozens of cameras were set up to record every one of his moves.

The Vice President of Rally Planning and Coordination read a short statement describing how Dr Girpade was sitting on a fast to show his support for the Great Leader and would only break it when the government apologized to the Great Leader for trying to defame him. Girpade didn't say anything. He simply folded his hands in a *namaste*, bowed to the assembled crowds, and held the pose for a minute to give time to the Media Circus so that they could click pictures, and then sat down on the mattress.

An hour passed. A second hour passed. Girpade was beginning to feel bored, though thankfully he wasn't too hungry. 'This is not too bad,' he thought to himself as one of the cameramen took a break from recording Girpade scratching his back and walked to the back of the stage to take a leak.

Suddenly, he heard the chanting of the ruling party's slogans. The slimy Panja was walking in his direction followed by a couple of lesser leaders and two dozen party volunteers. The volunteers were shouting slogans praising Badi Sarkar and Chhote Sarkar as Panja walked towards the stage.

Not aware of Panja's counter-fast, Girpade smirked and thought, 'this was quick. I didn't even have to skip lunch!' His thoughts wandered back to the delicious *paranthas* his wife had made in the morning. He couldn't wait to get his hands on a few more.

He made a quick gesture to his supporters and they started chanting slogans in favour of the Great Leader. Panja looked up and his eyes met Girpade's. Surprisingly there was no repentance in them but instead, he raised his eyebrows as if throwing a challenge. He turned around to his supporters and muttered something, following which they fired a round of slogans much louder than before.

Girpade's supporters took on the challenge and returned heavy rounds of louder slogans, reaching into the depths of their lungs for the extra decibels.

Neither side was willing to give in. The exchange of slogans lasted ten rounds, by the end of which Girpade had started biting his muffler because his ears hurt and half of his volunteers had collapsed to the ground clutching their throats, exhausted from the shouting. Panja looked on, smirking. His team had won the match and they all seemed perfectly fine, despite the exertion.

'Bloody non-veg eaters,' Girpade thought. He had not noticed that they had brought along a Boom Box to belt out the slogans and they had just been raising its volume after each round.

Panja walked off with the arrogant demeanor of a Sri Lankan cricket captain shortly after hitting India's best medium-pacer off-spinner left-arm batsman-bowler for a six and Girpade noticed that another stage was being set up a short distance away from his own. The Media Circus quickly wrapped up and ran towards the new stage.

Girpade panicked and exhorted the Media Circus to come back but nobody heard him. In desperation he even performed a moonwalk on the stage but the only people that witnessed the epic dance step were a bunch of boys whose cricket match had been disturbed to set up the stage and they were eyeing him like vultures waiting to go for the kill. Girpade noticed stones in their hands. 'Ruling party agents,' he gasped in a low voice and quickly slid down on his mattress, careful to avoid any eye contact.

To make matters worse, he now felt thirsty.

Girpade noticed Panja reach his stage and shout some instructions to his men, and they immediately got down to work. Girpade was wondering why they were knocking down the entire structure when he noticed that they were carrying the parts to another location of the park.

Panja was moving his stage right across Girpade's podium!

They would sit facing each other, eye-to-eye, man-to-man. This was even worse than having to stay hungry. Girpade was aware of his parched throat again and looked miserably at a member of the Media Circus downing a bottle of Trite, the newest soft drink in town. 'Trite will make your lives bright,' its ads used to claim. Girpade made a mental note that when Badi Sarkar came to the park to convince him to break his fast, he would insist that she personally opened a bottle of Trite for him. Nothing else would do.

Panja's stage was ready. It was luxury compared to Girpade's sparse setup. It had a roof to keep away the wind, a crystal chandelier hanging proudly from it directly on top of Panja's seat, which was a luxurious Hazy Boy recliner-cum-bed-cum-foot massager-cum-back-massager-cum dental-flosser-cum-clothes-dryer. There were only a handful of these in the entire country. Girpade gaped at Panja's ostentatious show of wealth. His own mattress couldn't give him a massage or floss his teeth. It barely provided enough cushion for his bony bottom.

'Bloody pretentious Punjabi,' he muttered to himself. A satellite dish had been installed in Panja's tent and he was now watching live images of his own fast on a 60-inch HDTV. The wall-mount was being arranged, so for now two men were holding up the TV for him to view. Panja didn't seem happy with his images and was shouting instructions at the Media Circus to change their camera angles.

Panja relaxed in his multi-purpose recliner, switched on the back massager using the remote control and let out a burp loud enough to be heard a mile away. An audio technician from the Media Circus howled loudly as his ears got fried inside his headphones.

He gently rubbed his belly, as if trying to remember the taste of his previous meal – three full *tandoori* chickens, a dozen *naans*, and a kilo of *gulab jamuns*. Who knew when he would get his next one?

He whispered something in the ears of his assistant, before dozing off. The assistant giggled and ran off the stage.

*

Giani Seth was pacing up and down the length of his office. The board had sent him a letter last night. He was amazed at their sudden brazenness. Everybody knew that Giani Seth could not read and they had made sure that they sent the letter typed in English, in a scented pink envelope. It was all Chaddha's doing, he was sure. He had been trying to influence them ever since the popular *Karodpati* magazine had published their annual rankings that had confirmed that Giani Seth had twice as much money as Chaddha, the cheap bastard who still travelled in a MerceDesi, a car that screamed upper-middle class.

He had to send his helicopter to fetch Alisha to his 100-floor mansion to read the letter. His wife had offered to read it to him but he trusted no one other than Alisha.

He had not even allowed Alisha the time to change her clothes and she had come in looking sleepy, her hair flying about in the wake of the chopper, a shawl wrapped over her semi-transparent night-wear. As she read the letter out to him, Giani Seth's eyes had nearly popped out. The board had called for an Extraordinary Casual Meeting, which was the worst of all the meetings they could call. It was far from casual and they clearly wanted to discuss a leadership change.

Alisha returned to her apartment and went off to sleep but Giani Seth hadn't slept a wink last night. He had started drinking as soon as she left and the glass hadn't left his hand since then. He reserved the best for such occasions and it wasn't any imported single malt but the cheapest *desi* available at any seedy corner of town. The *narangi* was what his body wanted and he was already through with a few bottles by the time he reached his office.

He called Alisha into his office. She entered and immediately screwed up her nose in disgust. The room was reeking of alcohol. Giani Seth was already in a very bad mood and her expression of distaste made matters worse. Before she knew what was going on, he picked up her 45-kilo body and flung her at the window, screaming with rage. She hit the glass which shattered on impact and plunged to her fate 500 feet below, straight into the windshield of his new Bentley, the car with the logo of a bird on it, the one he wanted. The car was not available at the Mumbai dealership when Alisha tried to place an order on behalf of Seth. She had painstakingly found the only dealer in the world who had one available in his favorite yellow colour. She quickly arranged for it to be flown in a chartered commercial flight from Buenos Aires. It was going to be her surprise to Giani Seth for the day.

He opened the door of his office and called the intern inside. 'Srinivas, come in.'

Day 8: Himalayan Problems

Venkat came in with a baffled look. While he had given up trying to get the rich snob to address him by his right name, he had never been called inside Giani Seth's office. This was a special day.

Giani Seth looked at him carefully. The guy was ugly and unkempt. He was wearing a shirt with red and blue checks on top of cream corduroy trousers; his hair was soaked in coconut oil and neatly parted right in the geometric centre of his skull, his appearance rounded up by the white sneakers. If anybody could have been the opposite of the carefully groomed Alisha, this was it. Giani Seth repented his impulsive action, looked out of the window, winced at the mess downstairs and turned his attention back to Venkat.

'You will be my secretary from now. I will give you five lakhs a month for the job. Okay?'

The young student was flabbergasted. Even Google didn't pay this much! 'Sure, sir. Thank you, sir.'

'Okay, then get lost and call up Chakraverty from Giani Cars.'

He looked confused but had the good sense to head out when Giani Seth looked at him with a murderous look, made the sign of a gun with his hands and kept it against his own head.

'One more thing, Aiyer. Make sure you send a bottle of *narangi* every fifteen minutes. A second late and you are fired.'

Giani Seth's phone rang ten minutes later. By now he had thrown the glass away and was drinking straight from the bottle.

He answered the call. '*Oye* Bengali, how much is the production these days?'

Ashok Chakraverty was the CEO of Giani Car Industries, makers of the popular Gianizer hatchback, the Gianist premium sedan, and the Gianinja SUV. All three cars outsold every other car in their respective segments and the company had recently hit the 20 billion dollar market cap. Giani Cars was one of the feathers in Giani Industries' cap.

'*Saar jee, bhot* an honour to hear from the great Giani Seth. It *eez* going great. *Khoob bhalo.*' He spoke in his heavy Bengali accent. 'We are going to *heet* ten million cars this month.'

'Shut it down. Shut down the plant. No more Giani Cars,' Giani Seth said.

'*Bhut saarjee?*'

'Shut it down, you Bengali. Don't make me say this again or you are fired.' Giani Seth slammed the phone down.

He then called up his broker. 'Patel, sell all of my stake in Badi Sarkar Power Unlimited, Badi Sarkar Fertilizers, Badi Sarkar Heavy Industries, State Bank of Badi Sarkar and National Highway Authority of Badi Sarkar. Leave a single share unsold and I will break your legs and feed you to stray cows.'

Many years ago, the Prime Minister had announced that all the public sector companies were a gift from Badi Sarkar to the nation, and they should be named after her to show the country's gratitude. These companies were among the biggest in the world and Giani Seth had a significant holding in each of them. They were all a part of Badi Sarkar National Stock Index and a bulk sale of the shares was sure to destroy the market.

'But, but, sir this is...' he stammered. Giani Seth disconnected the call.

The board wanted to send him an ultimatum? He was sending an ultimatum to the government. Giani Port had to be approved. He was going to give them no other option. He was Giani Seth. He told the government what to do, not the other way round.

He switched on the TV and waited. After 20 minutes it began. The Badi Sarkar National Stock Index was down by 10,000 points. The financial markets were destroyed. All foreign investors were going to exit. The opposition would use this to tighten the nails in the government's coffin.

Giani Seth let out a hearty laugh and gulped down the remainder of the latest bottle. Ten years ago, one of the junior ministers had signed over all of the country's coal and iron-ore resources to him by mistake. He had naturally made the most of that opportunity and grown to be the richest man in the country. Having reached this far, he was not going to let it all go so easily.

They wouldn't dare reject his phone calls anymore.

*

Day 8: Himalayan Problems

'Chhote Sarkar, did you hear the Great Leader's speech this morning? He said that Badi Sarkar is responsible for creating rapist monsters like Neemacharya?' The lady in purple sari said.

He looked up from his French fries at the woman peering intently into his plate, gesturing to the cameraman to record what Chhote Sarkar was eating. He had come to McDammit for his weekly trip. Badi Sarkar only allowed him to eat their French fries once a week, insisting that she would make them herself on all other days.

'Oh, you followed me here? You are Jagriti, aren't you?'

She smiled at him, her fangs sharp like knives. Years of reporting dangerous stories as India's foremost investigative journalist had done that to her. 'Yes Chhote Sarkar, I am Jagriti. Tell me, does your mother have any connection to Baba Neemacharya?'

He took a deep sip of Trite before answering. 'Yes, she talks to Neemacharya about me. He says that I should hold a Neem leaf under my armpit while passing urine to make me smarter.'

'Please, take a seat,' he offered. She sat down on the chair opposite his. They were eye to eye. Chhote Sarkar found himself staring at her dimpled cheeks and slender neck but checked himself soon and turned his attention back to his food.

She threw her head back giving her well-rehearsed disarming laugh, the one that had made many of her interviewees fall in love with her. 'Really? Armpit? How fascinating! Tell us more, Chhote Sarkar?'

'There is nothing more to tell. She consults him for my problems.'

'Problems?' Her eyebrow was raised.

'Oh, no...nothing,' he realized that perhaps he shouldn't have said that.

'So Chhote Sarkar, you think the Great Leader is right in saying that Badi Sarkar is in a relationship with Neemacharya?'

He sputtered in the midst of a sip from his bottle and ended up spitting out a mouthful of Trite into Jagriti's blouse.

'Relationship? He said that?'

She flashed an evil smile as she tried to wipe the damage using a paper napkin, 'Yes, Chhote Sarkar. He even suggested that you might be his son.'

Chhote Sarkar got up, enraged, and threw all of his French fries on Jagriti's face. 'You are lying. This cannot be. He cannot be my father.'

'I am sorry for hurting your emotions Chhote Sarkar, but this is what he said.' She smiled as she picked out the French fries from her sari and wiped the ketchup off her neck, and the cameraman zoomed in on the hair inside Chhote Sarkar's nostrils.

'The Orchid party has been screaming all of this on Twitter all day today. You should check out their tweets.'

'Twitter? What is that?'

'What! You don't know what Twitter is?'

*

The party top brass rushed inside the conference room, swiping their ID-cards at the entrance as they got in. As per the protocol for the We Will We Will Rock You party Working Group meetings, there were 21 attendees and 20 chairs. The last one in would not get a chair and would be removed from the working group, with a promotion candidate replacing him in the next meeting. Badi Sarkar had started this tradition to weed out the low performers and bring in fresh talent.

Panja couldn't come as he was busy going through a fast-unto-death but he had sent his wife as a deputy. She let out a blood-curdling scream and jumped from the door, landing straight into her husband's chair of choice – the first one at the table, the place where the leader should be. Chamcha Das did what came best to him – bend over and sneak under the table to reach a seat. Bhakt Lal just punched everybody he came across in his pursuit of a seat. 'Survival of the fittest', Badi Sarkar had said when the leaders had initially protested against her new way of running these meetings.

Panja's wife dialed him in over Skype. His voice crackled over the phone and he soon appeared. He had now been without food for a few hours and already seemed thinner. His missus broke into tears looking at his malnourished state but managed to compose herself.

The scramble lasted a minute and everybody was soon seated,

Day 8: Himalayan Problems

though some people were rubbing their jaws gingerly. The one without a chair turned out to be Chhote Sarkar, who walked in casually after all seats were taken. Chamcha Das immediately got up from his seat, as did Bhakt Lal, both insisting that he take their seat. Chhote Sarkar took Bhakt Lal's chair and gestured to his companion, the young teenage driver of the auto who had driven him here, to take Chamcha's seat.

Everybody gasped. Only Badi Sarkar had the power to nominate new people into the working group. Bhakt and Chamcha left the room to suppressed murmurs. Chhote Sarkar looked at everybody and said, 'Badi Sarkar always says that we need to induce fresh blood in the party. This guy here, Chotu, just drove me here in a record time without jumping any red lights, without hitting any pedestrians and didn't overcharge me.' He smiled at the group and said, 'And, wait for this, his meter was not tampered with.'

This was truly special. An honest auto-rickshaw driver was unheard of. The room applauded young Chotu and a few of the senior leaders came up to him to shake his hands.

Badi Sarkar's voice boomed into the room. 'Good morning boys.'

'Good morning, Badi Sarkar,' the party leaders got up with folded hands and responded in a sing-song chorus. Panja got up from his recliner in the Ram Leela ground. Chotu stared on, looking at the TV screen, which was blank. Badi Sarkar's voice was coming over speakers installed in the roof and there was no video link, so he wasn't quite sure why all the men were standing.

Badi Sarkar never came into these meetings but dialed in through the audio conference number. Half the members in the working group had never even seen her. There were rumors that she was bed-ridden; some people said that she was a devil with two faces; some people said that she had got too big for her shoes by a sudden spurt in height that had made her seven feet tall; the latest rumor was that she had been living in the equatorial rainforests of Congo where she fed on fast diminishing tribes. As a result, none of her portraits and statues in the newly opened Badi Sarkar museum looked alike.

The list of Badi Sarkar rumors was long. According to one

particularly long-standing urban legend, her most trusted lieutenant was a 30-year-old parrot who stood guard outside her office and anybody who wanted to meet her had to answer a question asked by the parrot. Only those who gave the right answer were allowed in and anyone who failed was supposed to take a bath in the filthy Yamuna river, which was as good as committing suicide. As a result, nobody ever attempted to visit her.

'I have a surprise for you boys today,' the voice boomed. All the men were still standing with their heads bowed.

Suddenly, the doors of the conference room opened and a gorgeous woman walked in, escorted by a security guard. She was wearing the sensuous yellow sari first worn by famous actress SariDevi in the movie Master India, her hair was tied up in an elegant bun, her face was glowing with the energy of a hundred incandescent lamps, her big green eyes seemed even prettier thanks to the thick helping of *kajal* and her skin was radiant like one of the ladies from a Fair & Lowly advertisement. The men watched entranced as she strode into the room, her fragrance filling up their hearts with joy, the click-clock of her pencil heels breaking the shocked silence. She was holding a phone in one hand and what seemed like a remote control in the other.

She reached the front of the room and sat on the throne made of a single piece of diamond, the 100,000 carat Queen of Hearts, found in a cave in the Himalayas by the Prime Minister last year and dedicated to Badi Sarkar.

'Mom, you're here?' exclaimed Chhote Sarkar. Everybody gasped. Panja's wife whispered softly, 'Must be Santoor.' Badi Sarkar looked at her and smiled. Her teeth were so white that for a moment everybody shielded their eyes.

'How are you all today?' She kept the phone and remote control on the table and asked the group.

'Very good, Madam. Very good,' one of the older gentlemen responded first.

She shook her head and nodded at her security guard, who promptly stepped forward and gave a slap to the distinguished party leader whose left cheek now bore the fingerprints of his punishment.

Day 8: Himalayan Problems

'YOU ARE GOOD? VERY GOOD?' She shouted. 'The party is going through a severe crisis and you say you are very good. You should be ashamed of yourself. Go stand in the corner facing the wall and think about what you just said.' The 85-year-old party veteran did as told, retreating to the far wall and standing with his head bowed with shame.'

'HOLD YOUR EARS!,' she screamed at him. The man sobbed but did as told.

She looked around the room. 'Does anybody else also feel very good at the attack on our party?' Everybody shook their head. The people sitting close to where the offending leader was standing reinforced their answer by walking up to him and giving him another slap.

'Baba Neemacharya is a good man,' she said, her voice faltering as she mentioned his name. 'He has helped us a lot by taking care of Chhote Sarkar and we will always be indebted to him for his help.'

She dabbed her eyes with a handkerchief and continued, 'The attack on Baba's character has given the Great Leader new ammunition to attack our party. This is appalling and I deeply condemn his shameful behaviour.

'We are being attacked from all fronts. The Great Leader is spreading all sorts of lies about our party, Baba Neemacharya has also been trapped in an opposition conspiracy and today the stock market was crashed by Giani Seth, who has long been a faithful supporter of our party. I hope you all know how much work he does for our government by telling us which policies will benefit the nation and which ones will get us more money. How did we let someone so important become so unhappy with us?'

Nobody dared attempt an answer. The last person who had tried to answer one of Badi Sarkar's rhetorical questions had been sent to spend a night at a police station in a remote village in Bihar and had never been able to sit straight in a chair ever since he returned.

She got up from her chair and started pacing the room. 'Who wants to help me win the elections?'

Everybody raised their hands immediately.

'Very good,' she smiled and patted the bald head of a 60 year-old youth-wing leader.

From his noisy stage at the Ram Leela ground, Panja raised his hands to speak, prompting his wife to raise her hand. Badi Sarkar looked at her, then at the phone screen, and asked Panja what he wanted to say.

'Badi Sarkar, turn on the TV. Bow Wow channel. HE IS BACK!' He gasped. He seemed to be choking and his skin was pale like the skin of a girl in a Fair and Lowly advertisement before she starts applying the magical cream.

Madam turned on the TV and switched to Bow Wow. She glanced at the TV screen and immediately shrunk back, all colour drained from her face. Fuming, she reached for the remote control on the table and pressed a few buttons but didn't see any change. Frustrated, she slammed the remote into the wall of the room.

The Prime Minister was addressing the nation. He had returned from the Himalayas and appeared on TV without her permission. 'Somebody's gonna get hurt real bad,' she mumbled threateningly, as the PM started his speech.

'Dear fellow countrymen, our nation is under threat of war. American warships are advancing towards our coast and there is widespread anticipation that the Americans want to strike at least two major Indian cities in retaliation for the inadvertent insult caused by one of our diplomats to the American president.

'It is extremely irresponsible of America to think that they can attack our peaceful country in this brash manner. I have ordered that our navy deploys its fleet in preparation for battle with the Americans. I want them to know that they cannot get away with insulting our great nation in this manner. We will banish SitarBucks and McDammit from India forever if they as much as enter Indian waters.'

There were astonished gasps in the room at the last line. SitarBucks was the official coffee partner of the ruling party. The Prime Minister could not behave like this with close allies.

His face was glowing, he had a long beard and it looked like his hair had not been shampooed in years but the Prime Minister was speaking with the calm poise of someone who has achieved nirvana. There was even a faint halo around his head.

Day 8: Himalayan Problems

Badi Sarkar stammered and sank in her chair in disbelief, 'This cannot be happening!'

Chhote Sarkar noticed the tickers at the bottom of the TV screen.

'#DevilPrincipal's son speaks up. Says Madam is innocent.'

'My mother has done nothing wrong @AdarshBharatiya.'

'#DevilPrincipal's son starts #InnocentMadam campaign on Twitter.'

'Who killed Nafisa? Tonight at 11PM.'

Someone retrieved the remote and handed it back to Badi Sarkar. 'Badi Sarkar, please try again. He is remote-controlled, with a 15-year money-back warranty. Probably he was out of range earlier.' Badi Sarkar pressed a few buttons but the PM kept speaking.

Enraged, she got up on the table, turned on a 60 Cent song on her phone and started doing a vigorous Hip-Hop routine. Everybody ducked under the table as she performed splits, somersaults, the Helicopter and popped every joint of her body in a performance worthy of the first prize at *India's Got Great Talent*. Dance was her expression of extreme unhappiness and the last time she was this angry, she had cut off the thumb of the first person she saw after her performance.

The Prime Minister was wrapping up as she started twerking vigorously on the table. 'Something amazing happened during my time in the Himalayas. *Kucchh adbhut ho gaya*, my friends. I have realized my powers and returned to serve the great nation. I will never leave you again.'

'*Theek hai?*' he asked the nation and the screen went dead.

*

BB looked on fondly as she nibbled on her cheesecake. They were at the exclusive Durbar restaurant of the posh Rajmahal hotel. BB's show had been preempted today by the sudden announcement from the Prime Minister's office that the PM would address the nation at 9 PM. BB had been surprised. He had almost forgotten about the existence of the PM, leave alone the fact that he still had the ability to talk. Wasn't he supposed to be praying for Badi Sarkar's health in some secret cave in the Himalayas?

Everybody at work had been very excited about the sudden reappearance of the Prime Minister. BB gladly took the day off. This was the first day in five years that he would watch the news at 9PM instead of making news. She also didn't have a shoot planned for the day so they agreed to meet over dinner.

'You look so pretty,' he told her. She was wearing a seductive red dress with a plunging neckline and a slit that ran up her legs all the way to her thighs. BB was seduced but then all he had to do to be seduced by his sweetheart of five years was to look into her eyes.

'Come on, finish fast,' he said, his leg playfully running up that slit in her dress under the table, feeling the smooth skin of her legs.

'Oh, so the super-honest BB is now engaging in under-the-table dealings?' she winked at him and blew him a kiss.

BB laughed.

'Where do we go next?' she finished the cheesecake and asked him. He handed her the key to a room.

'You took a room?' She exclaimed.

'The executive suite, baby. The real dessert awaits there.'

'Ooh, I love it.'

'Anything for you, my love.'

They didn't waste much time getting to the room, or in getting on with business. Clothes were ripped off bodies, the bedcovers were thrown onto the ground and ten minutes later they both lay on the bed, panting from the exertion, she resting on BB's strong arms, and BB staring at the painting on the wall that depicted two horses galloping about happily.

'I love you, baby,' he said.

'I love you too, my honeybun,' she turned to him and gave him a kiss.

'No seriously, I want to get married to you.'

She squealed with delight and hugged BB. 'Then you will have to meet my dad.'

'Oh speaking of that, when are you going to tell me who your dad is? I don't understand the point of keeping it a secret.'

Day 8: Himalayan Problems

She sighed. 'I will let you know soon, BB. I am just worried that you will not like his name.'

'What?'

'No, nothing. I will try talking to him first.'

'I don't know what you mean. I will do anything to get married to you. You are my life. You are my soul-mate. I cannot live without you. It is as simple as that.'

She smiled at BB and gave him another kiss.

DAY 9

BETTER THAN BB

PatliiKamar@PatliiKamar

OMG the Prime Minister looked so hawt last night I could barely breathe.

Jagriti@JagritiRules

Finally #DevilPrincipal is arrested. Happy to see our efforts succeed. Hyper News is proud to be the first to break the news.

Chhicchora@Chhicchora

So the Prime Minister did not go to the Himalayas but was working out at a gym all these years.

FerozWriter@FerozWriterIIMA

'The Return of the PM. My column on ten things the PM can do to improve the state of our economy, in today's Crimes of India paper.'

Swamy@Swamy1959

I have got confirmed news that the Prime Minister was in Switzerland counting all the cash in Badi Sarkar's accounts for the last ten years.

TheOrchidParty@TheOrchidParty

The Great Leader expresses deep anguish about the ruling party supporting criminals like Baba Neemacharya and #DevilPrincipal

BowWowBreaking@BowWowBreaking

BREAKING: #DEVILPRINCIPAL IS IN JAIL. BOW WOW BROKE IT FIRST. WE THANK OUR VIEWERS FOR MAKING IT HAPPEN.

Adarsh picked up the newspaper and went through the headlines. The Prime Minister had made a surprise reappearance from his voluntary exile in the Himalayas and delivered a strong message to the arrogant Americans. The stock market had crashed following Giani Seth's decision to shut down the Giani Cars division. There was speculation too that he was behind the panic selling of stocks of several top public sector companies, all of which had made the stock index fall by ten thousand points to reach an all-time low.

The third news story on the front page was of the arrest of Madam from her school on charges of murder. Adarsh read the story with dismay. It was full of lies and exaggerations. The story claimed that Madam had herself tried to set the girl on fire because she didn't touch her feet. Yesterday the same paper had reported that the girl had eaten poison and run off to jump into the lake after Madam threatened to sever her neck with a butter knife.

Page 5 had comments from some prominent celebrities who had their own outrageous observations to make. Big Bee was quoted as saying that he was having second thoughts about sending his grandson to any school if this was the condition of our teachers. The writer Aparajita Sharma had written a scathing editorial on how India was a country where women should not be born at all because all Indian men were rapists.

Madam had been produced before a Magistrate yesterday and he had remanded her to custody. She had been taken to Central Jail by the police team, where a team of feminists waiting at the gate had shouted slogans against her and another group of ruling party volunteers had held up placards protesting her contempt for minorities. The court had refused the plea for bail, instead admonishing Madam for the terrible crime she had committed.

Adarsh had tried to clear the air through a blog post with details of all that had transpired between Madam, Rafi and Nafisa and tweeted a link with the #InnocentMadam hashtag, asking people to forward the link to prominent politicians and news channels, to put some pressure on them. The world needed to know the truth rather than fabricated lies being circulated by the Media Circus. Soon the link started getting some hits and he started getting responses on Twitter. There were those who lashed out at him for defending a brazen murderer, while some others supported him and helped spread the word.

As he put down the newspaper, Adarsh heard the sound of a notification on his phone. Somebody with the handle @ChhotaRustam had responded to his blog post.

He said, 'The story of your mother's troubles in unbelievable. The Media Circus painted a completely different picture yesterday.'

Adarsh responded with, 'Thanks buddy. Do me a favour and forward the blog to all news channels and prominent leaders. Help spread the word.'

His campaign was gaining traction. Ironically, his mom had always said that his obsession with Twitter was a waste of time.

*

It had been a full day since the fast started. Girpade was in pain. On normal days, he started feeling dizzy if his lunch got delayed by 15 minutes past noon and here he was, 24 hours later without any food or water. His mouth felt dry and flaky, his stomach was burning, his head felt dizzy and he barely had energy to wave at his supporters when they chanted slogans every 30 minutes. He glared across the stage at Panja, lying on his fancy contraption of a chair, watching TV. He seemed to be taking it quite well, occasionally getting up to mingle with the supporters, taking frequent washroom breaks and posing for the Media Circus whenever they asked.

The supporters were getting bored though. Girpade's supporters had been smarting since the previous morning when Panja's people had let loose a snake on Girpade's stage. There had been a massive scare as Girpade ran around the stage trying to get away from the

Day 9: Better than BB

slimy reptile. They had managed to chase it away but then Girpade had made them change every single carpet and bedsheet on the stage.

A few of them were anxiously looking at their watches, hoping for the fast to end fast. India was playing a cricket match later that evening with China, the undisputed world champion, who had won every match in the last year.

A little past 1 PM, Panja's supporters started taking jibes at Girpade, who was by now beating the stage in his frustrated state. His stomach was rumbling loudly and he was finding it hard to even stand up.

A fight broke out. The two groups of supporters charged at each other and soon it was a free-for-all, with arms, legs, sticks, chairs, anything that could be thrown being thrown around, as Girpade and Panja watched their armies slug it out, like Ram and Raavan did every year during Dussehra at this very venue. As if on cue, a few monkeys also appeared, surveyed the scene and ran off with a bunch of bananas from Panja's stage.

Chhote Sarkar climbed up the stairs leading to Panja's stage staring at the carnage in front of him. The Media Circus was out in full force and the fast and counter-fast had quickly escalated into a scene akin to one in the *Fast and the Spurious* movie series. Panja was alone on stage as reinforcements had been sent to the battlefield to the aid of their army. He appeared to be talking to someone on his phone.

'Where are you?'

'Thank God. I was beginning to get worried that maybe the reports are true.'

Chhote Sarkar quickly hid in a corner out of Panja's line of sight, who was quite occupied between the phone call, watching TV, and his in-progress back-massage. He listened on in amazement and couldn't believe his ears.

Panja completed the call and got up to go to the portable toilet installed by the side of the stage. Chhote Sarkar approached him and touched his feet, like Badi Sarkar had always insisted he do. Panja didn't look too happy to see him. He patted his back casually and proceeded in the direction of the toilet.

Five minutes later Chhote Sarkar was startled by a loud flash of lightning in the afternoon sun and soon he heard Panja screaming. He looked up to see the Prime Minister dragging him out of the toilet by his ears, a chicken leg in Panja's hand. He was beating up the old man as he dragged him back towards the stage.

Before he went into the Himalayan exile, the Prime Minister was over 70-years-old, diabetic, a heart-patient and a timid person who had got the top job after a draw of chits in the working group. His biggest power had been his support for multiple remote-control frequencies and the fact that his range extended into the tens of thousands of kilometers, which was unheard of in past remote-controlled PMs.

The transformation to this present person was uncanny. Now he looked like a Greek god, his shoulder-length shiny tresses free of dandruff, his face free of wrinkles, a soft halo around his head and his clothes whiter than those washed by the newest High-Tide detergent with oxy particles, nano-tubes technology and a rare extract of Yeti's fur that was supposed to keep the clothes white for a longer period. Chhote Sarkar looked at him beating up Panja whom he had caught red-handed, tomato ketchup dripping over his hands, and heaved a sigh of relief. Finally, some sanity was being restored in the world.

The Media Circus took over from the Prime Minister, snapping up pictures of Panja sprawled across the stage, unconscious from the blows, the offending piece of chicken leg lying at his feet. Jagriti walked to Panja and placed the chicken leg in his free hand, and the cameras started shooting the hapless victim, like an execution squad in a dictatorial regime punishing a citizen who didn't announce his undying love for their undisputed awesome leader.

The ticker on Hyper News would scream, in size 44 font, 'Panja Caught with Chicken Leg in his *Panja*.'

The Prime Minister looked up at Chhote Sarkar staring at him and came to him. As he approached, Chhote Sarkar felt an immensely strong force field draw him to the PM. His eyes exuded a warmth he had never seen before. His smile had the disarming power to fill the world with peace, yet a minute ago he had seen in those eyes the fire that could burn anything that came in the way.

He stared at the PM with a curious look in his eyes. The Prime Minister kept a hand on Chhote Sarkar's shoulder and said, 'I had no idea the Media Circus would be here in full strength. Thank God I got my hair cut and shaved off my beard before I arrived.'

'Walk with me, my child. There's one more thing we need to do.'

He led the young leader to Girpade's stage where the Orchid party Chief Rally Officer was lying flat on his stomach, howling in pain, his head about to burst from one day of no food or water.

'Get up, son,' the Prime Minister commanded.

Girpade got up and looked at the godly figure in front of him. 'Am I dead?'

The Prime Minister laughed and helped Girpade to his feet, lifting him by his shoulders. With that touch, Girpade felt his body getting enervated. Suddenly his head didn't feel so heavy, his stomach felt sated, the fever was subsiding and his throat was not on fire anymore.

He stared at the Prime Minister for a few minutes, curious about this new person whose mere appearance seemed to fill him with hope. He looked in those eyes and suddenly it struck him, and the Orchid party leader lay down prostrate on the floor, his hands folded in front of the Prime Minister. 'Oh my god, you ARE God. Never leave us again.' He grabbed the Prime Minister's feet and started sobbing. 'We waited for so many years.'

The Prime Minister asked Girpade to get up. 'I am no God, silly. I just feel like my head got a bit cleared up after all those years of solitude and the pent-up energy I had saved over the many years of staying silent found a release.'

'Gosh, I feel so strong,' he said, and gave a round-house kick to one of Panja's supporters who had crept up on stage holding a microphone intending to slam it on the Prime Minister's head. Girpade and Chhote Sarkar watched spellbound as the man fell a good 100 meters away.

'Sir, you are almost as strong at Pehelwan Singh,' Girpade said, referring to the Bollywood star with biceps bigger than a small car built by Giani Industries. In his recently released movie, he had summoned all of his power to throw a knife while standing next to a *vada pav* vendor in Mumbai and it had flown across oceans and mountains to strike the chest of a bad guy taking pictures of New York's Empire State Building.

He laughed, turned in the direction of more Panja supporters trying to launch another attack and let out a loud scream – the sound waves were strong enough to transport the bulky men all the way into the garbage dump at the other end of the park.

There was only one thing left to do. 'My dear Girpade, you are a good man. You wanted an apology from the government? I apologize to you for all the evil deeds that my government has done in the last few years. I promise that I will fix everything.

'Now break this stupid fast and let's go get some *masala dosa*.'

*

'Sir, two people from the government are here to meet you.'

'Thank you, Nagarjuna. Send the bastards in.' Giani Seth smiled at his new secretary and waved at Venkat to get lost.

'One more thing, Rajni. Regardless of how many sounds you hear, don't open the door until I call you. I don't want to be disturbed when I am with these two.'

Giani Seth grabbed his cricket bat and stood near his desk. The two entered and noticed the billionaire staring at them, his eyes full of rage.

'Turn around,' he ordered them.

They sighed and turned their backs on Giani Seth, who immediately walloped each of them with the bat, and continued hitting their backsides while they cried out in pain after each blow.

'You motherfuckers, I will hit you today till your backsides flatten out. I will teach you a lesson that you and your government will never forget. *Saalon kutton!*'

And it went on and on. He would hit Bhakt and remark, 'You wouldn't take my phone calls?' He would hit Chamcha and comment, 'The board threatened to kick me out of my company.' He would bang their heads together and say. 'I paid 5,000 crores to you bastards in advance.' He would kick them in the groin and say, '*Kameenon*, now you will know who the most powerful person in this country is.'

Day 9: Better than BB

An hour later, he had enough. Bhakt and Chamcha were smarting from the ruthless punishment handed out to them but were hopeful that it would be worth the pain.

'Okay, I am done,' he said and threw away the bat. 'Now let's talk.' He called up Venkat and asked him to bring two ice-packs and a bottle of scotch.

His anger somewhat controlled, he turned to his two visitors with a sudden change in demeanor and smiled at them. 'So my friends from the government, how are you? It is so good to see you.' The two cowered, half afraid that he was going to assault another part of their body next. Their hands immediately went to their cheeks, as a sort of instinctive reaction to the prospect of a slap.

'*Arre* come on *yaar*. I am not going to hit you. You have come from the *sasuraal*, after all. How is Badi Sarkar?'

'Err, she is fine.' Bhakt Lal replied and immediately got up, folded his hands and shouted 'Long live Badi Sarkar.'

Chamcha Das lied prostate on the ground, and said, 'May Badi Sarkar live for a thousand years.'

Giani Seth laughed loudly. 'You two ass-kissers are such clowns. How does she even tolerate you?'

The two noticed Venkat return with the icepacks, immediately grabbed one and started massaging their behinds. 'Ooh, this feels so good,' Bhakt said.

'Sit down, you rascals.' He handed them a glass each and poured out a generous helping from a bottle of scotch.

The still smarting Bhakt and Chamcha finished their drinks in a single gulp while Giani Seth had barely taken a sip. 'You politicians always have to behave like beggars, no?' He poured another drink for them. This time they sipped more slowly. They were here on a mission and couldn't afford to annoy the already upset businessman.

Badi Sarkar had found the two lying at the door of the working group meeting after it ended. They had their arms outstretched and were lying in a pool of tears, sobbing uncontrollably. She had taken pity on them and promised that she would take them both back into the working group if they managed to secure a deal with Giani Seth. They had happily taken up the offer.

'Okay Giani Seth, while we get the issue of your port settled, we can work out an alternative arrangement. What if we name a street after you?' Bhakt Lal offered.

Giani Seth got up from his seat, walked to him and gave him a slap. 'A street? What the hell is this? I am no two-penny *neta* that you will offer to bribe me with a street name. Save those for them.'

Chamcha got up from his chair. 'Sorry, Giani ji. We mean we can give you an entire city. You can do whatever you want with it – develop buildings, hotels, anything. All yours.'

'Hmm,' Giani Seth mumbled. 'I want two.'

*

Baba Neemacharya lay on his bed surrounded by his girls. Padmini sat right next to him, holding on to one hand and running her other hand through his dense hair. The Baba had not gone for his morning sermon today saying that he didn't feel like it. In fact, ever since he found out about Girl 45's betrayal, he had stayed in his room, tossing and turning in his bed, occasionally getting up to cry loudly. Some of the older faithful girls were also sobbing. They had been taking turns to soothe the Baba. At this time two girls were massaging his legs, one was applying neem paste on his chest to keep the blood pressure under control and yet another one was performing the *Lungi Dance* to keep his spirits raised.

All their efforts didn't seem to be producing any results. He was mumbling incoherently.

'They will come and take me away.'

'*Jail ki roti khani padegi, jail ka paani peena padega.*'

'Wait,' he looked at Padmini with innocent eyes and asked, 'do they have Bisleri water in jail? I get constipated if I drink normal water.'

The *Lungi Dance* girl switched to the more energetic *Chikni Chameli*, hoping it would help get the Baba out of his stupor. It didn't.

'Why did she have to do this to me? I was gentle with her. I even gave her a box of cherries to compensate for taking hers.'

'Baba, you need to be brave. Don't lose it,' Padmini chided him. 'Nothing will happen to you.'

Day 9: Better than BB

The intercom buzzed, breaking the calm of the room with its loud sound. Padmini answered. It was the control room and the security in-charge seemed in a state of panic.

'Padmini ji, I have received news that the area police inspector is coming to arrest the Baba with three constables. They should be here in an hour but tell the Baba to not worry. We can easily handle four men. They may enter the ashram but they will never get out.' He had ordered his security staff of 18 to gather their *lathis* and swords. Surely, the police couldn't just walk into the ashram and arrest Baba Neemacharya.

She gasped. Everybody in the room was looking at her face, waiting for the news.

Baba shook her. 'What happened, Padmini? Are they here?' He started wailing loudly now.

'Yes, Baba,' she replied, her eyes lowered but angry. Despite Girl 45's issues, the fact was that the Baba had taken good care of her over the last many years. He had given her an interest-free loan for her brother's engineering degree at a time when she was desperately looking for funds to pay his admission fees. He had given her a profit-sharing agreement where she got two per cent of the daily collections at the ashram. Yet, she had gotten him into all this trouble. She had been feeling miserable about betraying the Baba's trust.

'Call her,' she handed him the diamond-encrusted Motaphone mobile and looked at Baba, who was crying like the actor Veerkhan Bhai did in his last movie, when his girlfriend married his son instead.

'Call her,' she repeated, her voice stern. 'She HAS to help you.'

Baba took the phone hesitatingly, looked at Padmini again, his eyes seeking reassurance, and dialled the first number in his favourites list. It rang for a minute before being answered by her assistant.

'Hello.'

'This is Baba Neemacharya. Where is Badi Sarkar?'

'Baba ji, just one minute. Badi Sarkar is applying the Neem conditioner to her hair.'

'GIVE HER THE BLOODY PHONE NOW!,' he shouted, the pent-up emotion bursting out.

'Sure, sir. I'll give it to her right away.'

There were sounds of footsteps scampering over a flight of stairs, muffled voices as he handed over the phone, and she finally spoke, 'Good Morning, Baba ji. How are you?'

'The Baba is dying and is sad to know that his most loyal followers no longer care for him.'

She laughed, her laughter soft like the gentle rustling of leaves on a cool spring morning. 'Of course not, Baba ji. May your enemies die. We will not let anything happen to you.'

'*Accha*? Then why is a police inspector coming to arrest me?'

'What?' she gasped. She had given clear instructions to her working group that nobody could touch Baba Neemacharya.

'You don't worry Baba ji. I will get this sorted.'

Five minutes later the police jeep got a message from the control room and was asked to turn back. The inspector would return to the police station only to get slapped by the Assistant Commissioner and be handed transfer orders to walk the dogs at superstar Loverr Khan's bungalow, as a punishment for 'reporting to duty drunk'.

*

The Great Leader lovingly admired his cap as he counted the number of feathers in it. The ninth one was a recent addition, thanks to the World Council of Great Leaders inducting him as a life-member.

He rubbed his hands in glee at the prospect of the next feather, his mind fast forwarding to when he would be crowned king of India and become the Prime Minister.

The maid came into his office and handed him his phone. 'Call for you,' she said and silently retreated to the kitchen. She was cooking Afghani chicken for dinner today.

The Great Leader saw that it was a call from Giani Seth, put on his cap with the nine feathers in it and spoke. 'Hello, this is the Great Leader.'

'Hello Sirji, dear Great Leader. How are you?' Giani Seth's voice crackled on the phone.

Day 9: Better than BB

The Great Leader had been unable to form an opinion on Giani Seth yet. He had found him loud, uncouth and a bit of a clumsy rich man with hardly any class. He rolled his eyes as he answered. 'EXPELLIARMO, you rich billionaire. Out with your secrets. What makes you remember this poor man today?'

Giani Seth laughed. 'Sirji how are you poor? We are all poor in front of you. You are the Great Leader. I am just the owner of a silly private jet.'

'Very well, Giani Seth. How have you been?'

'*Arre* sir. It is like the entire world is out to get me. My port is still nowhere close to getting approved. My board wants to kick me out of my company. Badi Sarkar wants my money but doesn't want to give me anything. Even my daughter makes a face every time she sees me. Things are getting harder these days.' He sighed. 'There is only one hope remaining for now. I have sent a proposal to Badi Sarkar. Let's see what she says.'

The Great Leader's voice dropped a few decibels at the mention of Badi Sarkar but he kept the door open, 'I doubt you should expect much from that woman. Let me know how things go. If not, we can always plan an agitation.'

'Thank you Great leader ji. How is everything with you?'

'Everything is shaping up nicely. We will surely form the next government. I am planning a *raj yagya* in a few days. If this goes through successfully, nobody can stop me anymore. Don't tell anyone please. This is confidential information and I am only telling you as a trusted friend.'

'Of course, Great Leader ji. Good luck with the *raj yagya*.'

*

'Ladies and Gentlemen, we have long talked about the nexus between politicians and businessmen. They say politicians run the country but in reality it is businessmen with their deep pockets, who actually tell the politicians what to do.

'Does there exist a businessman-politician nexus that makes sure that the benefits of our nation's growth fail to reach the common man? Does there exist an implicit mutual back-scratching that goes on between the political and business leaders of the nation?'

'You are watching B for Buddhi, brought to you tonight by Scream, the energy drink that will leave you screaming for more. I am your host Buddhiman Buddhiraja. Tonight we will look at the richest man in the country and the true story behind yesterday's stock-market crash. The crash whose sound reverberated throughout the country as its fallout affected not just investors but everybody in the nation as the prices of everything from tomatoes to rickshaw fares jumped steeply in its wake.'

BB shook his head in disbelief as he shuffled the papers in front of him, damning evidence of the involvement of some respected names in perpetrating the worst day for Indian stock markets ever.

He stared into Camera #5 for three minutes as the title soundtrack from the disaster movie *Titanic* set the mood for viewers.

'Ladies and Gentlemen, we don't have any panel today and neither do we have any interviewee. Just you and me – the common man – the same common man who bears the brunt of the games that are played by the rich and the powerful of our country; the common man who struggles to find ways to save some income tax while filing his returns when the rich have their fortunes stashed away in their Swiss accounts and sleep on beds made of real dollar notes, soft to the touch and possessing the exact firmness that the human body needs for a rejuvenating sleep.'

Giani Seth's picture came up on the viewer's screen as BB continued his monologue. 'Look at this man. He is the richest man in India. He is the owner of factories, hotels, skyscrapers, Hairbus jets and countless television sets, all of which receive about three thousand channels while you and I barely get 200. Rumor has it that,' and there came the sound of a slight gasp from BB, 'he even eats a real apple every day. A real apple, ladies and gentlemen. At Rs 4000 a piece, most of us can barely think of eating an apple once a year at best, and he eats one every day. Such is the extent of the problem facing our nation.'

He continued, 'Look at this man closely. *He* is capitalism. He is the reason why the country is still poor. *This* man is the face of crony capitalism.

'It doesn't stop here. We have got leads to confirm that he

colluded with the government in fixing the price of bicycles because invariably we are going to run out of petrol and then everybody will be forced to buy one and he will multiply his wealth at the expense of desperate Indian citizens who need a vehicle to commute to work and will pay through their noses to get one.

'As for the nexus with politicians, we have got unconfirmed reports of ruling party leaders visiting his office to consult on strategy matters regularly. It is said that he is the government's unofficial sponsor.'

BB's face was back on the TV screen. He stared hard at the camera and said, 'We will take a break here, after which we will look at how his daughter killed five people in broad daylight and the case got buried under a truckload of currency notes that were delivered in the middle of the night to the Commissioner's residence.'

Suddenly there was a flash of bright light and viewers were surprised to find the Prime Minister seated next to BB.

BB squinted as he tried to look at the ball of fire sitting next to him but it was too bright. 'Is that you, Mr Prime Minister? Sir, can you turn down that halo?'

The Prime Minister smiled and pressed a dial on the watch he was wearing. The brightness went down a notch. It was still incredibly bright and hot but BB could make out the outline of his face now.

'Mr Prime Minister, sir, what a pleasant surprise. How are you, sir?'

'I am very well, my dear Buddhi. How have you been? Have you been keeping an eye on the criminals while I was away?'

BB smiled nervously and whispered, 'Of course, sir. Every night, one round of the country right after the show,' careful lest the sound carried to the mikes.

He looked at Camera #6 and flashed a warm smile, 'Ladies and gentlemen, the Prime Minister is here.

'It is such a delight to have you on the show, sir,' he looked at the PM, his eyes having got adjusted to the brightness now.

'It is my pleasure, Buddhi,' he smiled back.

'So sir, do tell us what happened in the Himalayas? Just look at you – you've ch ch changed so much,' BB stammered as he stared at the Prime Minister. He had bulked up, his body rippling with muscles, his body-language assertive, the benevolent smile and that halo spreading warmth around him.

'Oh Buddhi, let's just say some special powers came to me one day while sitting in that cave praying for the long life of...,' he coughed loudly. BB held up a hand to stop him, 'no need to complete that sentence sir. We can understand.'

'So Buddhi, do you want to see what I can do?'

'Of course, sir.'

The Prime Minister looked delighted and said. 'Carefully watch this.' He then sat on the ground with his legs folded under him, started chanting what sounded like a secret mantra and soon his body was floating a few feet above the ground, his eyes level with BB's.

'I don't need to take a flight ever again,' he said.

'Wow,' BB said and applauded his levitation.

'Hold on, there's more.' He then stared at one of the cameras and it came flying through the air straight into his hands. He then did the same with the expensive German pen in BB's shirt pocket.

'Now watch me bend this pen.'

'Sir, sir, one second.' BB took the pen back and handed him his other diamond-studded pen. 'This one was a gift from the girlfriend. She is very sweet, sir. I love her and want to get married to her soon.' He smiled nervously as he kept the pen back in his pocket. The Prime Minister proceeded to bend the second pen from the centre, to form an L shape, by just looking at it for a second.

'Mind boggling, sir.'

Two swords suddenly came flying through the air. 'I am a master at sword-fighting, Buddhi. I suspect I might be even better than you now.' He grabbed one and Buddhi playfully took the other. 'Oh sir, I doubt that, sir. I am the BEST at word-play and sword-play.'

The two men engaged in a vicious sword-fight for the next half hour. It was a veritable storm in the studio as the two lashed at each other, jumping in combat, evading a deadly strike from the other,

Day 9: Better than BB

jabbing, lunging, giving it their best, no one giving an inch to the other. Stuff soon started flying around in the studio and the lights started dimming, when the producer stepped in and requested them to stop.

The Prime Minister still looked the same as before; not a single hair out of place, while BB's face was sweaty and a lock of his hair had strayed onto his forehead. He shook hands with the Prime Minister and said, 'Good fight sir. You are quite amazing.'

He had more.

'Get a keg of beer,' the Prime Minister ordered and the producer sent one of his men scurrying to the pantry to find one.

The PM got the 100litre keg, smiled at it, looked at BB and said 'Bottoms up!' He then picked up the aluminium keg and drank straight from it, taking only two minutes to empty it out. He finished with a loud burp.

'Sir, you are amazing. You are incredible. You are even better than...' BB went silent for a minute, pondering over something, before speaking again.

'Sir, I want to confer on you the 'Better than BB' award today.' BB touched the PM's feet in respect and ran off into the darkness to emerge a minute later with a large trophy featuring a man holding a massive bull by its testicles above his head.

'You are the worthy owner of this trophy, sir,' BB cried for the first time in his life for finally finding a man who could match up to him.

The Prime Minister took the trophy and hugged BB. The two sat down on their seats and resumed their discussion.

'You know what, Buddhi. I have resolved to fix all the problems affecting our country. Suddenly I feel so empowered and strong.' He flexed his biceps to reveal arms that looked like Himalayan peaks. 'I promise that I will personally do whatever is required to make our country a superpower.'

'So what were you saying, Buddhi? Crony capitalism? Giani Seth, you said?'

DAY 10

ONE THOUSAND PUSH-UPS

RightToTroll@RightToTroll

The Prime Minister went to the Himalayas and got two LED lights fitted behind his head for a fake halo? Well played.

AdarshBharatiya@AdarshBharatiya

MY MOTHER IS NOT GUILTY. #SaveInnocentMadam

PatliiKamar@PatliiKamar

The Prime Minister's sword is so longgg!

MeeraKaamJoker@MeeraKaamJoker

@PatliiKamar #TWSS

FerozWriter@FerozWriterIIMA

From bending over to bending pens, the Prime Minister has come a long way.

TheOrchidParty@TheOrchidParty

The Great Leader's raj yagya will spread peace and harmony in the nation and restore our past stature in the world.

BowWowBreaking@BowWowBreaking

Breaking: BB confers 'Better Than BB' award on the Prime Minister

Adarsh spent the night tossing and turning in bed. Madam was still in jail, sleeping on a cold, hard floor in inhuman conditions. He had gone to meet her yesterday and she was a mess – depressed and frustrated. She had thankfully taken the lunch and change of clothes from him. 'This place is hell. Get me out of here,' she had said between sobs as she ate the homemade *paranthas*.

Adarsh had returned home with a heavy heart. His #SaveInnocentMadam campaign was gaining traction and he was beginning to get support from people. Even the Big Bee had retweeted him yesterday, as had the writer Feroz Daadiwala. He hoped that the judge would see reason during the bail hearing in two days. After hearing about the inefficiencies of the Indian judicial system, he had always wished that he never had to make the rounds of courts but here he was, his worst fears having come true. He felt helpless and lost. Dad had also been trying to round up his contacts but they had all said that no amount of influencing could help and everything was up to the judge during their hearing.

He had called his manager yesterday morning saying that he would be working from home for the day, at which he had given him a tongue-lashing, calling him careless and asking him to start showing a greater sense of ownership to his work. After that tiff, he had taken leave for a week. He couldn't afford any more headaches at this juncture and he just felt that he had to be home, doing everything he could to get Madam out of jail.

His sister cooked breakfast while the maid swept the floor and dad read the newspaper, sipping his tea.

The neighbour's security guard rang the bell just as Adarsh was in the midst of posting a tweet. 'Your car is blocking eight inches of our driveway and *sahab* is very upset. Please move it.' Adarsh nearly slapped him. This was the fourth time this month that they had sent the guard to squabble over parking.

Dad came over quickly before Adarsh could let out his frustration on the guard. 'Go tell your *sahab* to come and talk directly if he has any problems. *Chal* now, go.' The poor guy retreated hastily.

Adarsh turned on the TV and hesitatingly switched to Hyper News. They had been the most venomous of them all towards Madam, calling her all sorts of dirty names. At this moment, they were showing a clipping of the Prime Minister dragging away Panja from his fast, chicken leg in hand. The clip had been all over the news the day earlier, with headlines ranging from 'He Is Back', 'Remote-controlled No More', 'Halo 4', to IndiHAHA TV's 'Did Aliens Inject Deadly Virus into the Prime Minister?'

Suddenly a massive 'Breaking News' symbol covering the entire screen appeared, and the star anchor Jagriti was on. 'Dear viewers, we have just received an update from a verified source about the identity of the missing girl, Nafisa. This news is so shattering and devastating that we strongly advise viewer discretion. The weak-hearted may please change the channel to something more wholesome, like *Saas-Bahu* TV or cricket.

'I repeat. This breaking news update is going to change everything. Your lives will never be the same again. You will not be able to eat the food you are eating right now after this, because it will remind you of this historic day. This event will be discussed at office water-coolers for months to come. This date will be marked on calendars for generations to come. This is not a story suitable for heart or kidney patients, so please change the channel. This is momentous. This is historic. This is…'

'Minister of Mining Mohammad Panja is Nafisa's illegitimate father.'

Her co-anchor had been watching her for the last few minutes working up the tempo for the news announcement but could finally control it no longer and blurted out the news. Jagriti cupped her mouth in shock, slapped her colleague and walked off the set. 'You were just an intern and I brought you to the newsroom but clearly now you've grown too big for your boots. I QUIT!'

Adarsh couldn't believe his ears. The girl Madam had been accused of murdering was Panja's daughter? He was 81, old enough

Day 10: One Thousand Push-Ups

to drop dead any moment and yet he had fathered an illegitimate child? What was wrong with the leaders of the ruling party, sowing their seeds wherever they went? Just last month there had been news of Sharif Chand, the 100-year old former minister, who had tried to molest one of his nurses when she tried to give the bed-ridden man a sponge-bath. Then there was one more leader who had been charged with giving her husband 50 Viagra tablets for a very unusual form of death, only because she wanted to run away with her lover, another party leader. The Twitter world had been unanimous in calling for a very 'stiff' punishment for her.

This announcement could change a lot of things for Madam, though Adarsh was also worried that this issue would become even more politicized now and Madam might actually be in bigger trouble because of Panja's connections.

His phone buzzed. There was a tweet from @ChhotaRustam. 'Congrats @AdarshBhartiya, that girl turned out to be Panja's illegitimate daughter!'

*

Giani Seth noticed his daughter eating a bowlful of *gulab-jamuns* and remarked. 'So have you decided that you are going to stop losing weight? That's like my good rolly polly.'

'No dad, this is the new diet plan devised by the famous dietician Mickey Tikki. He generally only works with Hollywood stars. I am the only Bollywood actress he has agreed to train.'

He laughed loudly. 'This is dieting? Eating so many *gulab-jamuns*? You are going to get loose motions.'

She replied, in full sincerity, 'That's just the idea dad. You see? They say this helps reduce weight by five-six kilos in just two days.'

'*Kucch bhi.*' He didn't have time to get into an argument. He was expecting a call from the We Will We Will Rock You party head-office. Those two idiots must have gone back and talked to Badi Sarkar by now. She was the only one authorized to take a decision.

As if things weren't bad enough, last night that loud-mouth Buddhi had talked about him on his show. Giani Seth gritted his teeth. He had half a mind to buy his channel, then get him run over by a rickshaw and throw his lifeless body into some sewer drain.

He started pacing the living room, muttering abuses under his breath.

She noticed her dad upset over something and came by, a *gulab-jamun* in her hand. 'What's up dad? You look worried.'

'Oh this journalist Buddhi has been talking about me. Help me decide baby. Should I kill him by getting him run over, get him shot by Yusuf *chacha* from Dubai, plant a bomb under his car, or throw acid on him, douse him in kerosene and set him on fire?'

Babli stopped in her tracks, the *gulab-jamun* still in her mouth, her skin pale, gasping for breath. Giani Seth thumped her back for a few minutes, after which she asked him to stop.

'Baby what's the problem? Why did you get so upset?'

She hesitated, before blurting out, 'Dad, I am seeing a boy.'

She paused, before continuing. 'It is Buddhi. I want to get married to him. I love him.'

There was a loud clap of thunder, followed by a lightning strike. It didn't actually happen outside but Giani Seth did see the flash, hear the thunder deep inside him and felt his insides burning.

'WHAT!'?!

*

'Sir, there is a phone call for you,' his assistant walked up to the Prime Minister and handed him the cordless phone.

'How many times have I told you not to disturb me when I am exercising?' The Prime Minister's bare chest was glistening with sweat, and he was currently doing one-handed push-ups. His trainer was keeping count.

'94, 95, 96...'

'Sir, it is the American President,' the assistant said.

Without breaking his rhythm, the Prime Minister told his assistant. 'Tell him I am busy and that I will call him in an hour.'

'97, 98...'

The trainer egged him on. 'Come on, sir. We also have to do one thousand pull-ups after this.'

'*Haan, haan* don't worry. I am not going anywhere.' The entire floor was wet with sweat. The PM had completed five sets of a

Day 10: One Thousand Push-Ups

thousand crunches each, two hundred surya-namaskars, practiced kicking a ten-feet high clay pot, rained punches on a punching bag until it exploded, and was now working on his shoulders.

'Ajit,' he called out to the trainer. 'We need to focus more on the chest this week. Been stuck at 55 inches for a few days now. I have to get to 56 as soon as possible.'

'Sure, sir. Let's increase the bench-press weight to 2,000 kilos from tomorrow. I think we are not pushing your body enough. Even small boys can do 1,500 kilos these days,' he laughed.

The PM rang a bell for the housekeeping staff to come and wipe the floor dry as he took a break to drink two glasses of bull urine mixed with a pinch of ginger powder and 15 egg-whites.

Workout complete, he showered and changed into formal clothes. As he put on the shirt, there was a ripping sound and the shirt got torn into pieces. Ajit the trainer, looked at him and said, 'Sir, I think 56 inches *ho gaye.*'

The PM gave him a chest-bump and called out to his assistant to dial the American President's phone number. It had been five hours since his call.

'Hello, is this the President?

The voice on the other end was a bit sleepy. 'Who's this?'

The PM glanced at his watch. '*Yaar* it is 1PM. Why are you sleeping, you lazy ass?'

'Excuse me, it is 2:30 in the night. Who is this? Do you know who I am? Do you know who my father is?' He sounded annoyed.

'I know. I know. No need to get so hyper. This is the Indian Prime Minister.'

'Oh hi, Mr Prime Minister. I tried calling you earlier but you didn't have time for me.'

'Yes, I was busy working out. You can't just call a man at any time you feel like, dude.'

'Oh that's great. Listen I called you because I hear there's some...'

'No, you listen. I am very angry with you. What do you think of yourself? You will send your navy to attack India? Do you know how many countries India has ever attacked in its 10,000-year-old history? Zero.'

The PM was so furious that his entire house had started shaking. An earthquake was forming deep below the surface, just like the fire burning inside him.

He continued, 'Zero. Do you know which country gave the world this fantastic number? India. Do you know that 88 per cent of the engineers at NASA are Indians, or that 96 per cent of doctors in your country are Indians? Do you know that Steve Jobs got his inspiration to create Apple in India? Do you know that beer was invented in India? What do you know, Mr President? What do you know?'

He handed the phone to his assistant and flexed his biceps, as if for the phone to see. 'Mr President,' he resumed his diatribe, 'we will not take any nonsense lying down. We will fight for our nation. We will fight brick with brick, tit with tat, missile with missile, Superman with Shaktimaan, but we will not let you cause any harm to our nation.'

'Whoa, whoa, whoa – what is going on, Mr Prime Minister? Whose navy is attacking India? What are you talking about?'

The Prime Minister was taken aback. He hadn't even given the most deadly threat yet, the one to banish SitarBucks and McDammit from the country and his opponent was already cowering?

'Let me reassure you, Mr Prime Minister – America is deeply committed to India and we want to be allies. I had chicken *tikka* for dinner, for God's sake. I am even talking to you on hands-free, with my hands folded in a *namaste*. Trust me, our navy is not out to attack you. In fact, we just found another African nation where there was violence between two tribes of a few dozen people each. We are planning to go in and get them sorted out. You know – slam bam thank you ma'am. That sort of thing.

'You want to join in? We will share some oil with you, too.'

Was it all a hoax? The Prime Minister was very confused at this sudden turnaround. The news of America attacking India was what had prompted him to return from the Himalayas and here it was all turning out to be a lie.

In reality, it had started with a prank call from a radio channel RJ to a Bow Wow news anchor who had taken it for real and the story of the US navy out to attack India had just exploded from there.

Day 10: One Thousand Push-Ups

'I don't know, President ji. Let me message you on Whatsapp when I decide.'

'Sure. Talk to you later.'

'Ok *chal phir*, bye.' The Prime Minister hung up.

His assistant shook his hand. 'Sirjee, congratulations! You have just made history by averting a big disaster. Now nobody can stop you from getting this year's Nobel Peace prize.'

*

'Sir, I beg of you. Don't do this.' BB was lying in Giani Seth's feet, on the terrace of his 100 floor residence.

Giani Seth spat on the ground. 'What were you saying? Crony capitalism? Your parents taught you a lot of English, *hain*? Now please tell me what does it mean?'

'Nothing, sir. Nothing. Forgive me. I didn't know Babli is your daughter.'

'*Chalo*, no worry. I am planning on marrying her to Chaddha's son. Chaddha is a bastard but his son is good looking, went to foreign for his education, and is going to run their 12,000-crore empire.' He chuckled. 'It's just 12,000 crore, and they call it an empire. *Saale* middle high-class people just don't have any class at all.'

'Sir, I was also educated abroad. I am also told that I am good-looking. Besides, I love her. Even more importantly, she also loves me and wants to marry me.'

Giani Seth picked up one of the juicy apples lying in a fruit basket next to his chair and threw it at BB's head. It missed the target and fell off the roof onto the pavement 1,100 feet below, where a stampede broke out as people rushed to take pictures of the exclusive fruit.

'Oh, Babli? You don't worry about her. Have you seen her diets? One week it is *gobhi* diet, then next it is *aloo parantha* diet, then it is *gulab jamun* diet. You are also a diet for her. She will adjust in a few weeks.'

BB started crying so loudly that even the birds sitting on the nearby electric pole stopped chirping. 'Sir, don't.'

'I didn't hear that.'

'Sir, don't.'

'Say please?'

BB hesitated. He had never uttered the word in his entire life. 'Please' was one of two words that were not in his dictionary, the other being 'impossible.'

'Come on come on, please *bol*,' the father of the bride ordered.

'Please, sir. Please. Please. Please. I want to marry Babli. Please,' he sobbed, his face red, heartbeat raised, his suit all soiled from lying on the ground for the last one hour.

It had all happened so quickly. He was preparing for the night's telecast when his phone rang. Giani Seth had simply said, 'If you want to get married to Babli, then come to Giani House in five minutes. We will have dinner tonight.' BB had run the three kilometers from his studio to Giani Seth's residence in four minutes flat, only to be told that he would not be able to use the lift, but would have to climb the hundred flights of stairs to reach the terrace. He had reached the top floor panting but hadn't even been offered a glass of water yet, leave alone food.

'Ok so nice of you to ask politely.' Giani Seth said as he sipped on his tenth glass of scotch. 'But why should I let my daughter marry the man who talks on TV against me, calling me a thief and what not?'

BB looked at him with deep hatred in his eyes.

'Look at you. Why should I let you marry my daughter?'

BB said nothing.

'WHY SHOULD I LET MY DAUGHTER MARRY YOU? HOW MANY TIMES DO I NEED TO ASK?' He shouted.

'Sir…'

'Sir *ko goli maar*, just say that you will never show any news against me. Say that you will post an apology today saying that what you said yesterday was all bullshit.'

BB shook his head.

Giani Seth called his assistant. 'Ramesh, call up Chaddha. Let's fix the date today.'

Venkat started dialing the number, when BB shouted. 'Okay okay, don't do it. I will issue an apology but Babli is mine.'

Day 10: One Thousand Push-Ups

'That's like a good boy,' Giani Seth finally picked up BB and offered him a glass of water, which he gulped down with gratitude.

*

The Orchid party office was abuzz with activity. The Media Circus was ready to present a live-telecast of the Great Leader's latest initiative to clean up India, reduce pollution and corruption, improve the cricket team's performance and increase his chances of winning the elections.

'The Great Leader is a learned man who knows all of our ancient scriptures by heart. The *Raj Veda* is one such lost ancient book whose knowledge was never allowed to go out to the common man by the ruling party. Unfortunately for them, the Great Leader was handed a copy by a guru who saw him solve complex astronomical problems on the ground as a small child in his village, got impressed and gave him the *Raj Veda*,' Girpade told the assembled journalists.

'According to the book, he who performs a rigorous *raj yagya* that lasts for 24 hours without a second's interruption succeeds in anything he tries – be it cleansing the system, winning an election, or even instantaneously clearing 500 levels in Candy Crush,' he explained.

'The Great Leader has thus suggested to the government that he be allowed to perform such a *yagya* but they asked for clearance from the Environment Ministry where the file has been stuck for two weeks now. I am told the Minister of State has been sitting on the file because his seat cushion got eaten up by rats. But we can't wait any longer, so we are going ahead with the *yagya* and will start tomorrow morning sharp at 9AM,' he said as he shrugged his shoulders.

The Great Leader came to address the gathering of journalists. 'My dear friends, I don't know why the government is scared. We are doing this *yagya* just to solve India's problems, and surely the government also wants to do that, no?

'We have noble intentions behind this *yagya*. It will only benefit the country. The government should not try to block such an auspicious event. I hope the Ministry of Dirty Tricks will not collude with the Environment Ministry to spoil the environment here.'

He bowed to the assembled Media Circus, folded his hands to seek their blessing and headed back into the building. He had to take a special bath for the *yagya* – starting with rubbing turmeric all over his body and honey on his bald head, massaging his entire body with coconut oil, letting it stay for two hours, going for a five kilometer barefoot run, drinking a glass of cow's unboiled milk, standing under a *peepal* tree for exactly six minutes and 20 seconds, washing off his body with Mother Dairy double-toned milk, climbing the same *peepal* tree and picking the ten greenest leaves and finally taking a bath with the popular GetLaid bodywash.

What had not been told to the media was that this procedure would make the Great Leader invincible and nearly-immortal, immune from most causes of death. Stress would no longer affect his heart, smoking wouldn't damage his lungs and liquor would not touch his liver or kidneys. The only thing that could kill him would be a fall from a helicopter, as that wouldn't be covered by the *yagya*.

*

'Ladies and Gentlemen, there comes a time in our lives when nothing seems right; when you just feel like there is nothing inside you; when you feel like you are waiting at the train platform and the bloody train is never going to arrive; when the satellite dish alignment goes off just before the cricket match starts and you can't watch the World Cup final on TV anymore.'

'Tonight is one such night.' BB said as he looked into Camera #5, his eyes cold and distant.

'You are watching B for Buddhi, brought to you tonight by Scream, the energy drink that will leave you screaming for more. I am your host Buddhiman Buddhiraja. Tonight I have some terrible news to share.' He wiped his eyes on his sleeve.

'The Indian Prime Minister spent 17 years in the Himalayas, meditating and praying. When we had almost forgotten about him, he suddenly returned. He was a changed man – a glow on his face, unheard of powers in his body and mind, a warmth in his eyes, and a determination in his demeanor. He came as a whiff of fresh air and a promise to set right whatever ails our country. He talked to the

Day 10: One Thousand Push-Ups

American President and got his navy to back off from an attack on India that would have surely caused massive destruction. He caught the despicable Mohammad Panja cheating during his fast and embraced the opposition leader, a rare gesture that sent shockwaves across the political fraternity. He brought along hope, something that the common man had long given up.

'Ladies and Gentlemen, it breaks my heart to tell you all tonight that...' words failed him and he kept his head on the desk and burst into tears, crying like nobody had ever cried before. His wails were louder than the loudest jet engines and Adarsh had to turn down the volume of his TV to avoid waking up his dad, sleeping in the adjoining room. He tore at his hair. He beat up his desk and slammed his face into it repeatedly until he could do so no longer, out of pain.

BB cried and cried for the next five minutes before he turned to the camera resembling a picture of wretchedness, barely able to open his eyes, his hair all over his face, his shirt soaked in his own tears. He tried speaking but was at a loss for words, waving a helpless hand at the camera asking it to be cut off.

The telecast broke and Adarsh watched with his mouth open as an ad for the latest deodorant that promised to help software engineers find onsite job opportunities played on TV.

After a ten-minute long ad-break, BB was back on the screen. He looked a little more composed now though his eyes were swollen and his chin seemed to be bleeding, perhaps from slamming his face into the desk.

BB stared into the camera, took a deep breath and spoke.

'The Prime Minister is dead.'

Adarsh couldn't believe his ears as BB broke the news. There were no details provided. BB just stared into the camera for an hour as a sad *sitar* played in the background and then the telecast ended.

DAY 11

THE TALKING PARROT

AdarshBharatiya@AdarshBharatiya

The girl came to Madam's school and she told her that she can't be admitted in the middle of the session. #SaveInnocentMadam

Chhicchora@Chhicchora

After the Panja revelation, Principal Madam should be given a fair chance. *Daal mein kuch kaala hai.*

RightToTroll@RightToTroll

BB realized that the PM is better than him and got him killed because he wants a monopoly.

PatliiKamar@PatliiKamar

OMG, just heard the news of the Prime Minister and I can't breathe. #RIPPrimeMinister

FerozWriter@FerozWriterIIMA

How could Panja ji father an illegitimate child when he has been busy buying groceries for Badi Sarkar?

TheOrchidParty@TheOrchidParty

The Great Leader is saddened by the sudden death of the PM and demands an enquiry by the Bureau of Botched Investigations.

Swamy@Swamy1959

I have confirmed news that Chhote Sarkar wets his bed every night.

'Upload complete.'

Chhote Sarkar saw the prompt on his laptop screen and smiled, his eyes glinting. All the hard-work had borne fruit. It had helped that he had friends at the right places who had been able to help obtain call records for Panja, leading Chhote Sarkar to her identity and eventually, the location.

The trip to that village in Haryana had helped clear his mind. He had spent the time thinking and now knew what he had to do. He had had enough.

It had taken some coaxing, some diplomacy, and some downright con to get her to talk. And she had talked, sitting under the tree, surrounded by mustard fields, that muscular *jaat* boy sitting by her side.

'We want to get married,' she said, 'but he doesn't let me. Says you are too young. He is not your caste. He is not your religion. Go to school. Go to college. Blah blah.' She seemed rather resentful.

'Who is he?'

She had shook her head, a mischievous look on her face. 'I can't tell you, but I can tell you he is an important man. He can get you killed and hide you someplace no one can find you, if you cause me any trouble.'

He had sniffed and begun to sob silently into the sleeve of his *kurta*. 'Oh why would I cause you any trouble? I am myself troubled by the opposition party. One of their leaders took away my sister forcibly.' Acting had never been his strong point even though Badi Sarkar had got him into the drama club at college but he had been convincing with his crying act, because it earned him her sympathy.

'Oh, then maybe my dad can help you.'

'I doubt. These are very senior people.'

She had answered with a loud scornful laugh. 'Senior? Are they bigger than the powerful Minister for Mobile Phones?'

'Dr Panja?' He had pretended to be shocked. 'Dr Panja is your father?'

'Yes,' she had replied, and immediately realized that maybe she shouldn't have said that. 'Don't tell anyone please. He will get into a lot of trouble.'

'Don't worry. Why would I?'

He had watched her run off into the mustard fields, hand in hand with the *jaat* boy who had watched Chhote Sarkar suspiciously all along, like he was going to steal his girlfriend.

Chhote Sarkar copied the link to the video and sent it along to some of his friends.

*

Adarsh read the newspaper with great interest. There was surprisingly little coverage of the Baba Neemacharya rape case but that was understandable given his political connections. There was news of the rumor that Nafisa was Panja's daughter and speculation that he was going to get kicked out of the cabinet after his humiliation at the hands of the Prime Minister.

Talking of the Prime Minister, it was another fascinating story. There was no confirmed account from the government but the *Crimes of India* reporters were quoting unverified sources for their story. Apparently the Prime Minister had gone to meet Badi Sarkar at her home. Adarsh found it hard to believe the following part. As against popular belief, Badi Sarkar, Chhote Sarkar and the Great Liberator Statue outside their home were not the only three people provided with the special XXX level security. In reality, there was one more – a parrot who was Badi Sarkar's confidant. He reportedly sat outside her office and anybody who wanted to meet Badi Sarkar had to answer a secret question whose answer was known only to a handful, the Prime Minister not being one among them.

As per the report, the Prime Minister had gone to her office only to be stopped by the parrot who asked him the question, thus infuriating him and he had in turn wrung the parrot's neck, killing him instantly. As soon as the parrot's XXX guards noticed this, they opened fire on the Prime Minister and a violent gun-battle followed between them and his guards. The Prime Minister survived the battle, even taking several bullets that seemed to have no effect on him but by the end of it he got so full of rage that his body just exploded out of anger, killing all of the guards instantly. Luckily there wasn't much damage to Badi Sarkar's office.

Twitter had come alive since yesterday's expose that Panja was the missing girl Nafisa's father, though it had been denied by the party office which had expressed grief that a dead girl's name was being linked to a senior leader of the party.

'There is no proof linking Dr Panja to the girl,' the party representative had said during the panel discussion on Galaxy TV. Of course, that had not stopped people on Twitter from having fun at his expense and #PapaPanja jokes had continued through the day.

Adarsh had wondered if there was anything he could do for Madam but felt helpless. @ChhotaRustam had said that he could find out Panja's personal mobile number to start a missed-call campaign but Adarsh wasn't sure what the benefit would be.

His phone buzzed. Another message from @ChhotaRustam. 'Check this out,' it said, followed by a YouTube link.

Adarsh opened the link and his eyes nearly fell out. It was the girl whose image the news channels had been flashing for the last few days. She was running through a mustard field with a guy, happy with her life and singing bollywood songs.

Adarsh couldn't believe his ears. Nafisa was alive and admitting that Panja was her father on video. He punched the air, shouted out the news to his sister and ran to the park to get dad who was out on his morning walk.

Just 30 minutes later, #SaveTheMadam was trending across India, as was #FraudPanja. Adarsh felt reassured. Nothing could stop Madam from getting released now.

The Big Bee tweeted the link to a blog post he had written about his love and respect for brave teachers such as Madam. @PatliiKamar announced that she would post a picture of her wearing only three tiny neem leaves if Madam got released that day. An NGO was coordinating a candle-march at Jantar Mantar. Another group mentioned plans for a protest rally outside Badi Sarkar's residence the next morning.

Things suddenly seemed better. Adarsh wiped the happy tears from his eyes just as the neighbour's guard rang the bell. A leaf from the Ashoka tree in their compound had fallen inside the enemy territory, infuriating his *sahab*.

*

Badi Sarkar watched the TV, her face expressionless but the first finger of her left hand twitching, as if trying to press a button on the remote. This was her standard reaction every time she was stressed and it normally ended in someone getting serious punishment.

Chhote Sarkar walked into her room and noticed the headline. 'Nobody killed Nafisa.' The anchor was shaking her head in disappointment. 'Poor Madam is suffering in jail while the girl she was supposed to have murdered is having a good time in a village with her boyfriend. How low can this government fall?'

She switched the channel to another one and they too had the same news running.

'BREAKING: NAFISA IS ALIVE. WHERE IS PAPA PANJA?'

He glanced at the TV and then at his mother and said, 'This is terrible news. Never thought Panja ji would do this.'

She looked at him, stood up and patted his head, 'Sit down, my son.' Chhote Sarkar noticed the twitching of her finger increase. She held her left hand in the right one but the finger just didn't seem to stop.

'My son, I think it is time.' She said.

'No,' he exclaimed. 'No. No. No. We discussed this earlier.'

She sat him down and held his hands. 'I am very sad, Chhote. First the PM's unnecessary behaviour and that sad end and now Panja. I think it is time for you to become...'

'No, mom, don't say it,' he kept his hands on his ears.

She didn't stop. 'Listen to me, Chhote. I think it is time you became the Prime Minister.'

'No, mom. I will not become the Prime Minister. I am not ready. It is too early.'

Day 11: The Talking Parrot

'Chhote, behave yourself. We will announce this tomorrow. You will be the Prime Minister and lead the country to its destiny. You are the future. We are all here to help you. Don't worry.'

Chhote Sarkar ran out of the room and towards the kitchen. He returned a minute later, holding a loaf of the oatmeal bread specially imported for Badi Sarkar every day from Brooklyn in New York.

'I will eat the entire bread right now,' he threatened.

'NO Chhote! It will make your face blow up. It could even,' she gasped, 'kill you!'

'I WILL EAT THE BREAD!' He began to tear out a piece.

Her phone rang. She looked at the number, let out a long breath, told Chhote Sarkar to hold on, and answered.

'What? They are coming? Don't worry, I will do something.'

'I just told you, didn't I? I will call him up.'

'Stop shouting. I am in the middle of something.'

'Go to hell. Do whatever you can. Did I ask you to do what you did?' She hung up. The twitching in her finger had resumed.

'Okay Chhote, I am very disappointed, but if this is what you want, then so be it. I will call the Working Group to pick a Prime Minister.'

*

The girls watched in shock as Baba Neemacharya threw the expensive diamond-encrusted phone on the ground, howled loudly in anger, and sank into his bed, his body curled up and voluminous tears flowing.

'What does she think of herself? Tells me that she is in the middle of something? I did so much for her and her stupid son and she hung up on me? May the wily woman go to hell one day for her misdeeds.'

He turned to his girls and said, 'We have to take matters in our hands. Nobody will come to help us.

'Form groups of four and take your positions. You have to stop them with anything you can find. Throw stones, throw boiling oil, lie down in front of their tanks, use your bodies if you need but make sure they cannot get into the ashram and defile it with their dirty presence. Remember they are coming to take away your Baba, the Baba you love so much.'

He further added, 'I will give one crore rupees to each of you if you stop them today. Now go and make your lives meaningful.' The girls ran out the room. Padmini stayed back, staring at the Baba.

'You too, Padmini. Go and protect your Baba from the evil forces who seek to silence us.'

'I will go to the Garden of Eden for a little walk,' he told her, referring to the private lawn behind his chamber. It had a small lake with blooming lotuses, a helipad for VIP visitors and rows of pretty tulips imported from Europe.

'Oh, can you lend me your phone for ten minutes? I have to make a phone call.'

She handed him the phone and headed out, her hands on her hips and her mind split about what she should be doing. Baba took the phone and dialled a number.

The Commissioner of Police had watched a Pehelwan Singh movie about an honest police officer who takes on the cement mafia single-handedly and had been inspired to go after the high-profile rape-accused Baba. As if the movie wasn't enough motivation, he had also got a phone call from the Prime Minister while watching it. The PM had told him that he was sorry about wasting so many years being a remote control but he was going to work double-time to fix the nation and needed his support in doing so. The Prime Minister had given the Commissioner clear instructions to do the right thing and that he would back him if he wanted to go after high-profile criminals who had until now been protected by their political backers.

The Commissioner had heard the news of the Prime Minister's tragic death with tears in his eyes and resolved that he had to make his vision come true. In the morning, he had collected a force of 100 constables and a couple of inspectors and marched off to Baba Neemacharya's ashram. Unfortunately for him, the Baba had followers in his office who leaked the news to him in advance and now the Baba was planning his strategy.

Baba walked into the garden and waited. Soon enough there was the sound of a chopper approaching, on time, as promised.

Baba mumbled to himself as he gathered his dhoti and got onto the helicopter, 'The neem is the truth.'

*

'Let's start the meeting.' Badi Sarkar addressed the Working Group. Nobody had got eliminated today as Chhote Sarkar was not attending.

'The first agenda item for today', she looked at Panja, sitting in the first chair next to her, alert and vigilant, his back straight, no expression of any guilt or remorse on his face, 'is you, Dr Panja.

'What is wrong with you? We all know that you had that daughter but how did you let that video get recorded? Didn't you teach the stupid girl anything at all? What is she, a dumb goat? How could she confess to a stranger with a camera that you are her biological father?'

'I am sorry, Badi Sarkar,' he said, his face bowed.

'Sorry is not enough, Dr Panja. You will get punished for this.' Her face was cold and her fiery eyes were threatening to melt the thick line of eyeliner accentuating them. 'As punishment for bringing such disgrace to the party, I want you to say ten good things about any opposition party leader, or be prepared to face the interrogation panel of Rowdies.'

Everybody gasped. This was the worst punishment she had given anyone in the 50 years she had been running the party. The last time someone got a punishment that could even be compared to this one was 20 years ago when she had asked a leader to eat ten live snakes because he had sneaked out of a meeting on the pretext that he was unwell, and had instead gone to watch a cricket match. The poor guy had died of hundreds of snake-bites on his face.

Panja winced. Choosing one of the punishments was like choosing between eating poison and starving to death. On the one hand, if he said anything positive about the Orchid party, rays of anger would erupt from her forehead instantly reducing him to ashes, while on the other hand, facing the Rowdies interview panel was a harrowing experience that had left millions of youngsters with scarred brains and a lifetime of counselling, thanks to the intense questioning that made them question the very purpose of their lives.

He got up from his chair and fell at her feet. 'I am sorry Badi Sarkar. Please don't make me do this.'

The others in the room nodded and a few feeble voices asked Badi Sarkar to show some mercy.

'Okay, then go to the ground outside and complete seven rounds in ten minutes, return and give me 40 push-ups.'

Panja got up delighted, changed into his Reebok dry-fit shirt and shorts, left his walking stick in a corner of the room, did a light stretch-up and ran outside, chanting verses from the Bible and Quran for inspiration.

'I am going to expel him from the party when he gets back. We cannot forgive him for bringing so much shame on our party,' Badi Sarkar announced to a stunned room. Bhakt and Chamcha shared glances and smiled. One of them could become the Minister of Mining now, or at least be assigned the responsibility of doing Badi Sarkar's grocery shopping, the additional portfolio currently held by Panja.

'Okay, this brings us to the more important agenda for today. We need a new PM.'

There was pandemonium in the room as soon as she said this, as all the *netas* raised their hands and started enlisting their reasons for why they should be appointed to the post. Scuffles broke out, faces were slapped, a couple of wigs were pulled off, and it was a scene out of WWE's Royal Rumble for the next 20 minutes, before Badi Sarkar took out her whistle and blew it, calling for order.

Everybody stopped and looked at Badi Sarkar. Bhakt Lal let go of Chamcha Das' *kurta* collar.

The one person who had sat through all of this silently stared at all the distinguished leaders around him, with their bloodied lips, ruffled hair and ripped *kurtas*, a few holding their *chappals* in their hands, ready to strike their opponent in the pursuit of that elusive seat of power.

'Is this a Working Group or the Parliament?' She shouted at the unruly politicians.

'Chotu, you are a Working Group member now. Don't you want to become the Prime Minister?' She asked the bewildered autorickshaw driver.

Day 11: The Talking Parrot

Chotu looked surprised. 'M...m...me?' He stammered. 'I have no idea what a Prime Minister is supposed to do. I studied only till 8th standard. *Nahi baba*, I don't know anything about the Parliament or Constitution, or running the country. The only thing I know is how to drive based on instructions given by the person sitting in the backseat.'

As Madam listened to him, her smile kept getting wider. 'This is perfect.' She walked up to him and kept a hand on his shoulder. 'Chotu, you are just what the doctor ordered for the party. You are our savior. You are THE one.'

'Now let's finalize this with a quick test. Okay?'

He looked at her curiously.

'Don't worry, we will just ask a few questions and then perform a remote-control adaptability test.'

'Okay,' he looked baffled.

'Members of the Working Group, fire away,' she beckoned. 'I throw open the interview of the next Prime Minister of our country.'

Chamcha went first. 'If Badi Sarkar asks you to get vegetables for her, what will you do?'

'I will get them,' he said.

Chamcha shouted. 'Wrong answer. We all have our portfolios. You step on mine and I will kill you.'

Bhakt went next. 'If a minister sends you a file to sign, what will you do?'

He said, 'I will read it and sign.'

'Wrong again. You never read. You are the Prime Minister, for God's sake. No need to act smart.'

Another leader asked, 'If a reporter makes some serious allegation against Badi Sarkar, what will you do?'

'I will ask for time, come back and check the facts.'

The leader's face went red and he screamed, 'WHAT? You will not slap the person and say that you will never tolerate anything against Badi Sarkar?' He turned to Badi Sarkar and said, 'This guy is a disaster.'

Meanwhile, Badi Sarkar hadn't stopped smiling. 'I think he is perfect,' she said. 'We just need to put him on a crash course and he will be ready.'

She took out her remote control and pressed a few buttons, looking in Chotu's direction. He seemed to get startled every time she pressed a button.

'Excellent. This boy is even compatible with the remote-control. He is going to be the Prime Minister.'

She rubbed her hands in glee. Her pretty face was lit up. The last time the Working Group had seen her this excited was the day they had finalized the location of Chhote Sarkar's first rally.

She pointed a finger at Chamcha and assigned him the important task. 'Set up a press conference for tomorrow. We will announce that Chotu will be the next Indian Prime Minister.'

Panja came running into the room, drenched in sweat, panting for breath, wheezing loudly from the exertion. He stopped in front of Badi Sarkar's chair and said, 'I did it, Badi Sarkar.' He then kept a hand on his chest and collapsed. 'I think I am having a heart attack. Somebody please get me to a hospital.'

Everybody laughed. Bhakt Lal said, '*Kya kar rahe ho,* Panja ji. This trick is for the media. We all know what this means.'

Badi Sarkar also giggled. 'Get up Panja ji. You are fired.'

*

Giani Seth was all fired up. Two days had elapsed since Chamcha Das and Bhakt Lal visited him and he still hadn't heard back from Badi Sarkar about the two cities he had asked for. As if this wasn't stressful enough, Babli hadn't eaten anything for a day saying that she was dieting, though Giani Seth was sure it was her way of trying to blackmail him into agreeing to her marriage with BB.

'Enough is enough,' he mumbled to himself sitting in his massive office, taking sips from the bottle. 'If they don't understand with smaller lessons, I will teach them a big one.' All attempts to make Badi Sarkar talk had failed so far but there was one more idea he could try. 'Madrasi, come in.' He picked up the intercom and called Venkat.

He was standing in front of him ten seconds later.

'Yes, sir?'

'Do you know Kalak Nath?'

Day 11: The Talking Parrot

'Sorry sir, no sir.'

'You are an idiot. Kalak Nath is the CEO of Giani Coal Mines. Got it? Who is Kalak Nath?'

'Sir, he is the CEO of Giani Coal Mines, sir.'

'Good. Call him up and tell him to send out a press release saying that looking at how hard life has become for the poor people in our country, we have decided to make some changes. We are going to start distributing coal for free to poor people from today and because of this we will be unable to supply any for the Badi Sarkar Power Corporation plants.

'Now get out.'

He took out his mobile phone and made another call.

BB was still in bed when his phone rang. His eyes were swollen, his face was pale and his hair was a tangled, unkempt mass. The news of the Prime Minister's sudden death had left him shaken. The Prime Minister had filled him up with hope; hope that things would be alright; that India would become a force to reckon with; that corruption would be a thing of the past; that nobody would go to bed on a hungry stomach ever again. Alas, that vision was too good to be true. BB was shattered by the news of the PM's death. He had barely slept all night, tossing and turning remembering that encounter with the Prime Minister in his studio, marveling at his sword-fighting skills, the delight on his face as he drank from the beer keg, the blinding light of his halo and just the incredible energy he exuded.

He answered the phone.

'This is your future father-in-law,' Giani Seth said, followed by the loud sound of a mouthful of *pan-masala* remnants being spitted out, before he came back on the line. 'How are you, dear BB?'

'Good morning, Giani Seth.'

'I thought you were going to apologize for insulting me on your show? What happened to that? Do you want to marry Babli or not?'

'I am sorry, sir. I can do anything for you but I don't think I can go on the show and say that it was false.'

'Oh,' Giani Seth answered, and shouted out to his assistant. '*Arre* Shankar, call up Chaddha. Let's fix Babli's wedding date and be done with it.'

An already shattered BB broke into tears and pleaded with him. 'Sir, please listen to me. I really want to marry Babli and would be willing to do anything for you, but I can't compromise on my duties as a journalist. If I hadn't been a journalist, it would have been a different thing.'

'*Accha*, what did you say? If you had not been a journalist...' Giani Seth repeated, thinking something. 'Okay then, you carry on. I will talk to you later.'

'Sir, sir, one second...please don't.'

'I have a call coming in. Bye.' Giani Seth hung up, stared curiously at the unknown number flashing on his screen and answered.

'Who the hell wants to commit suicide by calling up Giani Seth on his private line?'

'Giani, it is me,' it was a frantic but muffled sound.

'*Kaun hai be?* What do you want?'

'Giani Seth, this is Baba Neemacharya. Have you now forgotten my voice?'

'Oh Baba ji,' he folded his hands in *namaste* over the phone and laughed. 'What's up? Why is your voice so funny?'

'Giani Seth, the Commissioner is coming to arrest me with an army. I don't know what to do,' he started sobbing.

'Oh,' Giani Seth said rubbing his chin. 'This is very serious. What are you planning now?'

'Giani Seth, remember I have done a lot for you. Don't forget the times I have come to your help. Let me not remind you how you acquired Madari group and became an overnight billionaire by giving a *supari* for the poor old man to Yusuf bhai from Dubai. Or the time you kidnapped that Sardarji's daughter and kept her hostage till he agreed to sell Ghar Ghar Builders for half the market price. If I go down, I will take you with me, Giani.' Neemacharya's voice was still muffled as if he was inside a closet but the threat in it was loud and clear.

Giani Seth smiled. '*Arre yaar* Neemacharya, why getting so senti? I was just kidding. I will send a helicopter to fetch you and send some *prasad* to the Commissioner to cool him off. He is also our own guy. Don't worry.' Neemacharya had already got his two per cent

Day 11: The Talking Parrot

cut for the Gian Port project, so Giani Seth couldn't let the investment sink now.

*

The Great Leader sat on the small stool, wearing a white *dhoti*, bare chested, pouring *ghee* into the fire, his back straight and his ears alert, diligently following the instructions of the head priest performing the *yagya*, his calm face belying the anxiety within.

They were four hours into the *yagya*. The brutal pre-work and the preparations had left him fatigued already but there was also the mental stress of ensuring that the event went off smoothly, because nothing could stop him if he succeeded.

The Ministry of Dirty Tricks was expected to create trouble and the Great Leader had taken due precautions. More than 5,000 volunteers including 300 from the elite commando corps had been flown in from all over the country to ward off trouble. There was a ring-based security set up, with ten tiers of defense around the party office and the Great Leader. Not even a fly would be able to get in, Girpade had promised.

'Sir, please don't stop. Keep pouring *ghee* into the fire otherwise the gods will feel offended,' the priest chided the Great Leader for losing concentration, as he swatted a mosquito sitting on his nose.

Girpade had showed up in full battle-armour borrowed from the National Museum in the morning. The Great Leader had smiled at his trusted lieutenant and blessed him with victory.

'We will die but we will not let this *yagya* fail, Great Leader,' he had said dramatically, brandishing his Blackberry phone above his head like a sword.

They had started on time but the enemy had soon approached, in the form of a police jeep en route to the venue to stop the 'illegal' activity, which had been taken care of by the brave men in the first tier who had stopped the jeep and removed all of its tyres, as well as the constables' clothes because they had dared to try and stop the Great Leader.

A second wave had been sent shortly after, this time comprising a convoy of five reinforced Mahindra Scorpios. This group too had been smartly broken up and each car 'managed' by a group of brave volunteers.

Girpade had marshalled the troops well, even anticipating an attack from the sparsely guarded woods right behind the party office. The monkey traps hidden amidst the fallen leaves had come in handy, and there were about two dozen ruling party volunteers hanging from the trees by their feet, their faces getting increasingly bloated as the blood rushed to their heads.

He got a message on his phone. It was from Girpade. 'Big army headed our way, sir, but we will not let them through. Don't worry.'

Soon enough he started hearing distant sounds of the clanging of iron rods, bats slamming into each other, the cycle-mounted cavalry charging into the approaching enemy formations, and the slogans being chanted from each side. 'Great Leader *zindabad*', one wave would pierce the silent skies, followed by 'Badi Sarkar, Chhote Sarkar. Great Leader *ki hogi haar*.'

It was a fierce battle. Both sides put up a brave fight but the enemy had the numbers. Out of the corner of his eyes, the Great Leader noticed Bhakt Lal and his followers, all wearing heavy leather jackets and helmets, run into the compound. They were protecting a group of men holding fire-extinguishers hidden inside their formation.

'Badi Sarkar *ki jai*. Chhote Sarkar is the greatest.' They shouted as the Great Leader slapped his forehead in dismay.

'Bhakt Lal, you will go to hell for this.' An enraged Great Leader shouted at his tormentor, as the fire-extinguishers got deployed. The fire was gone. The *yagya* had failed.

'No, I will get into the cabinet for this,' a delighted Bhakt Lal broke into the chicken dance, just as Girpade came running to the Great Leader and fell at his feet.

'I failed, Great Leader. Allow me to burn myself right here at your feet to repent.' His armor was gone and his clothes were torn in places.

'Not yet, dear Girpade. We just lost a battle. There is still the war to be won.'

He glared at Bhakt Lal, picked up Girpade in his arms and

Day 11: The Talking Parrot

stumbled into the building, Girpade holding on to the Great Leader's massive shoulders. He had fallen from his cycle as he led his troops into battle.

*

BB parked his SUV in the basement and ran up the five flights of stairs, two steps at a time, like he did every day. The guard on his floor gave him a weird look that surprised BB but he didn't have time to stop for small talk. He probably had a fight with his wife, the story of all married men, he thought to himself.

He reached his cabin, changed into a suit, threw a few jabs at the punching bag to get the adrenalin pumping, watched five minutes of *Tiger Bahu* – the show that never failed to get his heart-rate spiked, and then headed to the studio.

As he approached the recording area, the ground nearly gave way under him and he felt dizzy. He quickly grabbed onto a spot-boy in time before he crashed onto the ground. Today's panel discussion had already started. Without him!

'The ruling party expelled veteran minister Dr Mohammad Panja, who has been in the news of late for all the wrong reasons, starting with cheating during his fast and getting busted by the former Prime Minister and then the scandal involving his illegitimate daughter Nafisa, for whose murder Principal Ambika Pandey was wrongly implicated, causing massive outrage on Twitter all day today. The party announced that Dr Panja had betrayed the party's trust by being involved in nefarious activities and that he had brought shame to the party.

'In a more serious accusation, the party also announced that the Prime Minister was felled by a bullet fired on Dr Panja's command, because of professional rivalry. BBI, the Bureau of Botched Investigations is expected to file a criminal charge-sheet against him shortly.

'Unfortunately, Dr Panja suffered a minor heart attack at the party Working Group meeting and one of the party colleagues rushed him in his autorickshaw to the hospital, where he is currently recovering.'

'Good evening, ladies and gentlemen, you are watching J for…'

'Jagriti!' he gasped.

His producer came running up to him, followed by two burly bouncers in tight T-shirts accentuating their big biceps and man-breasts.

'Sorry BB, I couldn't tell you in the hustle-bustle today. The channel's new owner wanted Jagriti to be the anchor.'

'New owner?'

'Oh yes, Giani Industries acquired our channel this afternoon, giving a cash-down payment of 2,000 crores. They wanted Jagriti to start right away. I am sorry, BB.'

The two bouncers escorted BB to the basement parking. His phone rang just as he was getting out onto the exit ramp.

'My dear son-in-law, you said that being a journalist is becoming a problem, so I solved it for you. Jagriti also mentioned that she was looking for a job.'

BB clenched his fists.

'*Arre jamai ji*, don't get angry. I have something better for you. Do you want to stop by for dinner?'

Giani Seth smiled at Baba Neemacharya sitting in front of him, nibbling at a chocolate bar, and dialled another number on his phone.

'Great Leader, how are you?'

'Yes, I saw what they did to your *raj yagya*. *Bahut bura hua*. Very bad.'

'Do you want to come over for dinner tonight? I have an idea.'

DAY 12

WHO WILL RING THE BELL?

AdarshBharatiya@AdarshBharatiya

The girl is alive. My mother is innocent. Please RT. #SaveInnocentMadam

PatliiKamar@PatliiKamar

Going on a candle-march tonight in support of Madam.

FerozWriter@FerozWriterIIMA

BB fired from Bow Wow? Congrats to @JagritiRules. You are filling big shoes.

RightToTroll@RightToTroll

Roses are red, violets are blue. If you are Principal Madam the government will screw you.

TheOrchidParty@TheOrchidParty

The Great Leader is deeply disturbed by the ruling party supporters disrupting his raj yagya.

BowWowBreaking@BowWowBreaking

Who will be the new Prime Minister? Tonight at 10.

Swamy@Swamy1959

I have confirmed news that Badi Sarkar secretly got married to Neemacharya five years ago.

'My friends from the Media Circus, we are very disappointed with recent developments in our country. The good Baba Neemacharya has been accused of a most terrible crime. The Great Leader's initiative to seek God's blessings for our nation's development was ruthlessly crushed by the government. I have personally been accused of being a selfish person who only thinks of his own benefit. Detractors have even said that I run the government.

'What nonsense is this?' Giani Seth said, his voice raised. 'We will not take this lying down. We will protest.'

The assembled Media Circus watched, took notes and beamed live images of the press conference being held on the lawns outside Giani Seth's house. They had been sent a notification late last night and were told to assemble by dawn.

The Great Leader stood up and took over from Giani Seth.

'Dear friends, we will march up to Badi Sarkar's house today to register our protest against the government's high-handedness. We demand that if we succeed in ringing the bell of Badi Sarkar's house, then the government should bow to our demands.'

Baba Neemacharya patted his beard. It had started itching now that he hadn't shampooed it for the last three days. The Great Leader was speaking well despite the fact that deep inside, he was heart-broken after his failed *raj-yagya*.

Some of the senior journalists rolled their eyes as they watched the proceedings. The irony was hard to miss. The Great Leader was throwing an open challenge to the government backed by an industrialist who was long known to be the single-biggest contributor to the ruling party's funds, and Baba who was reputed to be close to Badi Sarkar.

The Great Leader was still smarting from the previous day's embarrassment. His party had spared no effort but the ruling party had still managed to disrupt his *yagya*. Giani Seth was upset because the board had sent him another letter last night reminding him that he had a few more days before they took a vote on whether he should be allowed to stay on as the group chairman. Baba Neemacharya had not forgotten her tone when she told him to go to hell, at a time when he most needed her. For years he had listened to her endless droning about that imbecile son but the one time when he needed her help, she had conveniently shrugged her shoulders. She was going to pay for this betrayal, he pledged to himself.

'We will start our march at 8AM. The ruling party has an hour to make preparations,' the Great Leader announced.

The announcement done, Giani Seth beckoned the journalists to the breakfast spread specially laid out for them. It had the choicest meat options, eggs being cooked to order in 50 different styles, North-Indian, South-Indian, Chinese, Italian, French and the latest fad, Sudanese cuisine. The longest line was at the fruit corner, where journalists were seen stuffing apple pieces into their pockets.

An hour later, the protesting leaders were ready to go. The Great Leader, Giani Seth, Neemacharya, Girpade and Venkat got into a huddle and the Great Leader asked all of them to keep calm and give it their best.

'They will throw numerous challenges at us. They will try to stop us at every step but we must persist. That bell has to be rung. We have to win today, or the nation will be finished.'

They broke the huddle with a loud cheer. The distance to Badi Sarkar's home was six kilometers and they would cover it on foot. Girpade had deployed his volunteers along the route. The ruling party had also been working on their 'arrangements', having taken up the challenge.

The Great Leader smashed a coconut outside the gate of Giani Seth's home for good luck before beginning their march. Behind them the Media Circus mounted their vans, scooters, or in some cases bicycles, checked their cameras and audio equipment and they were ready to go.

As soon as the group headed outside the gate, they encountered their first obstacle. They took the first steps of the march and a herd of howling stray dogs came charging at them.

Day 12: Who Will Ring the Bell?

Giani Seth looked at the six dogs that were barking loudly with froth coming out of their mouths, and he remarked. 'They are not from the neighborhood!'

Then it struck them.

'The ruling party!' They shouted and started running, panting and huffing. The just-consumed heavy breakfast wasn't helping. Baba Neemacharya was the most troubled, weighed down by the five *aloo-paranthas* he had consumed. To make matters worse, he kept tripping over his dhoti.

They ran for nearly a kilometer before Girpade realized that it was time to resort to the least-preferred recourse of the Great Leader. Violence. He took off the bow from his back and shot six perfectly aimed arrows, each one killing one rabid dog. The Great Leader looked at the dogs, then at Girpade, and gave him a high-five.

'I wonder what the next obstacle would be,' Girpade remarked.

They reached the next traffic intersection when they were surrounded by hundreds of beggars who wouldn't let go of them.

'I'll handle it,' Giani Seth said. He then took out bundles of hundred dollar notes from his pocket and threw them in the wind, in the opposite direction of their destination.

As the notes flew in the air, all the beggars sprinted behind them. Even the apparently disabled ones picked up their crutches and dashed on perfectly healthy legs. One of the beggars approached Giani Seth. 'Good thinking, Seth. We would have never gone for rupees, only dollars. You can rightfully proceed to the next hurdle.'

From there, the group had a relaxed run for the next 30 seconds when they noticed the Commissioner standing by the roadside, leaning by the side of his official car, one foot rested on the rear wheel. He gave a quick salute to Giani Seth and made the gesture of a gun being shot at Neemacharya, who immediately recoiled, terrified.

The Commissioner meant no harm. His Swiss account had been bolstered by a hefty amount the previous night, after Giani Seth reminded him that the Prime Minister was dead and he should bury that vision with him and enjoy the money. In turn, he had promised to Giani Seth that he would not arrest Neemacharya for the rape case and would get the girl declared mentally unstable. For the day's run, he had declined any active help but promised that he would let them cover the first half of the distance unhindered, before the ruling party took matters in their hands.

Soon they were at the halfway mark, a quiet street lined by trees and a few cars parked on the sides. Surprised that the ruling party was putting up no resistance, they were happily jogging when something hit Giani Seth in the stomach and his *kurta* turned red.

'He has been shot. Giani Seth is DYING.' Jagriti screamed into the camera from her perch atop the Bow Wow van.

The ticker on Bow Wow changed to, 'BREAKING: THE END IS NEAR FOR GIANI SETH. R.I.P. GIANI SETH.'

To everybody's surprise, Giani Seth got up and ripped off his *kurta*. He had been shot at but it was not blood that stained his *kurta*; it was a water balloon. Soon a massive attack was underway with Giani Seth and his buddies being pelted from all corners with water balloons of various shapes and sizes.

Suddenly, someone came running past all the vans screaming like a jet engine and reached his battered team. He quickly handed out helmets and Springbok shoes with the latest super-smooth Glidemax Water-Cooler Jet-pack technology.

'Put these on,' he said, and the group hurriedly wore the shoes and helmets.

'Now run. Run. Run. RUN!' He shouted.

'Thanks BB.'

BB had come to the rescue. Giani Seth had wanted to keep him as a trump card for the last minute, but the young journalist had been unable to see his side under such duress and had been forced to step in.

They quickly outran the water-balloon execution squad. Girpade glanced at the Great Leader and exclaimed.

'It's a sign, Great Leader!'

He looked down at his clothes and gasped. His clothes were colored like the Indian national flag from the damage inflicted by the water balloons. The entire Media Circus applauded at the divine message that was clearly indicating God's choice for who should lead the country.

Day 12: Who Will Ring the Bell?

'Let's go, friends!' the Great Leader plodded on.

They started running but soon came across a massive crowd on the road. There were jostling men and women all over the road, all of them frantically heading in their direction, unmindful of the presence of the important people they were about to trample. The men quickly hurried onto a pavement just in the nick of time. One of the journalists who got on the road for a close-up picture wasn't so lucky and got crushed by the stampede.

'They announced a Zaara sale! The sneaky bastards,' Girpade remarked.

They were held up at the stretch for a good 40 minutes before the road cleared up a little and they were able to proceed.

The Great Leader spotted Bhakt Lal and his army standing in the distance. They were holding cricket bats and hockey sticks.

'Looks like Bhakt is shooting for the sports ministry now,' Giani Seth said over the loud wheezing sound that he was producing. The last time he had run was five years ago and today he had already done about four kilometers. On days when his wife insisted that he exercise on the treadmill, he would make Venkat run for five miles and send her a picture of the treadmill report. The only thing that Giani Seth considered worth running after, was money.

'Great Leader, I cannot do this anymore. This is killing me,' he said.

The Great Leader and BB turned back to look with dismay at Giani Seth, now sprawled on the ground. The two were running ahead of the others, both looking fresh like they had just taken a shower using the GetLaid bodywash.

Meanwhile Baba Neemacharya also looked as tired as Seth. Girpade had been limping all along, thanks to the battle he had bravely fought yesterday. The two sat down next to Giani Seth.

The ticker on Bow Wow news changed to 'Have They Given Up Already?' Jagriti was egging the group on. The Great Leader was still due to give his first major interview to her. Giani Seth had handed her the prestigious Bow Wow channel on a platter when she was wringing her hands in frustration after walking out of Hyper News on a whim. She had to support him in this hour of need.

Bhakt's army advanced upon the protesting group, their bats and hockey sticks at the ready. The Great Leader and BB took positions, bracing themselves for a bloody fight. Suddenly a scooter approached out of nowhere. On it was a young man wearing a brown monkey cap so they couldn't see his face.

'Get on,' he said.

'All of us?' the Great Leader exclaimed.

'Well, that or get beaten black and blue by Bhakt Lal.'

Bhakt had started running towards them now, his bald forehead appearing bigger as each second passed and he came closer.

The Great Leader and Giani Seth climbed onto the backseat of the scooter and Girpade stood in the empty section in front of the driver, crouching on his knees so that he would not block his vision. Giani Seth asked Venkat to stand on the side foot-rest and held on to him from his waist.

'You are already housefull. You go. I'll manage,' BB said. The scooter was struggling to contain all the heavyweights perched on it.

'What should we call you?' Girpade asked the scooter driver.

'Umm, just call me Chhota Rustam.'

'Why do I think I have heard your voice earlier?'

Bhakt Lal was almost upon them. The scooter took off and the young rider deftly manoeuvered it into a narrow side-lane that led to another side-lane hidden from the main road.

Five minutes later, they were outside Badi Sarkar's door. The scooterist had taken them through an intricate network of hitherto unknown roads that had bypassed all of the defenses employed by Badi Sarkar's men.

BB was already standing there, his face slightly flushed.

'How did you…' Giani Seth asked him as the passengers on the scooter got off and stretched to get their bones back in place.

'Don't worry, sir,' he pointed to the doorbell awaiting them.

Baba Neemacharya grabbed the Great Leader's shoulders and blessed him. 'Go forth, Great Leader and meet your destiny. Go and ask the woman inside to stop her corrupt ways; tell her to protect the weak and the poor; make her understand that the *dharma* of a

Day 12: Who Will Ring the Bell?

ruler is to be firm but gentle, democratic yet decisive and just but judicious. Go forth, o great man, and show others the path they should follow.'

The Great Leader pressed the bell.

He was surprised to find that Badi Sarkar herself answered the door.

'Come in, Great Leader. I was expecting you.' She spoke in a seductive voice. She was wearing a delicate floral sari carefully draped around her slender frame.

He entered the room. The others tried to follow him inside but she gestured to them to stop.

Bhakt Lal's men reached the building just as the Great Leader entered inside. A disappointed Bhakt looked at the skies and screamed so loudly that the waiting men had to cover their ears, lest their eardrums burst. He immediately doused his body in petrol and set himself on fire, wailing about letting Badi Sarkar down.

*

'Dear people of the Media Circus, we have called you for this press conference today to share some very important news.'

Badi Sarkar peered over her glasses at the Great Leader sitting next to her on the dais, with Giani Seth occupying the adjacent seat. The last few hours had been hectic and despite her decades of experience of running the party, she had been stressed. However, she was happy with the outcome now.

Adarsh sat glued in front of the television.

'Mom, come on. Badi Sarkar and Great Leader sitting on the same dais! Never thought we would see such a day.'

Madam came into the living room holding a cup of tea. She had appeared before the judge for her bail hearing in the morning. The judge asked them if they had any defense and before they could respond, he was quick to mention that he had seen the video that was being aired on news channels, suggesting that Nafisa was alive.

'But,' he asked them, 'the court of law does not work on the basis of YouTube videos. How do I know that it was a genuine video shot by a real person?'

At that instant, two people had walked into the courtroom. The first was Chhote Sarkar, followed by the *jaat* boy in the video. Everybody had gasped when they saw Chhote Sarkar. He had walked up to the judge and asked for permission to speak.

'Of course, Chhote Sarkar. What a pleasant surprise? What brings you here?'

'Your honour, I was the person who shot the video.'

The testimony of the boy had proven enough. Nafisa had dumped him and moved to some secret location after the scandal broke. The heartbroken boy had called up Chhote Sarkar, who had handed him his number on a piece of paper before leaving the village.

The aging judge had looked benevolently at Madam before ordering that the case against her be dismissed and she be released immediately. Adarsh had shaken Chhote Sarkar's hands and invited him to tea but he had just put on a brown monkey cap and dashed out the door saying, 'I have some important work to do.'

Badi Sarkar addressed the Media Circus. 'My dear friends, I am pleased to announce that we have found a replacement for the post of Prime Minister.'

She then looked at the Great Leader with a fond smile. He stood up and folded his hands.

'Everybody, please meet the new Prime Minister,' Badi Sarkar spoke, carefully emphasizing each word, leading to pandemonium among the assembled journalists.

Badi Sarkar spoke into the mike. 'Relax everyone, we will answer all questions but please maintain calm. The Great Leader is going to join our party and will be appointed as the Prime Minister, following the recent unfortunate death of our honorable Prime Minister.'

Adarsh was stunned. After all the hateful things said by both parties about each other, the leader of the opposition party was to become the Prime Minister?

The Great Leader spoke.

'My dear friends, after speaking to Badi Sarkar earlier today we realized that there are a lot of possible synergies that we can build upon to lead our nation to greatness. This is a chance for us to make a difference. This is the chance to reduce poverty. This is the chance

Day 12: Who Will Ring the Bell?

to improve the standard of living in the nation so that everyone can enjoy the delicious taste of SitarBucks and McDammit. We have fought many vicious battles between the parties but we want to stop that now and focus on building the nation.'

'But Badi Sarkar, what about Chhote Sarkar?' Jagriti shouted from the front row where the media were seated.

Badi Sarkar grinned. It had been a long and hard bargaining session with both sides looking to maximize their benefits. The Great Leader had offered to join the party to save her the humiliation of losing the next elections to him, in exchange of his becoming the Prime Minister immediately. She would be called the honorary queen of India, though the Prime Minister would no longer respond to her remote control that was soon to be taken and sunk in a deep part of the Bay of Bengal.

Chhote Sarkar had been a problem. If only he had agreed to be the Prime Minister, she wouldn't have had to entertain the Great Leader. However, he was insisting on going to France to study art, still holding on to that loaf of bread with which to blackmail Badi Sarkar. She had given up on convincing him, so she had requested the Great Leader to provide an honourable exit for her son.

The Great Leader answered the question. 'Chhote Sarkar has left us.' All the journalists gasped, and some of the ones on the party payroll started crying.

'Sorry sorry, that's not how it was meant to come out. Chhote Sarkar has decided to go to the Himalayas to devote himself to God for the betterment of our lives and we hope that he will return ten years later blessed like the ex-Prime Minister and then lead our nation to bigger things.

Badi Sarkar wiped her eyes. She had given him ten years to live his life before he came back and took his rightful seat. Until then, the Great Leader would stay on probation, with Badi Sarkar reserving the right to fire him on a four-month notice. The Great Leader had not been happy with this clause but had accepted it after she added the rider that the decision would need to be ratified by the judges on *India's Got Great Talent* show and he would be given a chance to show his talent before she could fire him.

'Sir, what about the Orchid party?' another journalist asked.

'We will dissolve the party as it is no longer needed but Shri Girpade will create a new company to research the many miraculous uses of the orchid flower. We hope to be in a position to start exporting Orchetrol in two years.'

Vajra got up and asked. 'Why is Giani Seth sitting on the dais?'

The Great Leader announced. 'Oh, we have come to realize that the government cannot function without close participation from the industry so we are proud to announce that the Giani Group of Industries has kindly agreed to become the official sponsor of the government. We will unveil the uniforms to be worn by all ministers and babus next week, once we finalise the design and placement of the Giani Industries logo.'

Giani Seth got up, folded his hands and bowed to the Media Circus.

The transfer of Rs 5,000 crores to Badi Sarkar had gone through last night. He had been the facilitator of the entire drama. The plan had taken shape over dinner at his place last night where he had brought together the Great Leader, Neemacharya and BB. The Great Leader had refused to look at BB initially but Giani Seth had got them talking and the Great Leader had eventually kissed him on the cheek and made up, promising to burn his differences and forget the embarrassment BB had caused him. In turn, BB had touched his feet and promised full cooperation to realize his vision.

The run in the morning was just a decoy to throw off the media. Later in the day, all of the details had got ironed out during the discussions at Badi Sarkar's house. The cow had asked for only the Great Leader at first, not knowing who was the real mastermind.

The plan had gone off like clockwork. The Great Leader got what he wanted. Badi Sarkar managed to save her seat. Giani Seth would no longer need to wait for government approvals for any of his projects. The board couldn't even touch him now, or ever. BB was all set. The marriage to Babli would need to be planned next.

The Great Leader had one more announcement. 'One more thing. We will appoint Baba Neemacharya as the Chief Faith Officer of the government. The kind Baba has done a lot for the people of

Day 12: Who Will Ring the Bell?

this country...' He was interrupted by a massive clamour in the room, though he could only hear the words 'rape', 'scoundrel' and 'that girl'.

'Silence!' He shouted. 'Baba Neemacharya has done no wrong. The Police Commissioner has confirmed that the girl who fled from his ashram was mentally disturbed and under the influence of drugs when she filed the complaint that has now been withdrawn.'

'*Great Leader ki...jai*' Girpade shouted and the specially set-up hydraulic pump arrangement showered orchid petals on everybody assembled in the room as the smiling Great Leader clicked a selfie with Badi Sarkar, an arm gingerly draped around her slender shoulders.

*

'Sir, the honorable Monitor of the Government is here to meet you,' the assistant told Giani Seth, sitting in his government office, staring at a piece of paper, unable to read out the contents.

'Send him in. *Bhej do.*'

He heard the loud clatter of footsteps and soon a smartly dressed man in an Armani suit and a purple tie came in. He was freshly shaved and his hair was smartly done for the first day at work.

'BB, my man,' Giani Seth got up from his chair and escorted BB in.

'*Yaar* first things first. Can you confirm that this is the paper approving the Rs 50,000 crore Gian Port project?' Giani Seth handed him the file he had been looking at before his future son-in-law came in.

He looked at the paper. 'Yes, sir. But why do you ask?'

'Oh, no nothing.'

Giani Seth signed the paper to approve his dream project.

ABOUT THE AUTHOR

Atulya Mahajan is a writer and satirist. His debut novel *Amreekandesi – Masters of America*, a look at the adventures of two Indian students new to the ways of American life, was published in 2013. He has been writing a popular satire blog at amreekandesi.com since 2007 and spends much of his free time on Twitter and Facebook as @amreekandesi. He has previously written humor columns for *The Times of India* and currently writes a blog for them.

Atulya is a technologist and works at an investment bank as a Vice-President. His Twitter addiction has got him into a lot of trouble over the last few years, mostly from his mother and wife, who threaten to forfeit his phone any day now. He suffers from a severe phobia of driving and has weekly arguments (which he loses of course) with the missus when she mentions her intention of going to the mall.

Atulya reads the newspapers with great interest every day and is often found banging his head on the table in frustration at the sad state of politics in India. He often day-dreams about a healthy democracy where votes are not bought, opposition party spokesmen are not beaten up for siding with the enemy on a job well done, and writers don't have to fear being sent to jail for silly spoofs on the ways of the land.

Blog: http://amreekandesi.com/
Twitter: https://twitter.com/amreekandesi
Facebook: www.facebook.com/amreekandesi
Email: atulyamahajan@yahoo.com

www.ingramcontent.com/pod-product-compliance
Lightning Source LLC
Chambersburg PA
CBHW060505090426
42735CB00011B/2115